FLOWS OF VIOLENCE

FLOWS OF VIOLENCE

Water, Infrastructure, and the State
in Buenaventura, Colombia

FELIPE FERNÁNDEZ

THE UNIVERSITY OF
ARIZONA PRESS
TUCSON

The University of Arizona Press
www.uapress.arizona.edu

We respectfully acknowledge the University of Arizona is on the land and territories of Indigenous peoples. Today, Arizona is home to twenty-two federally recognized tribes, with Tucson being home to the O'odham and the Yaqui. The University strives to build sustainable relationships with sovereign Native Nations and Indigenous communities through education offerings, partnerships, and community service.

ISBN-13: 978-0-8165-5588-8 (hardcover)
ISBN-13: 978-0-8165-5587-1 (paperback)
ISBN-13: 978-0-8165-5589-5 (ebook)

Cover design by Leigh McDonald
Cover photo by Sasha Marie Runge
Typeset by Sara Thaxton in 10.5/14 Warnock Pro with Alternate Gothic No1 D and Helvetica Neue LT Std

This publication was made possible in part by funding from the German Research Council (DFG) project IRTG 2445 "Temporalities of Future in Latin America" (Institute of Latin American Studies, Freie Universität Berlin).

Library of Congress Cataloging-in-Publication Data
Names: Fernández, Felipe, 1989– author.
Title: Flows of violence : water, infrastructure, and the state in Buenaventura, Colombia / Felipe Fernández.
Description: [Tucson] : University of Arizona Press, 2025. | Includes bibliographical references and index.
Identifiers: LCCN 2025011788 (print) | LCCN 2025011789 (ebook) | ISBN 9780816555888 (hardcover) | ISBN 9780816555871 (paperback) | ISBN 9780816555895 (ebook)
Subjects: LCSH: Water security—Colombia—Buenaventura. | Buenaventura (Colombia)— Social conditions—21st century.
Classification: LCC HD1702 .F47 2025 (print) | LCC HD1702 (ebook)
LC record available at https://lccn.loc.gov/2025011788
LC ebook record available at https://lccn.loc.gov/2025011789

Printed in the United States of America
♾ This paper meets the requirements of ANSI/NISO Z39.48-1992 (Permanence of Paper).

For Nico and Saskia

CONTENTS

ILLUSTRATIONS

FIGURES

MAP

ABBREVIATIONS

ASIB   Asociación de Ingenieros de Buenaventura (Association of Engineers of Buenaventura)

AUC   Autodefensas Unidas de Colombia (United Self-Defenses of Colombia)

FARC   Fuerzas Armadas Revolucionarias de Colombia (Revolutionary Armed Forces of Colombia)

INFOSPAL   Instituto Nacional de Fomento Municipal (Municipal Development Institute)

PTSP   Plan Todos Somos PAZcífico

SAAB   Sociedad de Acueducto y Alcantarillado de Buenaventura (Sewage and Water Infrastructure Society)

UNGRD   Unidad Nacional de Gestión de Riesgos y Desastres (National Unit for Disaster Risk Management)

FLOWS OF VIOLENCE

Introduction

In Buenaventura, water comes and goes every day, people tell me. It comes only for a few hours and then it goes again. But what do they actually mean? When people say "se fue el agua" (the water is gone), they mean that the water supply has been cut off and are referring to the intermittent nature of the service. This water (the water coming to and going from the pipes) seems to be so different from those *other waters* in the city: the surrounding rivers and the estuaries, the sea water, and the nearly omnipresent rainwater in one of the regions with the highest precipitation levels in the world (Taussig 2003, 51–56; Oslender 2002). These waters seem to be abundant, even infinite, while the liquid that comes from the pipes is scarce. The modern urban promise of available water seems to have failed in Buenaventura. Infrastructure as a technological project has not fully succeeded in its attempt to capture water, regulate its flux and pressure, and distribute it to households (Swyngedouw 2004; Gandy 2017; Bakker 2014; Linton 2010). Water flows for a few hours through the pipes, and then it stops. As a result, people construct small-scale infrastructures to store water during the cut-offs (Lawhon et al. 2018; Furlong 2014). Some water tanks and domestic pipelines are provisionally installed on the rooftops of dwellings in order to bypass the outages and generate an *effect* of constant supply. But these fragile and often improvised assemblages fail sometimes too, and then the water goes away again.

Water pipes in Buenaventura are very leaky. They have holes, fissures, and cracks, caused mainly by accident—that is, by unstable topologies, by the weather, and by aging materials. There are many leakages, and they are extremely difficult to measure and repair (Anand 2015a). Some people access water through improvised, "illicit" connections, causing leaks unintentionally. Water pours out from the gap between the hose and the bore, generating losses. Indeed, leaks lead to "unknown and uncontrolled flows of water" in the city, making the aqueduct difficult to govern (Anand 2015a, 308). Leakages "depress" the system, an engineer working for the municipality in Buenaventura told me. The term is borrowed from medical jargon, meaning that the pressure needed to provide for all supply pipes is insufficient. Consequently, water flows must be sectorized using valves, which means that water is supplied in some neighborhoods for only some hours of the day—four hours, on average—while it is cut off for others. A water schedule: the only way the necessary pressure in the system can be guaranteed. Usually, people *know* when water is coming to their neighborhood. However, the flow can vary, and water can be gone for days. The utility service company announces it through social media and the radio. Sometimes flooding cause damages in the system; sometimes there is construction work to be done. Uncertain flows alter and define everyday life in Buenaventura.

"Come, I will show you," said Yeison, one of the friends I made during my fieldwork stay in Buenaventura, leading me to a tap installed in an improvised kitchen in his dwelling. He turned the tap; no water. Spooky sounds came out, as if the pipeline were coughing. A few drops dripped from the tap. "You see? Water is gone," he told me. The water tank installed on the roof of his dwelling was empty. We went back to the hardware shop where Yeison worked, sat behind the counter, and continued chatting about water infrastructure. It started to rain heavily, and customers became rare. "It is not a coincidence that there is no proper water supply for Black people like me and my family. The state has abandoned us," Yeison stated. He told me about the construction process of his house: how he and his father built it from scratch with scraps and wood they brought from a junkyard next to the port, and how they extend it by building new stories every year. "This will be a castle someday," he told me, laughing. He explained how they improvised a connection to the main pipeline with a hose and water storage system, which they must constantly repair. I asked him whether I could write everything down. He agreed. The rain became torrential, creating streams that dragged plastic, gravel, and dirt. That day, an acquaintance of Yeison had been killed nearby, he told me. Just like the water, violence comes and goes.

What does it mean to live amid precarious and dysfunctional infrastructures? Anthropological literature has addressed infrastructural systems in urban areas of the Global South by analyzing the legal, political, and sociomaterial processes that constitute, maintain, and transform the built landscape in contexts of deprivation and constant breakdown.[1] Further, urban scholars have approached the ways in which the urban poor tackle the deficient provision of public goods and the ways of improvisation and informal practices developed amid precarious infrastructures.[2] Beyond the dichotomy of connected/disconnected subjects (who have also been conceptualized as haves and have-nots), these studies have shown how malleable and porous networked infrastructures can be, and how the material arrangements of these infrastructures create a potentiality to sustain life in the city despite the precarious and unequal distribution of public goods.[3] The *excess* of infrastructural systems—that

---

1. See, for instance, the work of Anand (2011, 2017, 2018, 2020) in India; Degani (2015) in Tanzania; von Schnitzler (2016) in South Africa; Mains (2019) in Ethiopia; Fredericks (2018) in Senegal; Larkin (2008) in Nigeria; Chalfin (2014) in Ghana; Schwenkel (2015) in Vietnam. For the Colombian case, see the dissertation of geographer Tatiana Acevedo (2018) on the water infrastructures in the city of Barranquilla, in northern Colombia.

2. See Simone (2006, 2015); De Boeck and Plissart (2014); Degani (2022); von Schnitzler (2016). For an overview on infrastructures as a subject of study, see Star (1999); Larkin (2013); Appel et al. (2018); Howe et al. (2016); Edwards et al. (2009) and Mitchell (2014).

3. Larkin (2004) criticizes the approach of science and technology studies scholars who argue that societies would be excluded from infrastructures. He asserts: "These arguments recur somewhat in debates over the so-called digital divide and the division of the world into technological haves and have-nots. My difficulty with this move is with the dichotomizing logic it promotes and its assumption that the economic and cultural effects of new technologies are absent from 'disconnected' societies. The

is, the multiplicity of entry points (Anand 2017) or the possibility of their "corruption" (Larkin 2004)—allow and enhance processes of tampering (von Schnitzler 2016) and adulteration (Degani 2022). While citizenship and urban belonging are extremely unequally distributed, urban subjects such as Yeison and many others develop mechanisms to make life possible in Buenaventura.[4]

Another sentence I repeatedly heard in Buenaventura besides "se fue el agua" was that things had gotten *caliente*—meaning "hot" in Spanish. This word is used to denote a worsening of the security situation and an increase of assassinations, robberies, and extortion, or simply the presence of armed actors. Buenaventura, located in the Pacific region, is host to Colombia's biggest port. It is also one of the municipalities with the highest rates of poverty, unemployment, and violence in the country.[5] Social leaders and grassroots organizations have labeled the city "un puerto sin comunidad" (a port without a community), pointing to the exclusion of the population from the port economies and the development agenda led by the state and the private sector alike (CNMH 2015; Bonet-Morón et al. 2020; Manos Visibles 2017). In the 1990s and the first decade of the 2000s, Buenaventura received thousands of immigrants and internally displaced refugees, who came to the city from the surrounding rural areas, fleeing from right-wing paramilitaries and state forces as the internal armed conflict expanded into the region, turning it into a "geography of terror," to borrow from the term proposed by

---

danger here is that this polemic looks through rather than at the object at hand and fails to examine the structuring effects that technologies and their failures—however dysfunctional—have in everyday life" (305).

4. Geographers and anthropologists have also addressed the construction of larger water infrastructure systems and have examined, at a macro-level, the relationships between nature, state, and cities. See, for example, Swyngedouw (1997, 2004), Gandy (2014), and Menga (2017).

5. Remarkably, few academic works have been published on the city of Buenaventura. Some exceptions are Zeiderman (2016, 2018); Jenss (2020, 2021); Lombard et al. (2021); Alves et al. (2020). In this book, besides my own empirical data, I draw on several sources to approach the city, including reports issued by NGOs and the state apparatus itself. See CNMH (2015); Díaz Vargas (2015); Moreno Monroy 2013; Rodríguez and Sánchez (2002).

geographer Ulrich Oslender (2008). From around 2005 on, emergent criminal groups known as *bacrim* (short for *bandas criminales*) established themselves in Buenaventura and the surrounding regions with the purpose of controlling security, drug trafficking, and taking over some businesses. New organized groups fought for control over large parts of the city. These confrontations led to an increase in violence, which peaked in 2012, with mass graves and even torture centers, as reported by the U.S. NGO Human Rights Watch (2014) after conducting research in Buenaventura. Myriad modes of violence proliferated in the city. *Fronteras invisibles* (invisible frontiers) marked the control of armed groups over neighborhoods and their populations. Extortions, assassinations, and enforced disappearance became part of everyday life. Violence and deprivation of public goods seemed concomitant phenomena.

Scholarly literature has coined the term "infrastructural violence" to denote ways in which vulnerable and marginalized populations are disconnected, expelled, and even attacked through the built environment.[6] Drawing from the terms proposed by Michael Mann ("infrastructural power") and Stephen Graham ("infrastructural warfare"), Dennis Rodgers and Bruce O'Neill (2012) developed the concept of infrastructural violence, arguing that infrastructure "constitutes an often-ignored material channel for what is regularly referred to as 'structural violence.'"[7]

---

6. See, for instance, Anand (2012); Appel (2012); Anand et al. (2018); Uribe (2020); Weizman (2017); Chu (2014).

7. Anthropologist Akhil Gupta (2012) addresses development policy and bureaucracies in contemporary India by pointing at forms of structural violence inflicted to the impoverished population. He notes that "the reason such violence is considered to be structural is that it is impossible to identify a single actor who commits the violence. Instead, the violence is impersonal, built into the structure of power. Far from being intended, violence in this sense does not even have to be caused by a particular agent" (Gupta 2012, 20). In a brilliant essay on the relation bureaucracy and structural violence, David Graeber describes structural violence as a "boring, humdrum, yet omnipresent" phenomenon "that define[s] the very conditions of our existence, the subtle or not-so-subtle threats of physical force that lie behind everything from enforcing rules about where one is allowed to sit or stand or eat or drink in parks or other public places, to the threats or physical intimidations or attacks that underpin the enforcement of tacit gender norms" (2012, 105–6).

The latter points to violence and harm as an effect of a "complex process of production whose outcomes are objectionable, in which all members of society are implicated and yet whose effects are ostensibly nobody's fault" (404). This means that state institutions, corporations, and individuals alike eventually contribute to the reproduction and maintenance of a "social machinery of oppression," as Paul Farmer (2004, 307) calls it. Rodgers and O'Neill split the concept into "passive" and "active" infrastructural violence. The former encompasses the social, political, and economic processes that have led to, for instance, the (partial) disconnection of communities from wider infrastructural networks, as in the case of Buenaventura. The latter points to infrastructures that are designed to be violent for, let us say, surveillance means. Stepping aside from the liberal axioms that frame suffering and responsibility at a scale of the individual, this approach critically engages with the material effects of oppressive social structures.

Urbanites in Buenaventura experience infrastructural violence in manifold ways. The electricity grid, water infrastructures, and sewage systems in the city are highly inefficient, affecting the bulk of the population (Fernández 2022). At the same time, the port as an infrastructural "enclave" of global trade has harmed urban citizens by means of exclusion and segregation. As other authors have recently shown (see Zeiderman 2016, 2018; Jenss 2020, 2021; Lombard et al. 2023; Alves et al. 2020), the expansion of the port in Buenaventura, as well as its development plans, have led to evictions, environmental damage, and an increase in violence. Furthermore, the port has economically marginalized local populations, employing very few *bonaverenses* and dismantling worker unions after it was privatized at the beginning of the 1990s (CNMH 2015, 130–45). Through licit capitalist practices linked to the liberal rationale, such as infrastructural expansion, contracting, and subcontracting, the port has established its power, significantly impacting the racialized and impoverished population (Appel 2019). In this way, the port continually "disentangle(s) the production of profit from the place in which it happens to find itself" and is removed "from the social, legal, political and environmental entanglements in which it is so deeply enmeshed" (Appel 2012, 442). At the same time, social leaders claim that the rise in violence in vulnerable neighborhoods next to the port is related to the economic interests of investors, firms, and the state itself (Jenss 2021).

The concept of infrastructural violence primarily focuses on the infliction of harm produced and maintained by the built environment. The dysfunctional provision of water as a public good in Buenaventura is one example of this, as I will demonstrate. However, violence in the city is not reduced to the effects of infrastructural disconnection and a deficient delivery of public goods. Violent acts such as homicide and extortion are endemic in Buenaventura. Consequently, subjects are exposed not only to infrastructural violence but also to the war-like and low-intensity "rhythms of violence" perpetrated by armed groups and criminal gangs (Jenss 2021)

I coin the concept of *violent flows* to point to the character of the sociomaterial phenomenon I study here. Like water, violence fluctuates in the port city of Buenaventura: it comes and it goes. Yet these two flows are inextricably entangled. When water supply becomes scarce, it is a reminder of long-standing relations of segregation, organized state abandonment, and neglect, and thus, a form of structural violence materialized in the city's leaky and deficient water infrastructures. Nonetheless, the hours of regular supply when water comes, and when the efforts made by the state become visible and tangible, create a sense of normalcy. Moreover, when crime pours into a neighborhood, sociomaterial relations become unstable, and water flows might be altered, since repair works and trust networks are widely jeopardized. This book seeks to elucidate the temporalities and convergences of these two phenomena.

The term *flow* gained prominence in the anthropological literature of the 1990s and the first decade of the 2000s. In the course of radical transformations (the fall of the Soviet Union, the end of the bipolar world, the liberalization of economy), anthropological and sociological scholarship theorized the novel forms and patterns of global interconnections, entanglements, and flux. Eminent scholars such as Arjun Appadurai (1996), Manuel Castells (1996), and Ulf Hannerz (1996), employed the term *flow* to denote phenomena of cultural, political, and informational movement and transformation across space. Opposed to conceptualizations of culture as spatially enclosed, *flow* sought to capture both the circulation of people, money, images, and commodities, and the dynamism of cultural identity.

Despite the reach of the term and its prominence, critique have arisen. For instance, Rockefeller contends that the flow metaphor, rather than accurately describe cultural processes, it is used as an image of "pure" and "agentless movement," which "align the observer with the perspective of a manager" (2011, 558). To equate complex forms of transnational movement with *flow*, a word commonly used to refer to the smooth movement of liquids, he continues, "makes it harder for us to understand the scale at which practice, and agency are manifestly important" (566).

Violent flows, as I employ the term here, point to the difficult legibility, murky agency, and unpredictability inherent to violence and urban water in Buenaventura. Rather than being pure, flows here are muddy—at least in metaphorical terms. They don't point to regular movement, either, but to disruption and interruption. Like hooded criminals, the directions and trajectories of these flows are difficult to elucidate. I approach in this book the mechanisms which *sustain* and *reproduce* a system of violence, quotidian and infrastructural. Consequently, I delve into the history of deprivation and abandonment of infrastructure and ethnographically explore how different forms of violence shape the population in Buenaventura.[8]

"What flows or does not flow out of this or that pipe," states Lisa Björkman in her seminal work on water supply in Mumbai, "depends on highly dynamic intersections among the multiple regimes of knowledge and authority that waters inhabit, as well as the ways flows are configured and reconfigured across space and over time" (2015, 12; see also Kaika 2005). In this book, I argue that water in Buenaventura is not only embedded within regimes of knowledge and authority but is further imbued with and mediated by violence. I thus examine the behavior of these two murky flows (of water and of violence), and explore their interconnections, rhythms, and pauses. Concretely, I do this by analyzing the history of the water supply system (chapter 1); the social mobilization and forms of resistance in the face of deprivation (chapter 2); the intervention of the state apparatus aimed to improve the water supply (chapter 3); the forms of daily improvisations to access water (chapter 4), and, finally, the

---

8. This book is inspired by the work of geographer Maria Kaika in following urban water flows and paying attention to its transformations and rearrangements: "As it flows from spaces of production to spaces of consumption, it undergoes changes in its physical, socio-political and cultural character" (2005, 6).

ways in which everyday crime alters and intercedes local sociomaterial practices (chapter 5).

Examining violence in both its (infra)structural and quotidian dimensions and further merging it with an analysis on water supply have allowed me to address certain logics of Buenaventura's urban landscape. As violence, infrastructure mediates life. To track the histories of these two and their entanglements evidences complex forms of the political in urban Latin America and beyond marked by deprivation and abandonment. Moreover, the fact that large parts of the population are Black racialized communities plays a central role here. Thus, infrastructural violence serves as a lens through which I analyze the constitution and maintenance of these racialized geographies.

Throughout Colombian history, race has been paramount to politics and power dynamics. During Spanish colonial times (sixteenth to nineteenth centuries), space, social mobility, and bureaucracy were structured along codified racial categories, widely privileging colonial elites. Indigenous communities, white Spanish colonialists, and enslaved people from Africa constituted the racial backbone of colonial and postcolonial Latin America. After independence, *mestizaje*, the term used to denote the racial mixture, was paramount to producing a modern national identity. Throughout the nineteenth and twentieth centuries, political and intellectual elites sought to circumscribe the racial profile of citizens and nationhood. Drawing on Ronald Stutzman, anthropologist Peter Wade defines *mestizaje* as an "all-inclusive ideology of exclusion, a system of ideas that appeared to include everyone as a potential mestizo, but actually excluded black and indigenous people" (2005, 241). *Mestizo* denotes the dominant (and majority) population, which is presumed to be the result of racial and cultural mixing and conceived of as the "proper" citizens of these countries.

Certain Colombian territories, most of them deemed marginal and underdeveloped, have been marked by dynamics of racialization. Literate white or mestizo men, both Colombians and foreigners, such as travelers, bureaucrats, geographers, and politicians (mostly a mix of all of these), actively participated in the production of geographical knowledge as part of the modernization project and state-making process, as historians have shown. As argued by Claudia Leal (2018) in her brilliant book on the Colombian Pacific, the production of these *racialized land-scapes* has been crucial to the cultural, political, and economic dynamics of the region. She further demonstrates that not only rural but also urban geographies were produced through racial segregation.

Yet race (*etnia*) as a social category has undergone significant re-configurations in the last decades. In the 1990s, a multicultural agenda achieved legal recognition of Afro-Colombians as a minority, conceding them rights of land tenure and self-government, and symbolically included Black communities to the language of stateness and nationhood. However, multiculturalism has not meant the end of racial inequalities for Black people, who are still condemned to spatial segregation, premature death, dysfunctional public infrastructure, and extreme poverty. As I demonstrate, despite the discursive reshufflings of race in contemporary Colombia, infrastructure and violence represent critical sites of producing racial difference. More than constituted by white-driven anti-Black violence and the eradication of Black bodies, as Jaime Alves (2018) shows in the case of Sao Pablo, I argue that the Colombian state produces racial difference in Buenaventura through neglect and abandonment, and a relationship of "inclusive exclusion." Everyday violence and the precarious supply of water as a vital public good in the city are the result of precarious politics, uneven development, and capitalist logics supported by a mestizo-driven state.

A Road Map

This book explores the politics of water infrastructure in the Colombian port city of Buenaventura, in the face of deficient supply, everyday violence, improvisation, and social struggle. By identifying and analyzing various forms of violence, coping mechanisms, and social protest, I ethnographically explore the ways in which violence and water infrastructures are embedded in the everyday life of urban citizens in this city.[9] I do

---

9. I use the term *water infrastructures*, plural, to refer to the variety of material entanglements, objects, and procedures that aim to capture, control, and distribute water as a public good in the city. By using the plural, I emphasize the heterogeneity and plurality of these material arrangements and avoid addressing them as a singular entity.

four things: I first examine how the state apparatus exerts infrastructural violence through the precarious provision of water. Then, I address the forms of resistance and protest in the face of the deficient public goods provision and endemic violence, discursively articulated and put in practice by social activists and local experts alike. Third, I study the material practices of construction of small-scale infrastructures to store water as a mechanism to cope with the malfunctioning water infrastructure networks. Finally, I focus on the ways in which crime and everyday violence alter social life and trust networks and shape sociomaterial practices.

First, I show how the state reproduces and maintains a system of deficient distribution of water supply by looking at both the institutional history of utility services and a recent (partly failed) state attempt to improve water infrastructures in the city. I argue that an "organized abandonment" (Goldstein 2012) of urban infrastructures by means of underinvestment and neglect resulted in institutional weakness and a massive deterioration of the pipelines, the water tanks, and the operation of the water supply system itself. A recent attempt to improve the water infrastructures has been materialized through a state-led development project called Plan Todos Somos PAZcífico (PTSP) which, at the time of writing in 2023, has not met its stated goals of improving the system and guaranteeing a constant water supply. Drawing on the concept of "complying incompliantly" proposed by Valentina Pellegrino (2022), I argue that the deferral and partial failure of this project responds to a mechanism through which the state apparatus appears to fulfill its responsibilities while at the same time failing to meet its stated goals. The mere existence of the project and its different forms of representation (through discourses, images, objects, and laws) allow the state to continuously reaffirm that it is making an effort to build and expand water infrastructures. Yet a proper water supply, the main goal and promise of the project, is still far from being realized.

I then move to the series of social mobilizations that took place in the port city at different points during the 2010s as a response to the infrastructural violence inflicted on the communities. By examining the discourses and actions taken by social activists, I aim to frame the spaces of struggle and negotiation that have recently shaped the politics of water infrastructures in the port city. The protest culminated with a twenty-two-day general strike in May 2017, during which the city's main road was blocked and the port had to stop operating. The strike ended with the signing of an agreement between the government and the Strike Committee. While other authors have analyzed social mobilization in Buenaventura (Jaramillo et al. 2020; Zeiderman 2018; Lombard et al. 2021; Jenss 2021), I will focus on the efforts made by experts of the Association of Engineers of Buenaventura (ASIB is its Spanish acronym) to mobilize knowledge, formulate solutions, and challenge the discourses of the central state. These ASIB members became key actors in the negotiations between the Strike Committee and the government. Moreover, I will show how the strike and the competing forms of expertise unpack historical tensions between the local and the central government in Colombia.

I then turn to the material practices implemented as means of coping with infrastructural violence: the construction of small-scale infrastructural systems of water supply. During my fieldwork, I witnessed the construction of domestic systems of water storage, which consisted of a hose leading from the public pipe to a water tank installed in the rooftop of the house that redistributes the water to the dwelling by means of gravity. I understand these practices as part of a series of mechanisms deployed by urban citizens to cope with the insufficient provision of water, and as a "quiet encroachment of the ordinary: a salient, patient, protracted, and pervasive advancement of ordinary people . . . to survive hardship and better their lives" (Bayat 1997, 57). Albeit deployed in a different register than that of social mobilization, I argue that these practices are also (political) ways of coping with everyday experiences of infrastructural violence.

Finally, I analyze the role of extortion and everyday crime in trust networks and sociomaterial practices. Shopkeepers in Buenaventura's neighborhoods are exposed to the so-called *vacuna*—a well-known form of extortion throughout Colombia, which criminal gangs claim is a fee paid to them to guarantee the security that the state cannot provide. I show how the vacuna further destabilizes security regimes and interferes in the social life of the neighborhood. I propose that, instead of being two concomitant phenomena that separately shape the everyday life of the urban poor, as argued elsewhere (Auyero and Burbano de Lara 2012), precarious infrastructures and crime are deeply intertwined in Buenaventura.

Infrastructure and Inequality in the Liberal City

How has deprivation of racialized population been historically constituted? Scholarly literature has pointed to the role played by liberal rule in the constitution of modern infrastructural systems (see, for instance, Appel et al. 2018; Anand 2017; von Schnitzler 2016). Historian Patrick Joyce (2003, 62–76) demonstrates how the emergence of urban infrastructure as a key technology in nineteenth century Britain responded to liberal axioms of governmental praxis (see also Anand 2017, 69). Under the liberal rationale, the technical and the political have been strictly divided. Hence, urban infrastructures were deemed to be mere technical objects. Elsewhere, Dirk van Laak (2018) characterizes infrastructures as "spaces of flow" (water, electricity, trains), and thus considers them to be the backbone of modernization and progress in a liberal sense (see Larkin 2013). However, and as several ethnographies have shown, the modern, liberal constitution of the built landscape is unevenly distributed along colonial, racial, and class lines: while it has guaranteed the flow and circulation of some, it expels, bypasses, and even attacks others (Graham and Marvin 2002; Rodgers and O'Neill 2012). As part of the liberal project, rather than representing progress and development, infrastructures are material arrangements that can "differentiate populations and subjects" (Appel et al. 2018, 5).

Liberal and colonial rule have been historically intertwined, especially in the nineteenth and twentieth centuries. Thus, infrastructures in (former) colonized countries emerged as vehicles not only of integration by means of flow, but also of segregation and marginalization. In his seminal work on water supply in the city of Mumbai, anthropologist Nikhil Anand (2017) shows how the modern water infrastructures of the city were built at the end of the nineteenth century at the same time as those of New York and London, but in a very different political context, namely British colonial rule. Colonial Mumbai water infrastructures discriminated between those deserving membership in the colonial city and those expelled from the promises of citizenship (14). This process was underpinned by fiscal restrictions—that is, underinvestment—in urban infrastructures for the delivery of public goods. While public works in (colonial) cities aimed to integrate and enhance capitalist networks, economic circuits, and productive subjects, they, at least in part, segregated and expelled the colonized others. Marginalized colonial subjects were largely excluded from the promises and projections of progress posed by the liberal rule. This legacy of colonial and neocolonial infrastructural segregation becomes evident in many urban spaces around the globe where people remain (at least partially) "disconnected" from infrastructural systems (Graham and Marvin 2002; Howe et al. 2016).

Like in Mumbai, water infrastructures in Buenaventura reflect the precarious development of the city. The unequal access to the water supply exemplifies the racialization, marginalization and organized state abandonment of large parts of Buenaventura's urban subjects (Appel et al. 2018, 3). Although urban infrastructures were not, like in Mumbai, modernized and transformed under colonial rule, Buenaventura was planned and designed after independence by a mestizo elite from the country's interior that had particular economic interests in the region, not aiming at modernizing the city and connecting the Black communities to public infrastructures.[10] While the then-village of Buenaventura played a subordinated role for the economic interests of the mestizo elites, the construction of a railroad at the beginning of the twentieth century started the gradual integration of the small village into the country's interior. From the 1940s on, the port infrastructures grew significantly, and the city experienced a migration wave both from the interior and the surrounding rural areas (CNMH 2015; Moreno Monroy 2013). Buenaventura's urban development was thus constituted by external actors and their interests to build and expand the port.

Historian Claudia Leal (2018) argues that the attempts to modernize Tumaco and Quibdó (the other urban hubs in the Pacific) by a mestizo elite were marked by the extractive economies of the surrounding rural areas on the one hand and the attempt to build a "civilized city" amid the "unruliness" of the Pacific rainforest on the other. In her book *Landscapes of Freedom*, Leal explores the modernization of these two cities, where an Afro-Colombian majority was relegated to low-income work, poor housing, and precarious infrastructures. As in the case of Tumaco

---

10. Peter Wade defines *mestizaje* as an "all-inclusive ideology of exclusion, a system of ideas that appeared to include everyone as a potential mestizo, but actually excluded black and indigenous people" (2005, 241). In this book, I use the term *mestizo* as a racial category of identification and intracolonial domination.

and Quibdó, unequal infrastructures and neocolonial planning strategies marked the production of urban space in Buenaventura throughout the twentieth century. Since the 1990s, the port infrastructures have increasingly expanded in order to meet the economic interests of the elite, while public infrastructures were not designed to properly deliver public goods to the large of the population (Alves et al. 2020; CNMH 2015).

The study of infrastructure and the built environment reveals the inequalities sedimented in the politics of city planning. Yet ethnographies of deficient and precarious urban infrastructural systems not only address the ways through which uneven development unfolds but further examine the complex material and political negotiations that take place between (infrastructurally) marginalized subjects and state apparatuses in order to gain "connections" to infrastructures. Studies demonstrate that access to public goods is achieved, for instance, through the mobilization of street-level bureaucracies (Anand 2011), tampering (von Schnitzler 2016), and adulteration (Degani 2015), as subjects tug, pull, and demand infrastructures from the state. By privileging ethnographic methods, scholars engage with the complex and multilayered everyday experiences revolving around urban infrastructures in different registers (Simone 2015a).

This book aims to contribute to these works and thus approaches the water infrastructures in Buenaventura as an "object of ethnographic engagement" (Appel et al. 2018, 4). More than a mere top-down technical object planned and implemented by a political agenda of liberal expertise, I define infrastructures, borrowing from Anand, as "flaky accretions of sociomaterial *processes*" (2017, 14), an assemblage that contains histories of violence and exclusion, ethical and legal regimes, materials, and techno-political procedures but also contestation, struggle, and piracy (Larkin 2013). Infrastructure is brought into being, represented, and negotiated in a myriad of ways and places, such as development plans, daily maintenance, informal chats, social struggles, figures, popular songs, and the press, as the case of Buenaventura well shows. Far from being invisible objects (Star 1999), water infrastructures are a "matter of concern" in the city and thus an integral part of people's everyday life (Latour 2004).

However, I do not pretend to encompass the wholeness of water infrastructures in the city. In focusing on a state-led developmental plan, the material practices developed in response to the deficient delivery of water, and social protest and the role played by everyday crime in the provision of public goods, I scrutinize four distinct yet intermingled domains in which water infrastructures unfold. In doing so, I seek to further demonstrate how violence and infrastructure are closely related phenomena in the city. In what follows, I theoretically elaborate on the role of the state apparatus.

The State's Inclusive Exclusion

During my fieldwork, people constantly complained about the consequences of "state abandonment" in Buenaventura and the Pacific region in general. The precarious delivery of public goods was interpreted as a form of state absence in many parts of the city, by social activists and inhabitants alike. Both water infrastructures and violence served as a lens through which to "see the state" (Corbridge 2005). It was not the first time I heard about this idea of the state in the Pacific region. The local and national press constantly reproduce images and discourses of underdevelopment, suggesting that many areas of the region have been abandoned by the state. Ethnographies on the state in Colombia have pointed to the dissemination of this idea of absence and abandonment (Ramírez 2015, 2011).[11] This, in turn, contributes to interpretations of the Colombian state as failed, weak, and precarious, caught in a perennial but unsuccessful state-building process.

Indeed, Colombia and the Colombian state have been widely depicted as fractured and divided, not fitting with the Weberian idea of the state as a comprehensive bureaucratic entity that successfully claims a monopoly of violence over the totality of a territory. In their comprehensive history of the country, historians Frank Safford and Marco Palacios Rozo (2002) argue that Colombia's diverse geography and climates have played a decisive role in its state-building processes and uneven economic development. Indeed, the centers of economic and political power are located

---

11. Anthropologist Margarita Serje (2012) demystifies the idea of the "absence of the state" in frontiers and marginal territories and scrutinizes the specific forms of presence of the state in these territories.

on the north–south axis of the Andean mountains, which encompasses the main rivers of the country (the Cauca and the Magdalena), the extensive Caribbean coast, and the inter-Andean valleys. Meanwhile, lowland regions such as the Amazon, the Pacific, and the Orinoco are deemed peripheral.

Other authors have not taken geographical fractures as a given condition for uneven development, instead examining the cultural production of difference within the Colombian state formation process and national identity.[12] Margarita Serje (2011) analyzes the discursive production and representations of the territories that constitute what she calls "the reverse of the nation," pointing to the country's no-man's-land and peripheries. In an "ethnography of a context"—a context within which colonial and modern representations are configured and maintained—the author traces the history of the production of the Colombian internal frontiers, revealing the power relations between the center and the periphery and demonstrating how the opposition between civilization and barbarism has been critical to modern state-building in Colombia. This production of difference is crucial not only to sustaining images and discourses of "savagery" and "unruliness" but to the very process of state-building, as Veena Das and Deborah Poole (2004) have shown. In their work on the margins of the state, they argue that the latter "is imagined as an always incomplete project that must constantly be spoken of—and imagined—through an invocation of the wilderness, lawlessness and savagery" (Das and Poole 2004, 7). Hence, the (re)production of frontiers has become a central feature of the state-building process in Colombia.

---

12. Uribe (2017) criticizes conceptions of Colombia as a fragmented nation-state, arguing that the "amputated map" of the country "strongly reflects and reinforces the dominant image of the frontier as vast peripheral zones falling within the country's geographical borders yet lying beyond the limits of the state." Hence, the fact that these territories have not been "integrated" would be related to the misleading idea that the "state has historically been too weak or simply unwilling to reach and control its peripheral regions." However, "the proliferation of all sorts of frontiers in the body politic of nation-states suggests . . . that the former constitute spaces whose role is central for the very existence of the state" (7). For further conceptions of the frontier, see Hansen and Stepputat (2005) and Das and Poole (2004).

Other scholars have examined the ways through which statehood practices unfold in the "reverse of the nation."[13] Ethnographies on local expressions of the state in Colombia have demonstrated the complex ways in which power is distributed among different state institutions and how, at the same time, nonstate actors such as political parties, NGOs, and armed groups converge in everyday forms of governance and state rule. A myriad of factors such as political membership, regional power, and alliances with armed groups shape the constitution and unfolding of local state practices.

Yet it is not only the local context that captures and reproduces this idea of the state. Interventions planned by the central government have also been critical to state-building processes but have been widely under-studied by scholars. In the case of the Pacific, centrally conceived and hierarchically structured development agendas directed toward the region have proliferated since the 1990s. Diverse programs of natural conservation were implemented as the new legislation regarding Afro-Colombian ethnic communities was promoted (Restrepo 2013). Take, for example, the Proyecto BioPacífico, funded by the Global Environmental Facility, a multilateral development fund, and executed by the Colombian central government between 1992 and 1998. This project was formed by an interdisciplinary group of experts (including biologists, sociologists, and historians) and aimed to collect data on the region in order to design an agenda on sustainable development in the context of the new paradigms of environmental protection and minority rights (Leal 2015). In a similar vein to Serje, geographers Asher and Ojeda (2009) have argued that this plan mobilized a set of institutional structures and practices through which the images and discourses of backwardness and marginality on the Pacific were (re)imagined and (re)fashioned. Thus, state interventions unfold within a context of frontier production in their attempts to integrate territories while reproducing logics and discourses of alterity.

But not only images and discourses are pivotal to these frontier-making practices. Infrastructural projects have been key vehicles of modernization and state-building processes at the internal frontier of Latin America states and beyond (Harvey 2014). Simón Uribe's (2017)

13. See Aparicio (2012); Ballvé (2020); Asher (2009); Ramírez (2011); Restrepo (2013); McFee (2019); Gill (2016); Burnyeat (2018).

work well exemplifies this phenomenon for the Colombian case. There, he addresses the construction and maintenance of a "frontier road" (the so-called trampoline of death) that runs from the city of Pasto in the Andean region to the town Puerto Asís in the Amazon lowlands.[14] The road was built (and rebuilt) during the nineteenth and twentieth centuries in an attempt to shrink geographical distances and integrate part of the Amazon lowlands while fostering a state-led civilizing process by means of colonization, bringing together a variety of nonstate actors such as rubber tappers (*caucheros*), Capuchin friars, settlers, and local politicians. The precipitous topography, the myriad dangers posed by the road, and the region's extreme weather all evoke images that echo the frontier as a space of fear, backwardness, and endemic violence, Uribe argues. Drawing on Agamben's "state of exception," he demonstrates how this infrastructure project perpetuated "feelings and memories of isolation, exclusion and abandonment from the state," while, at the same time, expectations of "smooth paved roads" embodied a "long-awaited promise of development and inclusion" (Uribe 2017, 3), which in turn has remained broadly unfulfilled. The frontier (the Amazon lowlands) represents a territory which has never been "excluded from the spatial and political order of the state, but rather incorporated to this order through a relationship of *inclusive exclusion*" (4, emphasis mine).[15]

---

14. Alexis De Greiff (2021) traces a material history of the Colombian state, focusing on infrastructure, and approaching the fragmentation of the country as a result of the interaction between institutions, infrastructure, and nature.

15. Uribe (2020) uses the term "infrastructural violence" to analyze the construction, repair, and representations of the road. He asserts that "infrastructural violence operates here in two imbricated and mutually reinforcing ways. On the one hand, it is inflicted physically against those who travel daily along the road by means of the material threats it imposes. Being to date the only road linking Putumayo with the neighboring province of Nariño and also the former's Andean and Amazon territories, the Trampoline of Death remains an unavoidable route for people and goods constantly moving back and forth between these territories. Exposure to death or injury is thus inevitable and relates to how people are connected across space. On the other hand, violence is also perpetrated politically through its representation as an intrinsic, hence inevitable feature of the region's 'savage' or 'backward' nature, thus perpetuating the social stigma historically attached to the frontier. In so doing,

Infrastructure projects such as the road analyzed by Uribe aim to enhance geographical integration as a key technology of the state-building
process while reinforcing the idea of an unruly frontier. This twofold
process of simultaneous integration and exclusion has been, for persons
inhabiting the frontier, "the norm rather than the exception" (Uribe 2017,
4). Yet it is not only infrastructures that aim to integrate the territory
that depict the material politics deployed at the frontier. As this book
demonstrates, infrastructures for the provision of public goods in an urban setting at, or rather within, the frontier reproduce similar discourses
and logics. Here, I understand the water infrastructures in Buenaventura
(and the institutional arrangement which aims to govern and transform
them, as well as the material practices that unfold) as loci of this long-
awaited expectation of development and inclusion which is not met but
mirrors specific forms of state-building processes at the Colombian frontier. I further turn to the term "state-organized abandonment," proposed
by Daniel Goldstein, to denote this state intervention. The author, in his
seminal work on Bolivia's urban margins, contends that state institutions
carry out a "negative inclusion" and a "perilous exclusion" of these marginal spaces marked by "poverty, underdevelopment and neglect" (Goldstein 2012, 5). As I show in chapter 1, Buenaventura's water infrastructure
is depicted in pathological terms (like the road analyzed by Uribe), even
as state interventions fail to accomplish their stated goals of development
and proper water supply.

Encountering the Field

The first time I visited Buenaventura was in 2015. I was doing an internship for a small, poorly funded NGO based in the city of Cali, ninety-
three miles from Buenaventura, in the country's interior, and where I was
born and raised in the 1990s in a middle-class mestizo family. During
my internship I accompanied a group of workers undertaking their daily
activities in the rural town of Sabaletas, two hours by car from urban

the violence of infrastructure is rendered normal, either by labelling it as 'accidental'
or 'nobody's fault,' or, in most cases, by making the victims guilty for the violence
inflicted upon themselves" (65).

Buenaventura. The NGO was promoting a project for entrepreneurs who were interested in setting up small-scale businesses for locals in the village. While preparing for the trip, I checked some facts about the Pacific in general, and Sabaletas in particular. I read about the massacres that took place there in 2000 and 2001, which were perpetrated by right-wing paramilitaries with the support of Colombia's army, leading to the displacement of the majority of the village's inhabitants. I also read about the massive contamination of the village's main river, Anchicayá, by the allegedly intentional dumping of residues by a hydroelectric power plant, which massively affected the livelihoods of the population. I read about the high amount of rainfall and the fascinating biodiversity surrounding Sabaletas. I was excited and looked forward to traveling there. I was expecting to meet the fascinating (and violent) realities of the region I had read about in Michael Taussig's experimental ethnography *My Cocaine Museum* as an undergraduate in Germany.

On our way from Cali to Sabaletas, we stopped in Buenaventura. "This city is really tough," one of the NGO workers said, grimacing in disgust. Indeed, I was impressed by the colossal chaos, by the overwhelming mix of people, sounds, dust, and (crumbling) infrastructures. After a while, we continued our journey. Sabaletas was sort of magical. Wooden dwellings are built alongside the river. The evergreen and thickly grown trees are lush; the river (though contaminated) is exuberant. The rainfall and the sunset I witnessed were beautiful. While accompanying my colleagues doing the boring bureaucratic NGO work, I decided to build contacts with local social leaders with a view toward undertaking further anthropological research. Two years later, in 2017, I returned to Sabaletas and carried out fieldwork for my master's thesis. There, I considered the presence of the state in the village by looking at both the development agenda directed to the region and the violent acts committed by the paramilitaries (and state forces) almost twenty years earlier. Every time I commuted from Cali to Sabaletas, I had to pass through Buenaventura. Nothing seemed magical in such an urban mess. If anything, it evoked images of slums and suffering (Robbins 2013). I thought that it would be nearly impossible for an outsider to conduct fieldwork there.

In 2018 I was in the process of preparing a dissertation project. I was still broadly interested in the southwestern Pacific and noticed that little had been written about urban Buenaventura. Scholarly literature had mainly focused on the rural Pacific due to the recent legislation regarding ethnic minorities and the emergence of ethnic and social movements. Renowned anthropologists such as Arturo Escobar and Michael Taussig had published ethnographies on the rural Pacific, while there were only few publications on the port city of Buenaventura, written mainly by Colombian scholars such as Boris Salazar and Óscar Almario. This gap seemed striking to me, since the majority of the population in the region inhabits the urban, not the rural, areas. I then decided that I wanted to turn my attention to that slum-like city I observed from the bus on my way to Sabaletas. I considered it a challenge.

In 2015 the Centro Nacional de Memoria Histórica, a state institution of social research regarding the internal armed conflict, published a report on Buenaventura, which I read as a sort of guide to the city.[16] Through this report, I learned more about the precarious provision of public goods and the endemic violence—the two main ills of the port city. I then turned to the literature on infrastructure in anthropology, urban studies, and human geography. The approaches appealed to me, given my desire to understand the (socio)material landscape (and chaos) I had observed from the bus. Furthermore, Filip De Boeck's ethnography of Kinshasa (Congo) and Rem Koolhaas's documentary on Lagos (Nigeria) inspired me to explore the possibility of entering and making sense of a city that at first glance seemed hermetic and impenetrable for a mestizo, almost foreign, researcher like me.

At that point, I was mainly interested in critically examining state action and presence in an urban space that appeared to be highly troubled. Water infrastructures seemed suitable for such a purpose. While rural

16. The Centro Nacional de Memoria Histórica was founded in 2011 as a continuation of the Grupo de Memoria Histórica, which was led by Gonzálo Sánchez and located within the Comisión Nacional de Reparación y Reconciliación, which, in turn, was led by historian Eduardo Pizarro. The Comisión Nacional de Reparación y Reconciliación was created during the Uribe administration (2002–2010). The Santos government founded the Centro Nacional de Memoria Histórica and, drawing on several reports made by social scientists, closed the commission, and took the Grupo de Memoria Histórica, which had already published reports, and made it into its own institution.

areas in the region are aquatic spaces, as geographer Ulrich Oslender (2002) puts it, the city lacks a water supply. What is the reason for the existence of inefficient infrastructures? Who governs them? Why are they crumbling and highly visible? Where is the state? Are there non-networked, improvised infrastructures that survive amid breakdowns?

I was aware that fieldwork would be difficult due to the security situation in the port city. I hoped I could rely on institutional support and carry out an internship for an NGO or a state institution and be accompanied during my stay. By the end of 2018, I traveled to Buenaventura to interview a group of hydraulic engineers I had contacted through a Buenaventura-born high state official in Cali. I then rented a room in one of the few safe areas in the city and continued interviewing experts, state officials and social leaders. I was warned not to leave my room in the evenings. I devoted my time to writing a field diary and reading reports on the city published by private and public institutions.[17] I sent several requests and applications to both state institutions and NGOs to find an internship position, but none of them considered it useful to employ a social scientist. I was an expert in neither the technical domains of water infrastructure nor in public policy. Then I was offered the opportunity to work in the social unit (*componente social*) of a construction firm that was subcontracted to PTSP. The social unit mainly employed social workers since its main task was to "socialize" (communicate and present) the construction projects with the "affected communities" living near the construction works. After the engineer on the phone explained to me that I would be "accompanying" the unit but would not have anything to do with those "boring technical things" regarding water infrastructures, I rejected the offer.

From the very beginning, I was interested on how "ordinary people" (Bayat 1997)—that is, neighborhood residents who are not directly involved in the political happenings of the city—experienced the water shortages. I was willing to enter a barrio to interview people there. I began to chat strategically with both taxi drivers and the service staff at

---

17. I read the reports written and published in the 2010s as the city attracted the attention of NGOs and supranational organizations for the increase in violence: CNMH (2015); Human Rights Watch (2014); Taula Catalana (2016).

the hotel.[18] I asked about the water supply in their neighborhoods, about the schedule and the leaky pipes. From their stories, I learned about how people deal with the deficient provision of public goods. I asked them if I could visit their neighborhoods (I was attempting to have a "proper" anthropological experience, after all); in response, most of them expressed reluctance due to the "security situation." As a stranger, they told me, I could be targeted by armed groups.

One Tuesday morning in January 2019, I met Iván. He was driving a *pirata* (a non–officially registered taxi) in Buenaventura after losing his job as truck driver. I was coincidentally sitting in his *pirata* on my way to a meeting with an engineer at a construction site. Iván is of mestizo ancestry, like me. He started asking about what I was doing in Buenaventura. I explained that I was conducting research on water infrastructures in the city. Without my asking him to, he then invited me to his neighborhood, where his wife runs a hardware shop. "I am an expert," he told me. "I know everything about water. People buy everything at the hardware shop to get access to the pipeline. Come with me, I will show you." When I expressed my concerns about the security situation, he told me that they would tell people I was their nephew, and that I would be safe. I agreed and rented a room in their house, in Ciudad Blanca.[19]

Upon my arrival, I met Claudia, Iván's wife, for the first time. She introduced me to her family and neighbors and told me that I would always be welcome. When I explained that I was a social anthropologist conducting research on water infrastructures, she told me that in the hardware shop she runs, people buy devices to construct water storage systems and connections to the pipelines and that I would learn a lot about water supply staying at her place and talking to people in the shop. She offered me a room in her house that she normally rented to truck drivers. I had finally found a safe site to start my fieldwork. Things were

---

18. I began to talk to taxi drivers whenever I traveled through the city. I was inspired by other ethnographies I had read in which chatting with taxi drivers turned out to be fruitful for grasping the everyday life and rhythms of the city. See, for example, Melly (2017) and Taussig (2003).

19. I have changed all names of places and persons to protect their lives or, at least, their identities. Some geographical references have been altered for the same reason, without influencing academic accuracy.

going well. It felt as though a sort of serendipity was leading me to an interesting field site. At that point, unplanned happenings were becoming constitutive of my fieldwork (van der Geest 2017).

Neighborhoods (locally denoted as *barrios*) have a different character in Buenaventura in terms of their history, as well as their social and material dynamics, and only partly overlap with the *comunas*, the administrative urban units. On the Isla de Cascajal (where the main port, hotels, and municipality buildings are located), many settlements were established throughout the twentieth century. Stilt houses on the low tide were built after people took land from the sea by piling up alluvial materials. These neighborhoods have come to symbolize the settlement patterns of people in Buenaventura who have migrated from rural areas, where stilt houses are built alongside the riverbanks (Taussig 2004, 160–64).

From the 1960s onward, an emerging middle class of workers and unionists employed by the port settled down in barrios such as La Independencia and Bella Vista, in buildings mainly made of concrete. These neighborhoods tend to enjoy better infrastructures, such as paved streets, as well as water and electric infrastructures, although even there, the provision of public goods is inefficient. Moreover, with new waves of migration and demographic expansion in the 1990s and the first decade of the 2000s, state-led housing projects such as Ciudad Blanca and San Antonio were built to offer housing to both impoverished and displaced persons from the rural areas and evicted inhabitants from the Isla de Cascajal, where the implementation of new urban development plans destroyed existing houses (Jenss 2021). Additionally, informal settlements (*asentamientos irregulares*) can also be found everywhere in the city. The self-built houses and "illicit" occupation of the territory locates these subjects at the margins of city planning and infrastructures. As I will show, these informal settlements are materially and economically intertwined and connected to other more "formal" barrios, as the case of Ciudad Blanca exemplifies.

For the case of Buenaventura, it is inaccurate to talk about urban racial segregation in classical terms. Throughout the twentieth century the port was rather an "enclave, a warehouse for commodities coming into and out of the interior of the country" managed from the interior of the country (mainly from the city of Cali) while the city grew "organically," led by Black local political elites (Leal 2018). There was no such thing as a white or mestizo neighborhood. Nonetheless, the city was conceived in order to serve the interests of mestizo capital. Segregation in the city is rather infrastructural. Still today, the development, maintenance, and security of the port mark the urban planning and development of the city, clearly shown by the Plan Maestro Buenaventura 2050, a public document crafted by urban developers (Jenss 2021). Meanwhile, public infrastructures remain precarious.

The day after I arrived in Ciudad Blanca, I spent a long time chatting with Claudia about the precarious water supply in the city. I learned a lot about the everyday maintenance, improvised connections and constructions, and what people do when water *goes* for several days. And I also learned about the story of her life as a middle-aged mestizo woman (locally called *paisas*). She had migrated in the 1990s, as a teenager, from the country's interior to try her luck in the Pacific region together with her then-husband. Initially, they lived in the town of Guapi, then moved to Buenaventura just after 2000.

Claudia showed me all the things she sold in the shop: hoes, tubes, pipes, hammers, sews, concrete, steel rods, gravel, and so on. She then introduced me to Yeison and Alexander, her assistants in the hardware shop. Yeison was born in the rural Pacific and fled to Buenaventura with his family as a child. Alexander moved as a child to the city from the Urabá region. Both Alexander and Yeison were raised amid violence and deprivation of many public goods, as they told me several times. Even though they knew I was carrying out research, they regarded me as a new friend and guided me through the enmeshed and troubled material landscapes of Ciudad Blanca.

I was privileged to have this kind of access to the hardware shop and to get to know people like Yeison and Alexander, whose everyday life is highly influenced by the construction, maintenance, and repair of domestic, small-scale infrastructures. I then started working at the hardware shop myself to learn more about infrastructural devices. I used the space to hold everyday conversations and interviews with neighbors, clients, police officers, and street-level bureaucrats. I did not record the conversations but kept a field diary with notes and drawings.

My identity as a mestizo was a key factor to entering the field. Iván and Claudia knew beforehand that I needed their assistance to conduct my research in Buenaventura. They were willing to help me and explain to me how water infrastructure and supply in their neighborhood worked. Further, they identified me as "one of them" in terms of racial and social identity. While most inhabitants in Buenaventura are of Afro-Colombian descent, shopkeepers, merchants, and entrepreneurs tend to be from the interior of the country, paisas. The paisas working in commerce tend to have a tight relationship with the big vendors in the main cities of the country's interior, have access to greater lines of credit in banks, and inherit a culture of commerce. Their identity and commercial activities also perpetuate racialized inequalities.

In general terms, I was seen as a paisa, an acquaintance or even a distant family member of Claudia—or "the hardware shop owner" as everybody knew her. I felt broadly comfortable and protected by this fact. As an (upper) middle-class mestizo young researcher, mainly educated in private schools in Colombia and universities in Germany, I did not feel that I quite identified with people like Iván and Claudia. They were from a family of peasants and shop owners (known in Colombia as *comerciantes*) and had not attended high school. While I openly talked about my privileges and my background, I sought to foreground our shared experience of being seen as paisas in an urban hub mainly inhabited by Afro-Colombians. My relationships with people like Alexander and Yeison were defined *through* the relationship they maintained with people such as Claudia and Iván. The fact that I was seen as an acquaintance (or distant family member) of the latter had a twofold effect. On the one hand, people kept a certain distance from me, seeing me as a paisa immigrant who did not understand the harm and realities of Afro-Colombians in the city. On the other hand, trust was built beforehand, since locals have had experience with shop owners and paisa immigrants for some decades. This is critical in Buenaventura since without this kind of trust network, subjects can be targeted by armed groups.

The idea of occupying dual roles during fieldwork has been widely studied in anthropology. The term points to the active participation and friend-like relationships that researchers and informants can develop in the field on the one hand, and on the other, the distance needed to remain an observer and researcher (Bell 2019). I constantly sought to make my position as researcher clear with Claudia, her family, and the assistants in the hardware shop, a sort of "boundary work." They asked me several times what anthropology and social research was about. We held conversations about the methods, the recording of interviews, and my field diary. Iván used to joke when people were chatting about water infrastructures: he would loudly scream "write that down" and point at me. Claudia admitted that she had secretly glanced at my field notes on the first day of my stay. She was afraid that I could be a covert state official reporting illicit connections to the pipeline.

Experts

Ciudad Blanca was not my only field site; I built a wide network of contacts with politicians, state officials, and engineers. I interviewed employees and consultants at the Sociedad de Acueducto y Alcantarillado de Buenaventura (SAAB), Hidropacífico, ASIB, and PTSP. I also interviewed prominent social leaders from the Comité del Paro (the Strike Committee). I took meetings with senior state officials of the Ministry of Housing, City, and Territory (Minvivienda), visited the offices of the municipality several times, and was invited to meetings and construction sites. In addition, I visited the headquarters of the PTSP in Bogotá.

My interviews with these people were generally highly formal and developed in a professional setting, mediated through the habitus of expertise. They were held mostly in restaurants, offices, or hotel lounges. However, I followed the recommendations of Boyer to "humanize" experts by "engaging the non-professional" (2008, 44). Boyer notes that an anthropology of experts should inquire into the (private) social worlds of experts, and not rest solely in the discourses of expertise and the object of inquiry. In this sense, I learned from the mestizo experts about their long stays in Buenaventura as trained engineers from Bogotá and Medellín. They complained about the humidity and the constant rain, shared their discomforts, and openly expressed their racial prejudices. Some of them stated that things will never change with "these people here" and that they did not feel comfortable at all living in such an "uncivilized" city.

On the other side, ASIB experts, born and raised in Buenaventura and its surroundings, defined themselves in ethnic terms as Afro-Colombians. While some of them have moved to other cities to find jobs, they maintain a close relationship with political leaders and activists in the city and engage in institutions and projects regarding water infrastructure. As I show in chapter 1, these experts borrow from discourses of social and ethnic movements to develop a political standpoint in the conflict of deficient water supply. During interviews, they claimed to *know* things better than external experts, noting that "hacer ingeniería" (doing engineering) was only possible if you knew the territory firsthand. These local experts were more willing to support my research and were flexible and reliable when it came to arranging interviews. They talked openly about their private lives and careers, but refused to invite me to their neighborhoods because of security issues.

Óscar, one of the leading members of ASIB, told me that he and his colleagues would help me to gather important data and expected, in return, that I would write papers that would contribute to the improvement of water infrastructures in the city. Most of them wanted me as a scholar to witness and learn firsthand the course things were taking in the port city in terms of infrastructure. After leaving the city in February 2020, I kept contact with members of ASIB via WhatsApp. They sent me invitations to online seminars organized by both the association and social leaders, and we arranged online focus group interviews.

Two prominent social leaders and members of the Strike Committee gave me several interviews. From them, I learned the history of the Comité por la Defensa del Agua y la Vida en Buenaventura (Committee for the Defense of Water and Life in Buenaventura), to which they belong. They also taught me a lot about social mobilization in Buenaventura. In chapter 2, I discuss the role social activists and local experts play as key actors in the political negotiations around the provision of public goods.

Other ethnographies on the Colombian state are based on fieldwork experiences within institutions (e.g., Pellegrino 2022; Burnyeat 2022; Vera 2017). My experience as a researcher from outside had a mixed effect on my data gathering. Whereas I could not gain insight into the everyday procedures of the institutions and its actors, I was able to interview different state officials and social activists while maintaining neutrality as a researcher. As it happened, this offered valuable insights; given that interinstitutional and personnel conflict contribute to the politics of water infrastructure in Buenaventura, I would not have been able to have the open discussions and dialogues that I had if I had been part of a state institution.

During the course of my fieldwork, I spent my days between the municipality buildings, restaurants, and hotels in the city center on the Isla de Cascajal or in Ciudad Blanca, where I stayed during most of my time in Buenaventura. Almost every day I wore loose-fitting shorts and T-shirts to help Claudia at the hardware shop. For the meetings, I put on a linen shirt and pants with leather shoes and took a taxi or a *pirata* with air conditioning to go from Ciudad Blanca to the city center. Late afternoon, I would take notes in a fancy café located in a recreational park recently built on the seaside from which people were evicted years ago.

Infrastructural Violence

When interviewing politicians and social leaders in the city center, mostly during lunches or official meetings, they warned me to stay away from neighborhoods like Ciudad Blanca, mainly due to "security issues." Although I knew that I was somewhat exposed to violence, I broadly ignored this advice. I could not imagine learning about the city only from the technocratic view of state officials or the politicized discourses of social leaders. I was seeking the morphologies and rhythms of everyday experiences amid deficient water infrastructures.

The very first day of my stay in Ciudad Blanca, Claudia told me that a body had been found near the hardware shop. It was found in front of a house rented by an NGO, fronted by a mural depicting the cultural and natural diversity of the Pacific. Day after day, stories of homicides, extortions, and forced disappearances became more frequent. Like many other shopkeepers in Buenaventura, Claudia was being periodically extorted. I also heard gunshots during my first week there. Young men installed illegal road tolls to collect money from cars and motorcycles. The police appeared occasionally, and Claudia chatted with them via WhatsApp to share pictures of the young men she thought were responsible for violent acts in the neighborhood. In chapter 3, I address the everyday violence in the neighborhood and the coping mechanisms Claudia deployed to protect the shop and herself from extortion.

Although my research was not primarily focused on violence, I started to record in my diary my everyday experiences with crime. Crime talk was omnipresent. People's daily chats were often directed toward making sense of violent events. Claudia told me one day that she was thinking about raising prices once again because of extortion. I started wondering whether these two phenomena, violence and infrastructure, could be in some way related. I decided to systematically gather material around everyday crime and began recording stories of violence as well.

My hunch was soon confirmed. As I spoke with a social leader in December 2019 about violence and infrastructure, he stressed that the two main rationales for the massive mobilizations in the 2010s, including the general strike, were the precarious infrastructures of water supply and the frightening increase in violence. "The city has grown in a disorganized manner. There is less planning and highly deficient infrastructures of water supply," he said. "And violence is everywhere, you know. They seemed to be two unrelated things [water supply and violence], but they are the consequence of bad planning, particular interests of capital and state abandonment."

This book explores the interweaving and overlapping of these two phenomena as well as the mechanisms deployed by social movements and ordinary people to cope with them. I adopt a twofold understanding of violence. On the one hand, I address the deficient water supply system as a form of (infra)structural violence inflicted by the state on marginalized urban subjects. On the other hand, I examine how everyday crime (in the form of violence) affects the circulation and commercialization of commodities which are crucial for the construction of water storage systems by locals in the face of deficient networked infrastructures. Furthermore, I interpret the construction, maintenance, and expansion of these storage systems as a sociomaterial strategy to cope with infrastructural violence.

Structure of the Book

This book is divided into two parts. Part I approaches the politics of water infrastructures through the lens of state-led development projects and social movements. It offers a macro-level perspective of what is happening in terms of water supply in the city by broadly drawing from ethnographic data and archival work. The infrastructures for the provision of public services in Buenaventura have become a political matter of concern in the last decades, turning into a highly visible object of discussion in both the public sphere and within state institutions. Moreover, social movements and local actors have become key to the processes of struggle and negotiation revolving around this issue.

Chapter 1 traces a recent history of Buenaventura, mainly focusing on the politics of infrastructure and violence. I illustrate the political, social, and economic morphology of the city in recent decades, marked by neoliberal rule, violence, migration, and social mobilization. I then demonstrate how institutional weakness and forms of state-organized abandonment have led to these precarious ways of inhabiting the city. The chapter provides context while presenting an interpretation of the city that underpins the overarching argument of this book.

Chapter 2 examines the Plan Todos Somos PAZcífico as a state effort to improve the water infrastructures of the city. I consider the formal intra-institutional dynamics, funding patterns, and implementation plans, as well as at the everyday practices of meetings, knowledge production, and conflicts. I approach the experts of the PTSP in their nonprofessional realms and address their prejudices, personal opinions, and perspectives on these conflicts. The argument I develop here revolves around the noncompliance of the Colombian state since the goals stated by the plan have not been reached.

Chapter 3 explores the discourses of social movements and local experts in Buenaventura, as well as their interaction. By looking at the ASIB as well as the Comité del Paro, I approach the articulation of locally rooted political standpoints regarding water infrastructures and violence in the city. I trace a brief history of the movement and show how technical and expert knowledge, social mobilization and ethnicity are tightly interwoven. Furthermore, the chapter demonstrates the concomitant appearance of deficient water infrastructures and violence in the political discourses that unfolded in the 2010s, which have been critical to developing the argument of this book.

In part II, I zoom in to the neighborhood of Ciudad Blanca. The ethnographic narrative aims to reconstruct the "texture of hardship" (Newman and Massengill 2006) by examining everyday life amid (infrastructural) violence. The hardware shop where I conducted fieldwork and worked as an assistant served as a vantage point from which I could identify and analyze the social and material dynamics of the neighborhood.

Furthermore, I explore the coping mechanisms deployed by urban sub-jects as technologies of inhabiting the barrio.

Chapter 4 addresses the construction, maintenance, and repair of water storage systems in Ciudad Blanca. Due to the interrupted water supply service, inhabitants throughout the city improvise small-scale infrastructures to store water and fill the temporal gap of nonsupply. Al-though the systems create an appearance of constant water supply, they are highly unstable and prone to breaking due to the materials used, the construction practices, and the extreme weather conditions.

Chapter 5 deals with extortion as a form of everyday crime. Everyday crime, particularly extortion, in Ciudad Blanca shapes the social and eco-nomic dynamics in the neighborhood. I argue that everyday crime and the shape of violence in Ciudad Blanca alter sociomaterial practices as well as trust networks, further affecting the flows of water.

Parts I and II represent different approaches not only in terms of scale and scope. As I show throughout the book, the field sites I have con-structed and studied are tightly interwoven. The ethnographic narrative I develop navigates different registers and artifacts, such as (oral) archives, memories, everyday conversations, jokes, formal interviews, and offi-cial documents and reports. Further, it aims to condense a phenomenon which fundamentally shapes the lives and rhythms of citizens, politi-cians, and social activists alike.

I include small, biographical vignettes of some of my interlocutors in between the chapters. These narrative portraits aim to pull the reader into the lived experiences of the people I met in Buenaventura, whose stories are highly marked by harm, violence, and precarity, but also driven by aspirations, beauty, and survival. These short biographies are inspired by Taussig's brilliant book *My Cocaine Museum*, which depicts life stories of people from the rural Pacific.

PART I

CHAPTER 1

An Ethnographic Approach
to Buenaventura

In 2013 Medellín, one of Colombia's main cities, was selected by the
Urban Land Institute as the most innovative city in the world. In the
following years, the city was awarded another two international prizes
for urban innovation, and it even hosted the UN-Habitat's 7th World
Urban Forum in 2014. Representations of Medellín in the media and
elsewhere created a narrative of a city that had allegedly overcome dark
times of poverty, violence, and inequality. Through assertive leadership,
skilled technocracy, and growing investment, the story went, municipal
administration and the private sector transformed the urban landscape
and dynamics of Medellín, enabling connectivity, offering opportunities for the urban poor, and fostering the empowerment of citizens. Indeed, Medellín's urban development has been showcased as an example
demonstrating that cities of the Global South could effectively transform
and become inclusive, sustainable, and productive while overcoming
inequality, unruliness, and insecurity (see Garcia Ferrari et al. 2018).

In the same decade, another Colombian city drew the attention of
national media and public policy institutions. In this case, the representations were not quite so positive. Narratives and images of horrific
violence, dispossession, and underdevelopment sought to capture the

everyday life of suffering urbanites in Buenaventura (figure 1).[1] Indeed, the port city, located in the southwestern Colombian Pacific and with a population of around forty-three thousand inhabitants, has throughout history been closely associated with urban dystopia. Planning and state intervention broadly failed, mainly due to corruption and mismanagement, according to journalists and politicians.

Such representations point to state abandonment as a cause of this wretched state of affairs. At the same time, local administrators are blamed for corruption and their alleged inability to properly govern. However, the proliferation of crime and the deficient provision of public goods were (and still are) seen as the two key crises of governance in the city. Alke Jenss (2020) argues that media and state narratives alike depict impoverished inhabitants in Buenaventura as an Other to the successful and steadily growing port economy. She contends that these characterizations of Buenaventura as a "badland" carry political consequences. Thus, negative representations of the port city have enabled the articulation of "discursive-spatial strategies which help governing social inequality through *racialized othering*" (Jenss 2020, 2, emphasis mine). Indeed, urban redevelopment attempts such as the ones contained within the Buenaventura Master Plan 2050 (2015), a development plan formulated for the city, propose to transform it by means of technocratic engineering, prioritizing the expansion of the port, and widely ignoring the everyday experiences of its people.

Cities in Colombia have been historically associated with urban dystopia. Only recently have urban centers such as Medellín been approached as laboratories of innovation in the context of emergent narratives of a "nationwide urban regeneration" (Zeiderman 2018, 6). Indeed, some cities in the Global South have been increasingly apprehended by Northern urban development agendas as hubs of (mostly privately led) innovation. Yet many others are still broadly depicted in pathological terms, pointing

---

1. See, for example, "Buenaventura, entre la pobreza y la violencia," *El Espectador*, February 23, 2013; "El salvaje Oeste de Colombia," *Revista Semana*, February 9, 2013; "Buenaventura, la 'joya' que se disputan las bandas criminals," *Vanguardia*, January 21, 2013; "Buenaventura: Entre la opulencia y la miseria," *El Tiempo*, July 30, 2015; "La pesadilla de la violencia en Buenaventura," *Verdad Pacífico*, March 9, 2014; "Buenaventura desmembrada," *Las dos Orillas*, November 13, 2014.

mainly to their lack of "proper" government and the deviations from ideal patterns of development reified by both Western cities and urban theory (Robinson 2002). African cities such as Lagos and Kinshasa have stood as global symbols of urban chaos, dysfunction, and mismanagement (Gandy 2008; De Boeck and Plissart 2014). Within this context, neocolonial imaginations are reinforced, while the embeddedness of these urban centers in an unequal global political economy as well as their imperial pasts remain nearly invisible (Roy 2011; Schindler 2017). Both anthropologists and urban scholars have critically engaged with these representations and have sought to contest and decolonize geographical imaginations revolving around the urban question.

In this chapter, I address the sociomaterial and political context of violence and water supply in Buenaventura. More than merely reconstructing hard facts and statistics, I approach the context as a hermeneutical tool to approach my object of inquiry. The state apparatus addresses water supply and violence as different domains of technocracy, namely as matter of infrastructure development on the one hand and security on the other. Here, I aim to look at the intersections. By engaging with the history of these two phenomena I elucidate how flows of violence and water intersect in the city: how the deprivation of public goods and the proliferation of everyday crime are the consequence of a political agenda guided by underinvestment, abandonment, lack of transparency, and neocolonial urban planning. The sources I critically engage with here (from reports and laws to interviews and fieldnotes) serve as a starting point to condense a narrative and set up a framework within which the arguments of this book unfold.

Moreover, I seek to weave a narrative that goes beyond romanticized representations on Afro-Colombian communities and social mobilization while avoiding and contesting pathological accounts. Indeed, infrastructural breakdown, everyday crime, and poverty are conspicuous realities in the city, not mere products of representation. Nonetheless, I highlight the everyday strategies and narratives deployed by urban subjects in encountering and navigating their difficult lifeworlds, as well as their "ways of thinking, feeling and acting that increase the horizon of hope" amid precarity (Appadurai 2013, 295; see Harvey 2000).

In Buenaventura, ordinary people and social activists weave discourses on the urban in different registers. While the latter act as key actors in offering critique and articulating politicized discourses of change, the former develop inconsistent, and sometimes contradictory and cumbersome, accounts that seek to give sense to their everyday experiences amid violence and the deprivation of public goods. However, many social activists are (or have been) ordinary, nonprivileged inhabitants of the city and know firsthand what sociologists Katherine Newman and Rebekah Peeples Massengill (2006) call "the texture of hardship." Here, I aim to bring together the narratives of these two different groups of actors. Although I engage mostly with narratives of social suffering, my ethnographic account resonates with what Joel Robbins calls an "anthropology of the good," the purpose of which is to "explore the different ways people organize their personal and collective lives in order to foster what they think of as good, and to study what it is like to live at least some of the time in light of such a project" (2013, 457).

The ethnographic narrative I present here is an interpretation of different accounts of the city (including my own field experience) and hence draws on several sources. I critically engage with accounts presented by state institutions and NGOs such as urban plans, reports, and laws. I also use my field experience and the interviews I carried out with local actors. Ultimately, I aim to contest "badland" representations of the port city.

Buenaventura: An Urban Hub in the Colombian Pacific

Buenaventura is located in southwestern Colombia, in the Pacific region, a historical and biogeographic strip extending from the border to Panama in the north to the Ecuadorian frontier in the south. On the western side, the region borders the Pacific Ocean, while it is delimited in the east by the Andean Mountain range. The Colombian Pacific is a highly biodiverse rainforest region, crossed by a myriad of rushing rivers and populated by rich flora and fauna (Oslender 2002; Offen 2003; Hoffmann 2007; Taussig 2004; Tubb 2020; Molano 2017; Restrepo 2013). Historically speaking, the region marks a so-called internal frontier of the Colombian nation-state. Internal frontiers have been represented since Spanish colonial times as impenetrable spaces of alterity, unsuitable to mestizo settler colonization and marked by harsh natural environments and hostile Indigenous communities. While the country's epicenters were geographically located in the Caribbean and Andean regions, these frontiers were deemed savage and nondomesticable, remaining at the margins of the national project of government and modernization.

Although the allegedly impenetrable nature of regions like the Colombian Pacific precluded mestizo settlement processes, that did not stop economic elites from establishing systems of extractive economy, in form of enclaves, as occurred in other frontier regions such as the Amazon. In the Pacific region, commodities like gold and timber were (and still are) broadly exploited (Taussig 2004; Tubb 2020; Leal 2018; Molano 2017). The labor in the mines during colonial times was mainly supplied by enslaved subjects, while economic elites from distant cities in the interior, such as Cali, Medellín, and Popayán, accumulated wealth. After independence in 1810 and the abolition of slavery in 1852, the exploitation of natural resources partially declined in the region. The freed Black population remained in the territory, living to a large extent beyond state regulation. In independent Colombia, attempts to either colonize or modernize the Pacific were broadly unsuccessful (Leal 2018).

The partial isolation and marginalization of the region notwithstanding, political and economic ties with the interior existed throughout the nineteenth and twentieth century. Three urban hubs rose as nodal points for commerce and government: Quibdó, Tumaco, and Buenaventura (see map 1). These were spaces planned and governed by mestizo colonizers and discursively represented as islands of civilization amid the "savagery" and the "unruliness" of the rainforest. Economic prosperity depended on the surrounding economies and the price of the exploited commodities, as Leal (2018) shows in the case of Tumaco and Quibdó. Rural–urban migration by former enslaved communities intensified during the twentieth century. In the case of Buenaventura, the completion of a railroad connecting the village with the interior of the country in 1915, as well as the modernization and expansion of the port from the 1940s onward, led to waves of migration as newcomers from the rural surroundings settled in the city and looked for employment (CNMH 2015, 120–50; Moreno Monroy 2013, 9–28)

Throughout the second half of the twentieth century, the city partly modernized, expanding the port infrastructures, and hosting migrants coming from rural areas year after year. However, city planning and public infrastructures were conceived not for the incoming population but

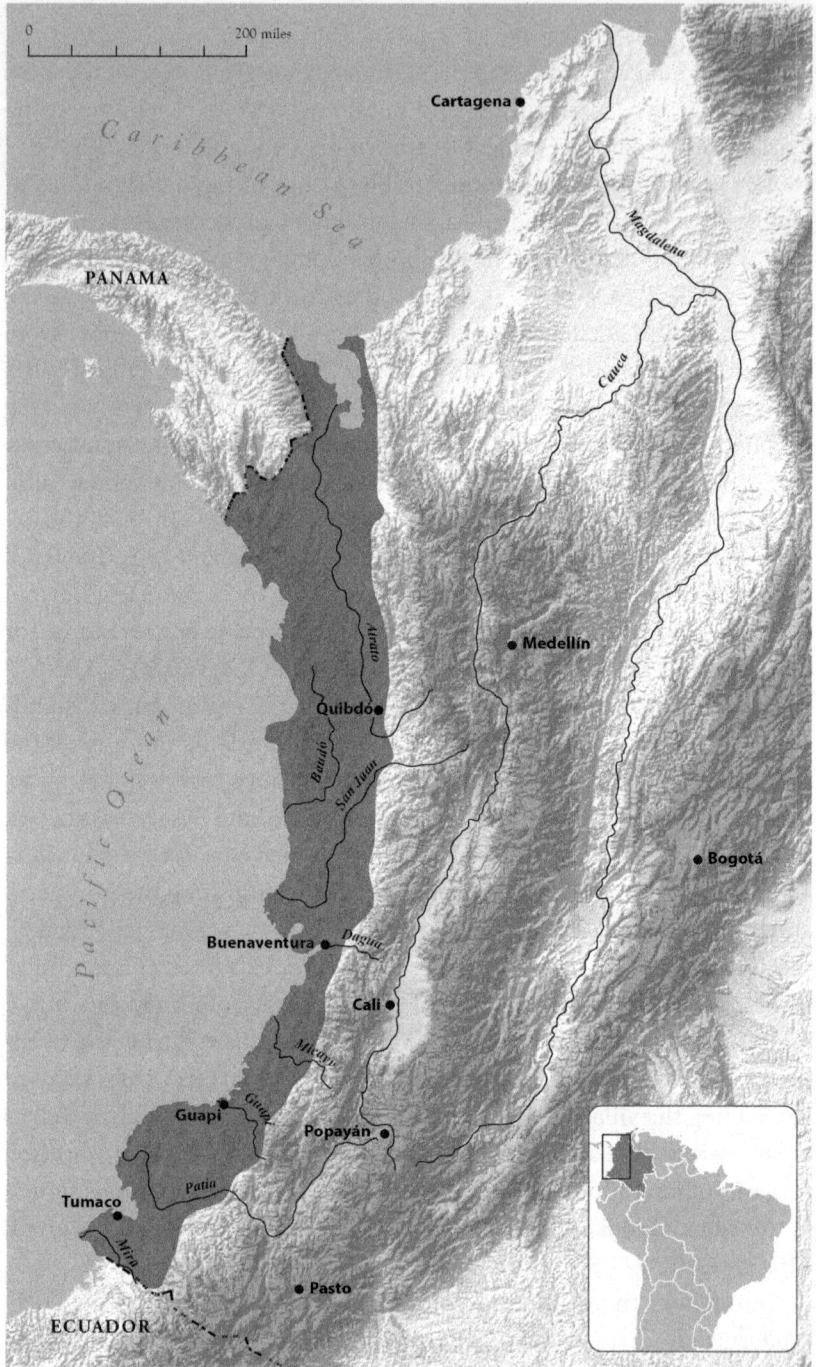

MAP 1 Colombia, with the Pacific region highlighted

for the port and a small mestizo and white elite. Although not legally framed or officially planned as such, the city was highly marked by racial segregation.

Toward the end of the century, the region experienced a turning point in terms of political and economic relations, making things for inhabitants even worse. One reason was the rapid expansion of the internal armed conflict and illicit economies into the region; the other was the liberalization of the economy and the subsequent wave of privatizations. Buenaventura grew rapidly during the 1990s and the first decade of the 2000s, hosting thousands of internally displaced persons after violence increased in the region. Consequently, poverty skyrocketed while state assistance for the displaced communities remained scarce, fostering informal urbanization.

Violence started to unfold as the FARC (Fuerzas Armadas Revolucionarias de Colombia, Revolutionary Armed Forces of Colombia), the leftist guerrilla, entered the territory in the 1980s looking for regions that had been abandoned by the state to build camps and establish illicit economies such as mining, smuggling, and drug trafficking. In the 1990s, the 30th Front, a military unit of the FARC, took over large parts of the rural and urban areas of Buenaventura, threatening local commerce and the economies of the port through kidnapping, extortion, and selective assassinations. Most of the *guerrilleros* were recruited among young men from the rural communities and were dispersed in small villages and camps along the rivers of the region. By the end of the 1990s, regional elites and some sectors of the armed forces requested the leaders of right-wing Autodefensas Unidas de Colombia (United Self-Defenses of Colombia, or AUC) paramilitaries build an anti-subversive block in order to regain control over the region (CNMH 2015, 60–70). Investigations by NGOs and human rights organizations have even demonstrated the active participation of the Colombian armed forces in the actions taken by paramilitaries. Several massacres were perpetrated by these groups in the rural Pacific from 2000 on, causing mass waves of displacement.[2]

---

2. According to the Centro Nacional de Memoria Histórica, between 1990 and 2013, twenty-six massacres took place in the rural and urban areas of Buenaventura (though only one of these took place in the 1990s). Between 1990 and 2014, 152,837 persons were forcibly displaced in the *municipio* of Buenaventura (CNMH 2015, 213).

At the same time, paramilitary armed groups took over illicit economies, which massively expanded during that time, pouring into the urban areas of Buenaventura.

By 2004 the first government of former President Álvaro Uribe (2002–2010) signed a peace agreement with the AUC, which brought about the dismantling of this umbrella paramilitary organization and a (partial) demobilization of mercenaries. Even though the organization's structures were partially dissolved, the "paramilitary phenomenon" did not vanish. New criminal organizations took over the region, leading to novel, murky patterns of violence and terror. The *bacrim* represented a sort of atomization of the former AUC, confronting each other to gain control over the territory and illicit economies. While displacement from the urban areas decreased a little, urban settlements were caught up in multiple cycles of violence due to disputes over territory and drug trafficking routes (Human Rights Watch 2014).

The increase in violence had a great impact on the social and political dynamics of the city, but economic liberalization also contributed. The 1991 Colombian constitution paved the way for new economic paradigms, leading to several privatizations of former state-owned companies. In 1993 Colpuertos, the company responsible for the administration of the harbors in Colombia, was fully privatized. In Buenaventura, Sociedad Portuaria de Buenaventura, a private company, was constituted to take over the operation of the port. This unleashed a transformation in labor relations in the city, leading to cost-cutting by means of the mass dismissal of port employees and the dismantling of the workers union, which had been a very important institution until then. Moreover, the rapid growth of the port economies and infrastructures was critical to the new urban development patterns that emerged. However, the enormous economic profit of the growing port did not have a positive impact on the city. Instead, it deepened the disentanglement between urban citizens and the port economies. Besides violence, the privatization of the port worsened the situation of Buenaventura's ordinary citizens. While urban development was mainly focused on the port economies, unemployment and rates of violence skyrocketed over the course of the following years. For this reason, grassroots organizations and social activists have referred to the city as "un puerto sin comunidad" (a port without community; CNMH 2015; Bonet-Morón et al. 2018; Jaramillo et al. 2020).

In parallel to the rise of violence and privatization of the 1990s, ethnic and social mobilization strengthened. In this particular case, social struggle unfolded in the context of a new global agenda on multiculturalism. The Colombian nation was constitutionally declared as multiethnic in 1991, legally recognizing the existence of Indigenous and Afro-Colombian communities and bringing about new political subjectivities (Restrepo 2013; Offen 2003; Asher 2009; Cárdenas 2023). In 1993 Ley 70 (Law 70) guaranteed Afro-Colombian communities a series of rights such as political representation and collective land tenure. Community councils (*consejos comunitarios*) emerged as new ethnic-governmental unities holding so-called collective territories, land forest areas conceded by the state. In these territories, the exploitation of natural resources became strongly regulated by the state, at least formally (Tubb 2020). Large-scale agricultural projects as well as industrial mining and fishing have been, with a few exceptions, forbidden de jure. Economic practices labeled "traditional" and "sustainable," such as artisanal fishing, were encouraged and even financed by state institutions and development plans (Restrepo 2013).

The global agenda on multiculturalism and the recognition of ethnic minorities overlapped with the political agenda on environmental protection. The deeply political concepts of 'biodiversity' and 'ethnicity' shaped a conservation agenda toward the region (Asher and Ojeda 2009; Escobar 2008). In fact, the development projects that emerged during the 1990s regarding the Pacific, and hence in the context of this new multicultural paradigm, were mainly based on principles of environmental protection and sustainability. The recognition of Afro-Colombians as new political subjects produced "spaces of alterity" in the Pacific region, which sought to guarantee the protection of the environment by fostering an "alternative development" based on traditional and local economic activities with low impact on the environment (Restrepo 2013; Escobar 2008).

Drawing on this environmental protection legislation and the new political paradigm of minorities, ethnic activist groups proliferated. The new multicultural agenda led these groups to articulate their demands in the new legal language of the state. The more visible ethnic activism had mainly been located in the urban areas of the Pacific and the interior alike and was led by both an Afro-Colombian intellectual elite—widely inspired by the civil rights movement in the United States—and worker unions. Yet during the 1970s and 1980s Black peasant and Indigenous movements as well as the Catholic church had created platforms for organization and political articulation, as Restrepo (2013) has shown. Indeed, they fostered the formulation of Ley 70 and the politics on Afro-Colombian minorities, directed at rural communities.

Throughout the 1990s and the first decade of the 2000s, activist groups such as the Proceso de Comunidades Negras focused on strengthening local communities in order to promote community councils and the land titling of "collective territories." Furthermore, these activist groups denounced the rise in violence and mass displacement and pointed to the contradiction between a new political agenda directed toward minorities and the increasing harm experienced by Afro-Colombian communities as the result of violence and the proliferation of armed actors and illicit economies in their territories during these decades. Aiming at calling attention the precarious living conditions of urban Black communities, the Proceso de Comunidades Negras has labeled Black displaced peasants *comunidades afro-urbanas*.

Besides ethnic activism, urban political mobilization has been key to the political landscape of the southwestern Pacific throughout the second half of the twentieth century. Social movements have formed in the port city since the 1960s; for instance, in 1964 and 1998, general strikes took place in the city (Jaramillo et al. 2020). However, in the 2010s, a series of protests took place in Buenaventura that marked a new era of mobilization. Due to the massive displacement from rural areas into cities, the precarious provision of public goods and the increasing violence at the beginning of the decade, in 2009 a broad alliance of left-wing social activists encompassing mainly unionists and ethnic social leaders created the Comité Interorganizacional (Interorganizational Committee) as a new platform for urban social mobilization. From 2013 onwards, a series of protests including marches and street blockades took place throughout the port city. Despite the efforts made by the first government of former President Juan Manuel Santos (2010–2014) to improve security policy and formulate a new development agenda for Buenaventura, the situation for large parts of the population did not improve. An example of these efforts was the Plan Todos Somos PAZcífico, a well-funded infrastructure project designed to build new water infrastructures and guarantee the provision of water supply in Buenaventura and other cities in the region, which was launched in 2014 (see chapter 2).

In 2017 social activists organized a general strike in the city. Thousands of people blocked the port entrance for twenty-two days, impeding its normal operation and causing huge economic losses for the private sector. Negotiations between the government and a strike committee were set up and led to an agreement, in which the state committed to create a special development fund directed to the city (Fonbuenaventura) and to design new policy strategies to achieve the provision of public goods such as water, health care, and education (Jaramillo et al. 2020, Manos Visibles 2017; Lombard et al. 2021; Jenss 2021).

At the time of this writing, however, the state has not delivered on its promises. Despite the announcement made by President Santos himself in 2014 that Buenaventura could expect a proper water supply system within two years, things have not improved significantly. Moreover, rates of violence did not decrease. In consequence, several disputes have arisen between social activists and the central government due to the failure to implement the accord. The development agenda of right-wing President Iván Duque (2018–2022) did not dismantle the funds and policies his predecessor had created to address the problems in the region. However, conflicts between activists and the central state have widely deepened. During my fieldwork in 2019, social leader and Strike Committee member Víctor Hugo Vidal was elected mayor of the city through his movement Buenaventura con Dignidad (Buenaventura with Dignity), allowing the social movement to participate in local government. The election of Vidal has offered a new platform for activists to articulate their demands to the central state.

In May 2021, amid the COVID-19 pandemic, which worsened the crisis of public goods delivery in Buenaventura, scarce rains and deficient infrastructures led to unusually large water shortages in the city (Acevedo 2021). At the time, a nationwide strike against police violence and the response of the government to the pandemic was taking place throughout Colombia. In Buenaventura, the port was partially blocked by a noncoordinated action of the Strike Committee. After some days, negotiations and a further agreement put an end to the blockade, and trucks distributed potable water to the neighborhoods. Furthermore, the sense of general chaos led to an increase in violence in the form of plundering and selective assassinations. Mayor Vidal even stated that the city was about to collapse entirely.

Water Supply in the Badland

In Buenaventura, much like the case explored by Uribe (2017) in Putumayo, people make sense of precarious infrastructures as forms of state abandonment. Deficient water infrastructures in an urban hub located in the Pacific region exemplify these sociomaterial processes enmeshed in discourses of exception, alterity, and violence. The press and state institutions alike broadly depict Buenaventura as a badland—a space imbued with the ills of poverty, violence, suffering and infrastructural breakdown, as Jenss (2020) points out (see chapter 2 herein). Dusty unpaved streets, crumbling pipelines, houses made of wood and roofs of zinc, building facades riddled with moisture, and tangled electrical wires portray the "nonfunctioning" and "backwardness" of a city where mass graves and torture houses can be found.

In fact, the history of Buenaventura's water infrastructure is a history of institutional weakness and underinvestment. Despite the city's rapid growth in the 1950s and 1960s, the aqueduct built at the beginning of the century was not properly developed (Acevedo 2021). Moreover, the city did not have a municipality-level institution to build and maintain infrastructures; it instead depended on a regional institutional arrangement to construct and manage aqueducts of mainly rural towns. Throughout the second half of the twentieth century, as one social leader told me, urbanites improvised water access through sources such as rivers and illicit connections to the main pipeline.

Since the 1990s the state has led (failed) attempts to improve the water infrastructure networks. For instance, in 1997 a Water and Sewer Master Plan for Buenaventura was formulated. The municipality pursued repair works with special funds provided by the central state to *finally* provide water to the population (Consejo Nacional de Política Económica y Social 2015). Yet these works were not completed due to a lack of funds and mismanagement. At the same time, a policy for the privatization of public service provision systems was implemented throughout the country. While infrastructures remained public, the operation of (and profits from) the system was broadly privatized (Guerrero et al. 2016). Indeed, a national law in 1994 (Ley 142) encouraged municipalities to privatize their water supply systems. Hidropacífico, a consortium of two firms based in the country's interior, won the tender to operate Buenaventura's water supply system for twenty years, from 2001 to 2021. This period was characterized by a demographic increase due to migration and mass displacement, as well as an escalation in violence. The SAAB, also founded in 2001, was the municipal institution responsible for overseeing the fulfillment of the signed contract between the municipality and Hidropacífico. Repair and maintenance work was to be executed and funded by both the municipality and the firm. However, several conflicts between the two institutions arose, leaving many important works undone. Hidropacífico was sharply criticized by both social leaders and local state officials for its cost-cutting measures in relation to the maintenance and expansion of water infrastructures.

Although my work concentrates on contemporary Buenaventura, where neoliberalism has profoundly influenced the political agendas on security and infrastructures, I do not argue that deregulation and privatization have been the sole reason for the deficient water infrastructures and provision of public goods. Responding to a global trend, the privatization of water supply was meant to improve the system by implementing knowledge and managerial practices developed within the private sector and in the face of the precarious provision of water (Bakker 2014). The fact that the provision did not improve significantly is certainly due in part to the profit-led practices of the consortium, which mainly focused on cost recovery, while infrastructures remained leaky and thus highly deficient. Hotels and the port itself were prioritized, while large parts of the city did not have proper access to water. Nevertheless, the state invested large amounts of money to improve the city's public infrastructures. Even though the state fostered the privatization of the system's operation, it did not fully withdraw from its responsibility to construct and maintain public infrastructures (Mains 2019). In fact, Buenaventura has undergone a series of "institutional experiments" to fund, develop, and improve water infrastructures (Fredericks 2018, 13).

The most recent and important of these state efforts is the Plan Todos Somos PAZcífico, launched in 2014. The political agenda of former President Juan Manuel Santos (2010–2018) considered the Pacific region a priority. In 2014 his government created an institutional unity within the presidency (Gerencia del Pacífico) whose main task was to formulate development plans on the Pacific. This initiative was driven by the social unrest that had taken place in the port city since the early 2010s and the alarming reports on violence and poverty that both international NGOs and national institutions had issued (see Human Rights Watch 2012; Taula Catalana 2016; CNMH 2015).

The PTSP was funded by loans from the World Bank and the Inter American Development Bank and executed by the central government, which framed it as a "state intervention." Its main goal was to build new infrastructures such as a main pipeline in the city and water tanks, as well as to repair the existing infrastructures. The institutional arrangement conceived to maintain and build water infrastructures—which had until then been limited to the SAAB and Hidropacífico—could now rely on another key and well-funded institution. Notwithstanding these efforts to construct the megaprojects, diverse institutional, managerial, and personal conflicts have impeded the timely fulfillment of the stated goals (chapter 2). Between 2018 and 2019, two water tanks were constructed on the eastern side of the city. Although not yet connected to the system, they were highly visible and served as a material symbol of state intervention. A huge billboard was erected next to the tanks announcing the presence of PTSP and describing the goals and timelines of the construction works. Acknowledging the partial progress of these construction works, state promises of constant water supply remain unfulfilled, while several conflicts have arisen.

I claim that the "organized abandonment" of the state, materialized in the ever-deficient water infrastructures and the precarious water supply, is interwoven with a phenomenon of state practice in Colombia, which anthropologist Valentina Pellegrino brilliantly describes as "complying incompliantly":

> Complying incompliantly is a type of governmental response to a problem that it is responsible for solving. It consists of the government ostensibly acting like it is solving a problem without these actions solving anything, and yet having the response favorably evaluated. Relative success is not related to solving the issue but to attaining appeasement. This is accomplished by creating a physical record of work presented using a language

and format known to be approved for monitored evaluations. (Pellegrino 2022, 80)

While Pellegrino addresses governmental responses to evaluations made by the judiciary such as the Colombian Constitutional Court, I point to the arrangement of representations and materialities of infrastructure that manifest themselves as construction sites, figures, timetables, decrees, speeches, and meetings, and serve to widely demonstrate the compliance of development plans (or at least the efforts made by the state) while failing to attain its goals. Representational forms of infrastructure have been addressed in anthropology by pointing to the myriad of artifacts (documents, reports, and figures) to which infrastructures are transposed and embodied (Larkin 2013, 335; Lea and Pholeros 2010). In turn, these artifacts ensemble representations which, as a whole, materialize evidence of compliance, while the goal of proper water supply is not achieved.

I contend that the noncompliance of the Colombian state sustains and reproduces infrastructural violence in the port city. The presence and mobilization of resources by the state through the PTSP well depicts what Uribe (2019) calls a relationship of "inclusive exclusion": a double movement through which state presence is precariously produced but that in fact reaffirms a form of absence. Violence is reenacted when the state cannot keep its promises and fails to achieve development goals, leaving the population without a proper supply of water. Infrastructural violence is thus materialized not merely in the city's leaky and deficient water infrastructures but also in the failed projects and the representations of apparent compliance.

When I confronted PTSP officials with the delays of the project, they pointed to the project's successes and showed me photos and figures as evidence. I insisted that the goals stated by the project were widely unmet, referring to the project plans and reports. They answered by pointing to the alleged local mismanagement and conflicts with social activists and engineers in Buenaventura. These mestizo state officials, employed by PTSP through the central government and based in Bogotá, stressed several times that "it's hard to work with people there," referring to racialized political actors and engineers from Buenaventura, reproducing images of unruliness and underdevelopment. Chapter 2 closely explores the discourses and practices of the project, traveling through the formal and informal domains that mold the state intervention.

Finding an (Oral) Archive

I first visited the public water management board SAAB in October 2018, looking for an archive I was told existed there that would be very useful for my research. There was little, if any, published literature on the history of the water infrastructures of the city. I was hoping to find key documents to at least roughly reconstruct the history of my ethnographic object, the city's water supply system. The SAAB is located in the principal building of Buenaventura's municipality, on Cascajal Island, in the very center of the city. The building's facade is covered by a huge and colorful mural representing the history and culture of Afro-Colombian and Indigenous communities, against the background of a rural landscape, colorful and quasi-magical. I met Mrs. Lara, the executive director of the SAAB, in her air-conditioned office on the eighth floor of the building. She, a middle-aged engineer, was one of the few non-Black persons working for the municipality, and one of the few women. During our brief but pleasant chat, she told me that she was the daughter of a Black woman and a mestizo father, born and raised in Buenaventura. Also, her thick Afro-Colombian accent was revealing. Among social activists and local experts, Mrs. Lara was perceived as a person *de aquí* (from here), whereas for the central state bureaucracies, she was rather a mestiza. This double racial identity puts her sometimes in very stressful situations, she playfully told me. "But, at the end, I am from here. I am half Black and I identify as Afro-Colombian," she stated. We drank a coffee while she briefly explained to me the technical conundrums the water infrastructures would put to engineers and urban planners. Then she stated that she would have to work, cordially introduced me to the institution's personnel, and offered to help me gather all the important information for my research. She finally led me to the small archive and offered to photocopy and scan any documents I considered useful for my research.

I was excited about the sources I would find in order to reconstruct the history of Buenaventura's water infrastructures. But once we entered the small, dusty room, I was disappointed. The archive was a mess. Unorganized folders were piled up in steel racks. I took a seat and randomly browsed through the documents, which were mainly legal and administrative. One of the main tasks of the SAAB was to oversee and track the terms of the contract signed between the municipality and the private operator of the water supply system, Hidropacífico. Indeed, most of the documents I encountered concerned delays in repair and maintenance works carried out by Hidropacífico. I returned to Mrs. Lara's office. She confirmed my suspicions that it would be nearly impossible to reconstruct the recent institutional history of the aqueduct by looking at the official documents of such an archive. She copied two important water management plans to my USB stick and gave me the phone number of a social leader, Nestor Romero, who, she told me, knew the history of the water supply in the port city very well.

A few days later, I met Nestor on the terrace of one of the biggest hotels in Buenaventura. Since social activists in Colombia are under constant threat of assassination, some of them—like Nestor—are accompanied by a bodyguard provided by the National Unit of Protection. The bodyguard took a seat at a table next to us. Nestor, like Mrs. Lara, is of Black and mestizo descent. He is in his mid-sixties and has an Afro-Colombian accent. We ordered coffee and I told Nestor about my project. He seemed very interested in my research and talked to me for more than two hours. His narrative navigated through political, technical, and academic domains. Nestor is not only an active and prominent member of Buenaventura's social activist groups and strike committees involved in the happenings of political struggle in the city; as Mrs. Lara had said, he is also an expert on the institutional history of water infrastructures in the city.

"The problem of water is infrastructural," he told me. He explained that the water sources that surround Buenaventura—at least eleven basins—would be sufficient to supply several megacities: "We could build infrastructures to have ten thousand liters per minute flowing through the pipes, can you believe that?" he said. "Instead, we have a water schedule to cope with low pressure caused by leaks. And on top of that, there are several households with no access to water. That is more than insane. The only reason to understand it is that the state is not interested in properly supplying water." He then added, quoting surveys conducted by important research institutions such as the Universidad Nacional (one of the most important universities in the country), that the quality of the surrounding water sources would be some of the best in Colombia, and even in the world. He went on to explain that the water infrastructures would work through gravity, since the water intake is located above the main pipelines. Motor pumps would not be needed for the system to function, which would significantly reduce the costs of operation. "We have optimal conditions: sufficient water sources, good water quality, suitable topology. The problem is the state," he asserted.

Nestor then started recounting the institutional history of the water infrastructures. At that point, the oral archive and the memory of an activist seemed to offer a much more comprehensive account given the lack of publications and the messiness of the archive at the SAAB and the municipality. I use Nestor's account to reconstruct an understudied research object. It is an ethnohistory since I approach it using the perspective of my interview partner. I later verified the key facts Nestor stated that sunny late afternoon on the hotel terrace, by reviewing governmental plans, newspaper articles, and the recent work of geographers Tatiana Acevedo Guerrero, Kathryn Furlong, and Jeimy Arias (2016), which all gave me important glimpses into this topic.[3]

A Brief History of Buenaventura's Water Infrastructures

In early independent Colombia, Buenaventura was a marginal settlement with almost no modern infrastructure. Throughout the nineteenth century, projects to expand road and railway infrastructures to the Pacific region in southwestern Colombia were conceived. The idea of expansion was bolstered by regional mestizo elites—mainly landowners who sought access to the Pacific Ocean and hence to global capital flows. The late nineteenth century saw the beginning of the construction of a railway system that would cross the Western Andean range and connect the Pacific region with the Cauca Valley. In her seminal work on the urban Pacific, Claudia Leal (2018) focuses on the urban centers of Tumaco and

---

3. I also reviewed the recently published essay by Tatiana Acevedo on the water infrastructures in Buenaventura (2021).

Quibdó. By the turn of the century, the city still played a subordinate role. She states:

> People familiar with the Pacific lowlands of Colombia might ask where the port of Buenaventura stands in this tale of emerging cities. At the turn of the nineteenth century, a unique dynamic brought this Pacific port to life. Unlike Tumaco and Quibdó, Buenaventura did not primarily export regional products; it exported coffee from the Andes and imported merchandise for western Colombia via the city of Cali. This port was an enclave, a warehouse for commodities coming into and out of the interior of the country. Its merchants belonged more to Cali than to the port. For these reasons, Buenaventura did not have as much of a local elite as Tumaco and Quibdó, and prior to 1930 it lagged behind them. Soon after, however, Buenaventura became the center of the Pacific coast and the largest city in the lowlands. (Leal 2018, 187)

To infrastructurally integrate the Pacific with the interior would allow connections to be made between international commerce and locally produced export commodities such as sugar and coffee (Nieto 2011). It was hoped that Buenaventura could become a counterweight to the existing ports of the Caribbean region (Moreno Monroy 2013). In 1915 the Cali–Buenaventura route opened after decades of construction. This coincided with the opening of the Panama Canal and with a resulting increase of shipping routes in the Pacific Ocean (Almario 2007). The emerging port infrastructures stood as a symbol of modernization and progress for the region and marked the beginning of Buenaventura's urban development.

Due to the demand of labor for the proliferating construction, as well as the hope for a better future, many Black peasants from the surrounding rural areas began to migrate to the city at that time. People lived in self-made wooden houses located mainly on Cascajal Island and had no networked water supply. "People went to *el chorro*, a stream running from the mountains, to collect water," Nestor told me. The railway company built a pipeline in 1905 to supply a small group of engineers and the steam engines of the trains. In the 1920s, alongside the construction of modern buildings in the city center and the demographic increase, three water tanks were installed in upper areas of the city. People went there to collect water for their households; only a few could connect to the network directly through the supply lines. Although an urbanization process was taking place around the railroad and the port, Afro-Colombian communities were largely excluded from urban development.

At the beginning of the twentieth century, water supply in Colombia was mainly sustained by private companies. Although a law in 1913 fostered the creation of public boards for the administration of certain public services, most municipalities lacked the funds to purchase existing private utilities. Only bigger cities such as Medellín and Bogotá could afford to create robust and independent public corporations to construct, expand, and operate infrastructural systems for public services supply (Furlong et al. 2016, 175–76). In the case of Buenaventura, the railroad company operated and maintained the water infrastructures until the 1950s. Meanwhile, the local municipal administration remained marginal and severely underfunded.

In 1950 the national government of Colombia founded the Municipal Development Institute (INFOSPAL). The main task of this key institution was to promote and oversee development plans and works for the several municipalities of the country. The creation of such an institution was aimed to strategically decentralize and modernize water supply systems throughout Colombia. INFOSPAL assisted the creation of regional public-owned consortia for the construction, expansion, and operation of the water supply systems at a regional level. However, there were many differences between an institution formed at a municipal scale and the regional consortium in terms of funding and expertise. While in cities such as Medellín and Bogotá the independent corporations could easily access public funds and expand the water infrastructures, other municipalities like Buenaventura depended on a regional institution with far less funding and experience.

In 1957 the national newspaper *El País* published an article on the city titled "Buenaventura Lacks Everything" ("Buenaventura necesita de todo") and listed the city's many problems: poor housing and sewage, electrical, and water infrastructures. Due to the increased activity and modernization of the port, even more people migrated from the rural communities, only to encounter highly deficient infrastructures for the supply of public goods. An assertive development agenda was urgently needed. However, the efforts of a group of congressmembers in 1958 to pass a law in the national parliament that aimed to create an independent regional corporation to foster the development of the city proved fruitless (see Moreno Monroy 2013; Díaz Vargas 2015).

Meanwhile, in 1959 a state-led company to administer all national ports was constituted: Colpuertos. In the same year, the public-owned consortium Acuavalle was founded by INFOSPAL and the regional government to promote and administer the water supply systems of the department Valle del Cauca, where Buenaventura is located. At the time, a new wave of migration due to the rapid expansion of the port impacted the demography of the city. "People settled down 'irregularly,' as the state likes to put it. With no urban planning and a concrete development concept for citizens, people moved from the rural areas to Buenaventura and were not connected to the infrastructural systems. The only infrastructure the state was interested in, was the port," Nestor said about this time. In the 1960s and 1970s, the extension of pipelines only slightly improved the water infrastructures, while only a few households were regularly supplied.

Although Colpuertos significantly bolstered the growth and modernization of the port economy, and also allowed the consolidation of a labor union (SINTEMAR), authorities did not achieve the desired development to integrate the port and the city. Indeed, the decades between 1960 and 1990 were marked by the establishment of stable labor relations and the constitution of an Afro-Colombian middle class (CNMH, 49–80). Notwithstanding this, there were still no encompassing networked infrastructures for public goods supply. The nonorganized settlement of rural migrant communities hampered the implementation of urban development plans. However, the proper functioning of the port remained the principal concern of the national government and the private sector alike. During the second half of the twentieth century, Buenaventura became a critical site for the integration of the Colombian economy into the global flows of capitalism. For this reason, port infrastructures were prioritized over the infrastructure for the delivery of public goods (Graham and Marvin 2002).

After sunset, Nestor and I continued chatting on the terrace. A transition of light had taken place. As the sky grew dark, city lights were gradually turned on, rearranging shadows and making buildings, houses, and streets even more visible. From the terrace, we could see them in

FIGURE 1 The port at night

miniature: messy streets, wooden houses, a roaring of zigzagging motor-cycles. And as the sea became silent and dark, a walled-off giant of steel and concrete became awesomely illuminated. Port cranes towered over-head; containers were loaded onto ships by highly precise movements. In this bright enclave of modernity and progress (figure 1), the breeze became slightly cooler. I felt happy to have finally found a sort of oral archive and to understand more about the city's infrastructures.

Nestor kept talking. "After 1990 things became messy over here. With the neoliberal agenda, you know?" In 1991 a new political constitution was issued in Colombia. Besides economic liberalization and the with-drawal of the state from many realms of society, this constitution fore-saw greater institutional de-centralization and the strengthening of civil rights (Ahumada 1996). For Buenaventura, the consequences of such a political agenda would have been rather adverse, Nestor told me. The disentanglement between the city and the port would widen. In 1993 Colpuertos was dismantled, and all ports in the country were privatized. Two mainly private consortia were constituted in the city to take over the operation of the port: the Sociedad Portuaria de Buenaventura and the Terminal de Contenedores de Buenaventura (CNMH 2015, 49–55). At the same time, the role played by the labor union was diminished. Mass dismissals followed as the port economy grew.

In terms of public utilities supply, structural adjustments had been made in Colombia in the 1990s. In 1994 Law 142 encouraged municipalities to privatize the operation of water supply systems, and it even required municipalities to justify themselves when they sought to keep public companies operating (Furlong et al. 2016, 181). In 1996 the National Council for Economic and Social Policy allowed a credit of US$17 million to finance and execute a Sewage and Water Master Plan in Buenaventura. The council anticipated an institutional rearrangement which encouraged the participation of the private sector in the operation of the sewage and water infrastructures. As a result, the SAAB was created in 2001 and an operation contract with the consortium Hidropacífico was signed. The private operator was constituted by two small water operators from the cities of Bogotá and Medellín (Conhydra and Hidroservicios; Acevedo 2021, 410).

"It was an onerous contract," Nestor asserted. With this new institutional arrangement and the expertise brought by engineers and managers of Hidropacífico (which had successfully operated water infrastructures elsewhere), some officials were optimistic that the problem of water supply would soon be solved. However, for the duration of the contract, which finished in January 2022, several conflicts between Hidropacífico and the municipality emerged. The contract set out a shared responsibility in the maintenance and expansion of the service between the operator and the government. While the local government criticized the private operator for not fulfilling its obligations to carry out maintenance work, Hidropacífico blamed a lack of public investment in the extension of the networks (Acevedo 2021, 411).

Social leaders and local experts remained skeptical about the envisioned improvements to the water infrastructures in the city. And they were right: things did not improve. In 2007 further public investments were planned, to be funded by a loan taken out by the municipality. Mismanagement and corruption within the local government led to fraud and embezzlement (Acevedo 2021, 412). As Nestor told me, "104 thousand million pesos [US$3 million] were squandered between 2000 and 2010. Scandalous!" The funds acquired by the local government should have been used to replace one of the principal pipelines constructed in the 1930s. "The contracting and construction process was disastrous. They only left ruins," Nestor continued. He wasn't exaggerating the state of the pipes; two of the three main pipelines have some 70 percent loss due to leaks. The replacement of even one of them would have improved the supply system, at least in part.

The profit-oriented management logics of Hidropacífico caused further problems for the population. Not only did the operator not comply with the maintenance works, but it prioritized the port as a consumer of potable water. Nestor and other social activists carried out a survey to clarify if the company was selling water to the port. They found out that, through opaque procedures, not only was the firm prioritizing the port, but it had even founded a bottling company.

Some days after the interview with Nestor, I visited the headquarters of Hidropacífico in the city center. After waiting for a long time, I was welcomed by its general manager. We sat in his office and chatted for a while about the water infrastructures in the city. While he appeared very open to talking to me, at some points he seemed not to like my critical questions. He stated that I was receiving information from social activists and that they were too radical in their interpretation of the state of things. "It is very hard to come to terms with them. They are absolutely rude," he stressed. In my desire to learn more about the company, I returned there several times. An employee in human resources, a middle-aged Black woman, was assigned to give me further information. I got her phone number. She never answered.

In the decade of the 2010s, the increase in the rates of violence and the evident deficiencies in the water supply system in Buenaventura strengthened both social mobilization and state interventions. In chapters 2 and 3, I address the political negotiations and happenings during this time. By 2018, as I moved to Buenaventura to carry out research, some material evidence of state interventions was visible. Two huge water tanks, shining with newness, stuck out next to the main road entering the city. A huge billboard depicted the progress of the PTSP construction site as a form of state action. But things had not improved then, and they still have not improved now.

"The water tanks should be connected to a pipeline which has not been built yet, can you believe that?" Nestor told me in the elevator of the hotel after our interview. "We acknowledge that the state has recently made efforts to improve things over here, but they are still not attaining the goals. We will continue struggling for a proper water supply system." At the entrance of the hotel, and before going on his way to a meeting in the municipality building, Nestor and I arranged another interview. I went in the opposite direction, holding my recorder (my tiny archive), and took a taxi back to Ciudad Blanca.

Infrastructural Landscapes

In a groundbreaking article, scholar Susan Leigh Star outlines the properties and aspects of infrastructure in an attempt to define this sociomaterial and technological phenomenon (1999, 379–84). Star states that infrastructures only become visible when they eventually break down: when, for instance, lights turn off due to power blackouts, or a bridge collapses, hindering regular mobility. However, urban places in the Global South are built upon and constituted through highly visible infrastructures and constant breakdowns (Trovalla and Trovalla 2015). Hence, urban anthropologists have repeatedly criticized the alleged invisibility of infrastructure. In the case of Buenaventura, where both networked and small-scale water infrastructures are leaky, troubled, and highly dysfunctional, breakdowns are not unusual events or spectacles but are instead discrete, quotidian, and intimate.

Elsewhere, Star (jointly with Geoffrey Bowker) has proposed that infrastructures should be studied through their inversion. By this, the authors mean the recognition of "the depths of interdependence of technical networks and standards, on the one hand, and the real work of politics and knowledge production, on the other" (Star 1999, 34). This responds to the analytical approach of figure-ground reversals through which enmeshed and complicated political and technological processes are addressed and scrutinized (Ballestero 2019, 23–24). By ethnographically reconstructing the political and institutional history of Buenaventura's water infrastructures, I aim to shed light on an important part of their (back)ground. But what about the water infrastructures themselves? Where do the material arrangements, the figures, become tangible? Where do these networked infrastructures begin and where do they end?

To ethnographically engage with infrastructures means to observe the sensitive, fleshy, and quotidian encounters between subjects and materials (Appel et al. 2018, 6–9). The everyday life of Buenaventura's citizens is shaped by daily interactions with water infrastructures. Brian Larkin stresses that, more than being invisible until they break down, infrastructures exist in a "range of visibilities that move from unseen to grand spectacles and everything in between" (2013, 336). Many of Buenaventura's leaky pipelines are buried and remain invisible, while water tanks are erected above the surface. Other supply pipelines are installed aboveground, and small-scale water storage systems are visible on rooftops and on house walls. Further, the hoses through which illicit connections are made can be seen sticking out on the surface, mostly tangled.

When I arrived in Ciudad Blanca, people repeatedly mentioned the pipelines and tanks installed in the neighborhood and the surroundings. I was eager to see these infrastructures, my ethnographic object of study. Yeison, one of the assistants in the hardware shop, took me on his motorcycle several times for "infrastructure sight-seeing," as we playfully called it. We first visited an old storage tank built in the 1930s on a small hill not far from the hardware shop. We rode there on dusty, unpaved streets full of potholes. Next to the tank, a small stilt house served as an *estadero* (a bar and restaurant) where criminals would sit around. Yeison warned me several times to avoid eye contact. The tank, made out of concrete, is an enormous cube with moldy green walls that has to be constantly repaired due to leaks (figure 2). It is vital for maintaining pressure in the pipelines and to store water for the inevitable shortages. When the tank needs to be maintained, water supply is cut off for several hours, and sometimes even days. A thirty-inch-pipeline is connected to the pipe, leading westward (figure 3). Unofficial settlements were erected around the tank. Hence, most households there are illicitly connected to the pipe through improvised and fragile hoses that generate (even more) leaks and are exposed to constant damage (figure 4). Water flows irregularly through the pipe, its pressure uneven.

A few days later, Yeison brought me to his home. It was located in a small, improvised settlement next to Ciudad Blanca. Between the two neighborhoods runs the *vía alterna*. This paved, modern, and well-maintained road leads to the port. Heavy trucks from international shipping lines drive by every minute (figure 5). There are parking areas and

FIGURE 2 An older water tank

FIGURE 3 A main pipeline

FIGURE 4 Hacking the pipe

FIGURE 5 Trucks next to vía alterna

gas stations on both sides of the road. Yeison and I crossed the vía alterna underneath via a tunnel, which is part of an abandoned drainage system. "Look, these are the hoses," he told me. Tied to the upper walls of the tunnel, several small, tangled hoses lead from Ciudad Blanca to Yeison's neighborhood. Once on the other side, they branch out to supply different households. While water supply in Yeison's neighborhood depends on small, improvised, fragile hoses, the port enjoys modern infrastructures (such as the vía alterna) that guarantee an uninterrupted flow of commodities. The port, considered to be of greater scale and importance, hinders the improvised, small-scale infrastructures used to supply water to everyday people.

Paul Edwards (2003) argues that infrastructures link different scales of time, space, and social organization. For instance, water infrastructures connect whole rivers and basins to households, shrinking spaces, and times. Moreover, highways and ports connect production sites with global markets linking different spaces as well. But what happens when the two become somehow intertwined? Are the different scales of time and space intermingled? In Buenaventura, the rhythms of global capital and immediate bodily necessities collide. While institutional weakness and urban segregation led to a highly deficient supply of public goods, private capital and logistical infrastructures were not only accelerated but prioritized (Jenss 2021). A tunnel full of hoses bringing water from one side of the road to the other is evidence of the infrastructural violence and material inequalities, which are in turn defined by the different scales of time and space these infrastructures seek to interlink. By traveling through these enmeshed material landscapes in Buenaventura, one can see firsthand the exclusionary politics of the built environment (Graham and Marvin 2002).

I learned even more about the small-scale infrastructures people build to store water during my shifts in the hardware shop. A hose is (legally or otherwise) connected to the grid and leads to a water tank on the rooftop of the dwellings. There, water is collected during the hours of supply. Once the water is cut off, people can access the stored water (Fernández 2022). At first glance, it seems to be an ideal solution to the unreliable provision of water. However, as I show in chapter 4, these infrastructural assemblages are precarious constructions exposed to the uneven pressure of the water flows and the extreme weather conditions of the city.

Hence, people are forced to constantly repair these self-built small-scale infrastructures. Further, and due to the lower incomes of people in the neighborhood, many cannot afford the PVC tanks and instead must use recycled materials such as nonfunctioning fridges or scrap cylinders to store water.

In addition to my motorcycle tours with Yeison, I also accompanied Dubier, an employee of Hidropacífico I met in the hardware shop as he came to sell surplus materials. As a plumber, his main task is to undertake minor repair works to the public infrastructures. Several times, I traveled with him to different households to install new water meters or to repair leaky hoses. To fix the entangled small-scale infrastructures (hoses, meters, valves), he always asked users to help him and sketched a figure in his notebook. Having found the problem, he would improvise repairs, trying out different materials. Users had to sign a form issued by the company, and the work would be done. Dubier told me that some materials were particularly vulnerable to the harsh weather conditions and that he would sometimes have to undertake repairs in the same households several times within a month. He also stated that illicit connections and improvisations would hamper the regular supply of the service.

Dubier and his colleagues are also tasked with cutting off water supply when payments are overdue. In these cases, a plug is introduced to the supply pipe. However, he told me that people usually either remove the plug or make an illegal, parallel connection to the supply lines. "When people are not skilled to do it, I do it to collect a bit of money," he admitted. In fact, his low salary as a subcontracted plumber is not sufficient to sustain his family. Both official and informal (even illicit) maintenance and repair works on public infrastructures at a domestic level are carried out by means of improvisation (Anand 2015a; De Coss-Corzo 2021). The lack of reliable infrastructures for water supply creates fragile assemblages which are reproduced through everyday material practices. Meanwhile, the pipes continue to leak.

Infrastructures accrete; they do not remain homogeneous. New adaptations are "innovated, installed, and brought into being on top of already existing infrastructures that both constrain and enable their form" (Anand 2015b). As I show in chapter 4, in Buenaventura, tanks, hoses, pipelines, and water storage systems at a domestic level are built and maintained in precarious forms due to institutional weakness and the

FIGURE 6 Entangled pipes and improvised connections

segregation of racialized subjects from urban development plans. To build upon existing infrastructures in Buenaventura means to weave the new into crumbling and precarious materials. Hence, the leaks that reduce pressure are embedded in the institutional history of water supply, reflecting long-standing dynamics of dispossession and violence.

To travel through these infrastructure landscapes, observe the crumbling materials, and see water pouring out of the leaks not only makes visible the political histories sustaining them; it also makes palpable the intimate experience of living amid precarious infrastructure systems. Constructing and tampering (as forms of resisting the exclusion from the built landscape) might not reverse the political processes which have excluded people from the water supply system. Nevertheless, it shows that infrastructures and people interact beyond the binary of haves and have-nots, and that marginalized urbanites should not be merely apprehended as suffering subjects of the cityscape. By ethnographically engaging with water infrastructures, I learned about everyday life amid exclusion, as well as the inventiveness of people.

To represent Buenaventura in pathological terms is to reduce urbanites to suffering subjects and fails to accompany them in their travels in and through the city landscape and infrastructures (de Certeau 2013). Instead, we need to zoom in, be present, and engage with the everyday life of people to enable fuller representations.

But not only precarious infrastructures are central to people's life in Buenaventura. Parallel to the deficient provision of public goods, people are affected by the everyday crime in form of territorial control by armed groups, extortion, assassinations, and forced disappearances. In what follows, I recount the social and political context within which violence in the region unfold and address the quotidian experiences of subjects with violence in Ciudad Blanca, registered in everyday chatting, jokes, and storytelling.[4]

For now, let us briefly zoom out.

Territories of Fear

Violence has been a constitutive phenomenon of Colombia's history since the nation's independence.[5] Throughout the twentieth century and up to the present, the country has been riven by a long-term (though mostly low-intensity) civil war. For large parts of Colombia's history, the conflict was mainly marked by political violence and waged by the two leading traditional parties: the Liberal Party (Partido Liberal) and the Conservative Party (Partido Conservador). While modern state institutions and a democratic system could be built and sustained, politics were defined by violence. In the wake of the assassination of liberal presidential candidate Jorge Eliécer Gaitán in 1948, violence escalated and led to a bloody civil-war-like conflict called La Violencia (1948–58). Following a military dictatorship led by the purportedly neutral General Gustavo Rojas Pinilla (1953–57), who sought to put an end to the conflict, the traditional parties agreed to rotate power and installed a system known as the National Front (1958–74), in which the parties alternated presidential terms and shared the bureaucracy.

---

4. In Chapter 6, I closer analyze violence "from below."

5. In Colombia and elsewhere, an academic group of so-called *violentólogos* have studied the causes, developments, and mutations of one of the longest internal armed conflicts in the world (see Palacios 2006; González 2014).

From the 1960s on, and against the background of a new world order after World War II, left-wing peasant guerrillas were constituted in different parts of Colombia.[6] The FARC was the biggest and most important of them. At the same time, both landlords and agribusiness companies formed and financed armies of counterinsurgents to combat guerrillas. By the end of the century, these regionally rooted armed groups came together under one umbrella organization, the AUC. However, the state and the army played a significant role in supporting the right-wing counterinsurgency paramilitary structures. During the 1980s and 1990s, guerrilla groups grew significantly in number and began to finance themselves through drug trafficking and kidnappings. In response, counterinsurgent paramilitaries expanded, committing several massacres and causing mass displacements from many rural areas in the country (Sanford 2004).

From the 1980s onwards, several attempts were made to put an end to the conflict between the state and the guerrillas by means of peace agreements. While some of them led to the reintegration of former armed groups into the political life of the country (as the case of the guerrilla group M-19, Movimiento 19 de Abril, shows), most attempts broadly failed. Not until 2016 did the FARC and the government of the then-President Juan Manuel Santos (2010–2018) sign an agreement leading to the broad demobilization of the former guerrilla group. However, the ongoing implementation of this peace treaty has been highly troubled and widely criticized (Cristo et al. 2019). Indeed, violence has not ended in the country—it has simply mutated and taken on new forms—and the dream of constituting a "post-conflict society" has not yet been fulfilled.

Furthermore, illegal economies have defined the rhythms and logics of the internal armed conflict since the 1970s. Whereas drug production and trafficking (mainly of cocaine) were originally managed and sustained by allegedly nonpolitical armed actors (the drug cartels), guerrilla and paramilitary groups rapidly engaged with the illegal economies. This underpinned the conflict and accelerated the cycles of violence. During

---

6. Guerrilla groups were inspired by Chinese communism (Ejército Popular de Liberación, Popular Liberation Army), the Liberation Theology (Ejército de Liberación Nacional, National Liberation Army), peasantry (FARC), and urban movements (Movimiento 19 de Abril, or M-19).

the 1980s and 1990s, the conflict escalated rapidly, leading to a humanitarian catastrophe (Aparicio 2012; Vera 2017).

While for larger parts of the twentieth century Buenaventura and the Pacific region played a subordinate role in the conflict, things changed dramatically during the 1990s. The biggest guerrilla group of the country, the FARC, poured into the region at the beginning of the decade as part of a new military strategy, widely expanding its zones of influence. By that time, the FARC was deeply involved in the illegal economies, which were flourishing in the region. New coca plantations as well as drug trafficking routes were built and sustained in the Pacific. The 30th Front and the Manuel Vargas Front, two military units of the FARC, took control over the rural areas of Buenaventura, eventually blocking the main road leading to Cali, kidnapping and extorting businessmen, and attacking the port infrastructures (CNMH 2015).

At the turn of the twenty-first century, the AUC sent troops to the region as part of a counterinsurgent strategy (clandestinely) supported by marines, local politicians, and parts of Cali's economic elites (CNMH 2015). The newly established Bloque Calima of the AUC took over the territory using violence. Several massacres were committed by the AUC during the first years of the 2000s in many rural areas of the Southwestern Pacific, leading to mass displacement to urban Buenaventura and elsewhere (Uribe 2007; Oslender 2008; Escobar 2008; CNMH 2015). In 2000, nine massacres took place in rural areas of Buenaventura. As a consequence of the broad alliance between paramilitary groups and drug cartels, illegal economies expanded massively: coca plantations and large-scale illegal gold mining spread as drug trafficking routes pierced the region. The partial expulsion of the FARC from the territory saw attacks on port infrastructures reduced.

At the beginning of the decade, the new political agenda revolved around environmental protection and the recognition of ethnic minorities, which mobilized several actors and gave hope to people of the Pacific. A new development agenda which broadly embraced local social and ethnic movements was expected to be implemented in the region (Escobar 2008). Instead, war expanded into the territory, harming social, environmental, and political dynamics. In large parts of the rural Pacific, the armed conflict forcibly displaced communities to urban areas.

After the 2004 peace agreement between paramilitaries and the state, murky alliances between local politicians, businessmen, and armed militias operating within specific local dynamics emerged, underpinning illicit economies (see Ronderos 2014). By the time the agreement was reached, paramilitary groups had already entered the urban areas of Buenaventura, broadly controlling commerce and imposing regimes of fear. Further, local politics were influenced by the armed groups. Neo-paramilitary groups took over many neighborhoods. Internal rivalry, a complex structure, and competing interests all led to an escalation of the conflict. The sea routes of drug trafficking, easily accessible from the tidal areas of the city, as well as the port infrastructures itself—which also serve for drug smuggling—converted Buenaventura into a nodal point of crime. Furthermore, as other authors have shown, the urban development plans and the expansion of the port itself (that is, the very interest of private capital) have led to an increase in patterns of violence (Zeiderman 2016; Jenss 2019, 2020; Lombard et al. 2021).[7]

A Violent City

In November 2013, the U.S. organization Human Rights Watch visited Buenaventura for around two weeks. A group of social researchers conducted more than seventy interviews with victims, judicial authorities, social leaders, police officials, and other relevant actors in order to gather and verify information regarding recent waves of violence in the port city (Human Rights Watch 2014, 6). Rumors had been circulating about

---

7. A good example of an exclusionary urban development plan is the so-called Master Plan 2050 (Esteyco and Findeter 2015) which Jenss (2020) defines in following terms: "This urban redevelopment plan, which the state commissioned to Catalan consultancy Esteyco, seeks to remake the city, and Cascajal island in particular, to match global port activities. The plan particularly targets Cascajal's next-to-port spaces and assigns different functionalities to Buenaventura's urban, such as a logistics-industrial zone, a tourist quarter, and upmarket residential spaces. It declares the Northern half of the city a future industrial complex, modifying its tax regime on berthing ships, quay dues, and storages" (6).

the existence of torture centers, dismemberments, intra-urban displacement, and other human rights abuses. In 2014 Human Rights Watch
published a report that made for sobering reading. It confirmed many of
the rumors, noting that disappearances, dismemberments, restriction of
movement and social control, forced displacement, and forced recruit-
ment had occurred.

The NGO widely condemned these crimes and recognized that, even
as many forms and modalities of crime and victimization were taking
place in the city, local authorities did not provide enough protection
to inhabitants. Furthermore, local and national state institutions were
blamed for "inadequate protection and accountability" (Human Rights
Watch 2014, 24).[8]

Colombian institutions such as the National Registry of Disappeared
Persons, as well as the Ombudsman's Office of Colombia, have gathered
data regarding the explosion of violence in the port city. According to
the Victims Unit (Unidad para las Víctimas, a state institution founded
in 2012 and responsible for the registration and assistance of victims of
the internal armed conflict in Colombia), in the municipality of Buenaventura, there were 308,809 victims of violent events between 2010
and 2021. This is the highest number of reported cases of violence in a
single municipality in all of Colombia.

After the formal dissolution and dismantlement of the AUC in 2004,
rates of violence in Buenaventura increased due to a sort of rearrange-
ment of emerging illegal armed groups (derived from the AUC itself)
such as La Empresa and Los Urabeños. These groups held (and still
hold) strong ties to regional drug cartels (CHNM 2015, 151–207; United
Nations High Commissioner for Refugees 2017), and other competing
groups such as La Local, Los Shottas, and Los Espertanos have since
emerged. Some leaders of the Bloque Calima were prosecuted and im-
prisoned after the agreement back in the early 2000s, but the logics and
structures of paramilitarism endured. The atomization of paramilitary

---

8. In 2011 a report by the North American Congress on Latin America had already
denounced the increase of violence in the city (Nicholls and Sánchez-Garzoli 2011).
However, that report did not have the same impact as the one published by Human
Rights Watch.

groups unleashed a dispute over the control of urban territories in the port city, leading to assassinations and mass intra-urban displacements. The aim to impose security regimes by the different groups in the neighborhoods of Buenaventura led to a dramatic increase of violent events. By 2014 the situation had spiraled out of control (CNMH 2015).

Although violence and crime are deeply related to drug trafficking and illicit economies alike, scholars and activists have mapped and analyzed the urban geographies of violence, proving a relationship exists between the port and city development plans on the one hand and specific sites where violence unfold on the other (Jenss 2020, 2022; Lombard et al. 2021). Anthropologist Austin Zeiderman argues that the informal seaside settlements have become a "vortex of the economic, ecological, and political forces of Buenaventura" due to the high violence rates and the plans to expand the port infrastructures (2016, 817). Notwithstanding the difficulty of demonstrating a direct relationship between violent groups and economic elites, the studies stress the interlocking nature of capital interests, development plans, and violence (see Alves et al. 2020).

The relationship between the port and the city points to a process of simultaneous dis/entanglement. This resonates with the arguments developed by Hannah Appel (2012) in her work on the offshore oil enclaves in Equatorial Guinea. Here, infrastructures such as walls and roads serve as boundary-making technologies between western production (or logistical) sites and the rest. However, these sites (including their structure, politics, and material relations) are deeply entangled in the everyday life of people beyond the walls by means of dispossession, colonization, and violence. Indeed, the racialized population of Buenaventura living beyond the walls suffers (infra)structural violence in a myriad of ways. In chapter 4, I demonstrate how everyday crime shapes the life of people in relation to water infrastructures.

Crime

While scholarly literature has addressed the terrifying proliferation of violence in the city, less fieldwork has been conducted in the affected neighborhoods, mainly due to the difficulty of carrying out field work in situ.[9] Indeed, interviews with relevant local actors, journalist sources and official documents offer reliable data for understanding the logics of everyday violence in Buenaventura. Yet by "go[ing] where violence occurs" to "research it as it takes place" allows us to understand the everyday textures of this "slippery" phenomenon (Nordstrom et al. 1996, 4). Indeed, this methodological imperative stresses the importance of bottom-up representations and allows the researcher to see the everyday strategies and mechanisms deployed by the population to cope with everyday violence and crime in Colombia (its rhythm, spatiality, and morphology), as Michael Taussig's (2004) extraordinary ethnographic account of a Black peasant village in Southwestern Colombia shows.

During my fieldwork experience in Ciudad Blanca, I witnessed crime as a social phenomenon mediated through words, images, and the plastic reality itself. My interlocutors and friends in Ciudad Blanca did not reproduce congruent accounts of violence relying on statistics, maps, or the logics of the armed groups. Violence was rather rooted in storytelling, jokes, and speculation. Although crime and violence in Ciudad Blanca is not as frequent and pronounced as in the seaside settlements, where mass graves can be found and people were displaced in massive numbers, the neighborhood has nevertheless been affected. The everyday crime talk offered me a lens to scrutinize urban life amid violence.

By the time I arrived in Ciudad Blanca, I had read some reports on violence in the city. Although I was aware that I would be confronted with everyday accounts of violence, the stories of extortion, assassinations, robbery, and intimidation frightened and overwhelmed me at first. At the same time, I realized that there was broad confusion about many facts revolving around the presence and absences of armed groups, their ways of operating, and their interests. In Ciudad Blanca and elsewhere, gossip, rumors, and storytelling help people to make sense of what they constantly experience. "You *never know* who is acting on whose behalf. There are guerrillas, paramilitaries, organized crime, thugs, but you never know," Claudia told me on the very first day of my field stay in the

---

9. In a paper on the port city, Austin Zeiderman points out that "long-term fieldwork in Buenaventura was deemed unfeasible due to the security situation" (2016, 1115).

hardware shop. By reflecting on the stories of crime, I sought to grasp the discursive and material strategies deployed by subjects to deal with quotidian states of fear and imminent risk and to examine in which ways they get (directly or indirectly) drawn into crime. Although murkiness and opacity are strategies deployed by armed groups to retain control over the population, these are strategies that are also apprehended and reproduced by the population itself (Taussig 2004; Penglase 2009).

From time to time, selective assassinations occur in Ciudad Blanca. The victims are mostly young Black men. The day of my arrival, a corpse was found a few streets away from the hardware shop, where I was sitting and chatting. Yeison and Alexander, Claudia's employees at the hardware shop, were guessing why the guy had been killed (they seemed to know him). They discussed whether he was involved in crime, saying that there had been rumors about his participation in a shooting some weeks before. "He was not clean," Yeison stated.

Furthermore, members of criminal gangs are known to extort local shopkeepers, a phenomenon I closely analyze in chapter 5. They also install illegal road tolls to collect money from motorcycles and *piratas*. I passed these toll checkpoints sometimes with Yeison, and we had to pay. People like Claudia and her assistants are constantly angry about the tolls. Gang members intimidate locals by walking armed and hooded through the neighborhood, as I witnessed on several occasions. Police patrolled the area sometimes; however, while in the neighborhood, they mostly remained in front of the hardware shop, drinking Coke and asking people about the "thugs." Claudia used to text those policemen via WhatsApp and send them pictures and names of young men she believed were involved in crime. From time to time, while sitting behind the counter in the shop, she would lower her voice and point to a passerby, asserting that he was a "thug" (locally known as *malandros, pinticas*, and *ratas*). "That's the motherfucker who was intimidating me last time," she said once. When things become caliente, as people use to say, the order of things is altered. Shots can be heard during the night as more assassinations take place.

After lunch on one hot Thursday afternoon, Claudia and I began chatting, once again, about violence in the city. Claudia stated that she would know exactly who is involved in crime in the neighborhood. "You can see how people behave, you hear stories, and then you can recognize them. The only thing is that most of them are hooded when they commit crimes." As I asked about Jeremías, the locksmith who was killed the night before, she said that she didn't know why he was killed. "At the end, you never certainly know who is behind the crimes," she stated. Yeison, her assistant, joined the conversation while piling up some bags of cement that had been delivered to the hardware shop. He said that he had been told that the assassination occurred because the locksmith got involved in a quarrel during a party and insulted the wrong person. "Danger is everywhere. Everyone can be a criminal. Not even the thugs know themselves for whom they are working."

As this example shows, stories about crime in Ciudad Blanca are framed twofold. On the one hand, people state that when it comes to violence, "you can never know" (*uno nunca sabe*). On the other hand, people argue that they "can tell" certain things because "everyone knows" (*todo el mundo sabe*). The former ("you can never know") evidences the murkiness and opacity of violence materialized in the uneven rhythms and flow of skirmishes, assassinations, and crossfire. The latter ("everyone knows") has been conceptualized by scholars as "public secrecy" (Taussig 2004), attempts made by the population to cope with violence's opacity by weaving a "fiction of predictability" (Penglase 2009, 59). Here, to know means to maintain (or create) order within unruliness.

After having built trust with him, I asked Don Pedro—a neighbor, the owner of a grocery shop, and a friend of Claudia—about La Empresa and Los Espartanos, the two main paramilitary gangs acting in Buenaventura. He talked about the threatening extortion notes he had received, signed by one or the other of the groups. "I think that some thugs sign on their own, that they are not part of bigger structures. That's why I denounce some of them." I was even more bewildered as I heard Yeison's version, that "gangs don't play a crucial role anymore. Criminals act on their own. They invoke a chief who doesn't exist. But to be honest, *you can never know.*" I wondered out loud, astonished, "So you don't think there are bigger structures of the organized crime here?" "There might be some structures, of course, but they are loose structures. People say there is one single big boss in Buenaventura. He may live abroad, somewhere in the United States. This is a fairytale. Can you believe that?." He laughed and continued, "Violence is everywhere, on every single corner of the city, so you just only need to be hooded and say you are a member of a criminal gang, and everybody is confused. Sometimes you don't even need a gun."

When things become caliente, that is, when gangs fight, and people are assassinated in the neighborhood, locals state that there is a confrontation between gangs. Once a conflict is framed as such, people make sense of these momentous states of exception and deploy mechanisms to protect themselves. "There are many invisible frontiers," a customer of the hardware shop told me. "And you know where they are." In fact, there are sites in the neighborhoods such as bars and gambling kiosks that "criminals" use to sit around and chat. I was told many times not to use the streets behind the gas stations, for example. As Jenss points out, people in Buenaventura deploy spatial strategies to cope with violence through, for instance, the "redrawing of cognitive maps of the city, following names of places, streets and blocks of houses where one can move freely" (2019, 8).

However, many young men from Ciudad Blanca and the surrounding neighborhoods become part of crime organizations or are somehow involved in illicit economies. Take Yeison, my friend. He (illegally) lends money at a high interest rate to neighbors and pays armed groups a sort of tax to be allowed to do so. To fulfill his dream, which is to open a motorbike workshop in the neighborhood, he needs capital, which he says he is collecting from lending money. Once in a while, Alexander, the other assistant of the hardware shop, takes selfies carrying a gun in his hand and posts them in his WhatsApp stories. And although he is not part of a gang, he likes to mimic gang culture: "You never know, maybe you'll have to act sometime." He borrows the weapon from his cousin, John Fredy, who is part of a criminal organization. When I told Alexander that I would like to meet his cousin to talk about his life in the gang, he just shook his head and smiled: "That's too dangerous."

Due to the high unemployment and poverty rates, the precarious education system and an ongoing exposure to the logics and rhythms of violence, young people see an opportunity for life and survival by (directly or indirectly) joining criminal gangs. In fact, everyday violence and crime deepen the uneven power relations in the city and are a consequence of the state "organized abandonment." However, engaging with crime appears for some as a path out of poverty, as a resource to cope with the different forms of structural violence they face. Ironically, by joining gangs and illicit economies, young people contribute to the perpetration of this structural violence.

Both crime and the deficient supply of public goods have been central to the constitution of people's everyday life in Buenaventura. Infrastructural breakdown in the form of damage and water shortages, as well as violence in the form of assassinations and extortions, have become quotidian events in this racialized cityscape. Subjects deploy shifting coping mechanisms to make life possible in such a harsh urban environment. When infrastructure fails and water becomes scarce, historically formed logics of state abandonment and frontier-making become evident: a form of infrastructural violence. Furthermore, when the tectonics of security shift—whose rhythms and logics people widely ignore—violence pours out. But it also happens when young men mimic criminals and pretend to be part of wider structures of crime. But *you never know*. Both water and violence fluctuate, mediating politics, the economy, and life in the neighborhoods of Buenaventura. The context I have traced here encompasses both the historical trajectories and everyday appearances of violence and water infrastructures in the port city.

Chapter 2 address ethnographically the PTSP and interrogates how relationships of *inclusive exclusion* are forged and reproduced through state-led interventions that have failed to improve the water infrastructures in the city.

Alexander

In July 2000 Doña Sandra announced that she was pregnant. Her siblings were sitting on plastic chairs on the second floor of their stilt house, on a balcony, just in front of the river. It was late afternoon and it started to rain heavily. Alexander would be the third of five children Doña Sandra would give birth to between 1999 and 2005. He was the last to be born in the house on the Naya River, where Doña Sandra grew up in the 1970s within a family of Black fishers and peasants. The day of his birth, frogs were croaking very loudly, Doña Sandra told me. A few weeks later, the whole family was forced to leave. On April 10, 2001, a military unit of the AUC entered the upper Naya River on speedboats, hooded, and killed people accused of cooperating with the guerrilla. Rumors of the massacre quickly reached the lower part of the river where they were living, and people embarked onto boats to flee. Doña Sandra put out a large blanket on the second floor of the house, laid some belongings on it, and tied it up with a rope. Alexander would cry the whole journey to Buenaventura, she remembers. Authorities estimate that around one hundred people were killed in the Naya River; some of them were even tortured. But only twenty-seven corpses could be found.

Upon arriving, the family moved to a small stilt house on Cascajal Island, in a very poor neighborhood known as Bajamar (low tide). Armed groups entered the neighborhood in 2004 to seek drug trafficking routes, and the whole family was forced to move out once again. At three years old, Alexander had already been forcibly displaced twice. Then the family moved to an *invasión*, an informal settlement that arose after the irregular occupation of land by forcibly displaced families. The *invasión* was next to the vía alterna. Sandra and Alexander's father divorced; a year later, she married Julio. Alexander calls him *papá*.

In the *invasión*, Alexander grew up amid violence, in a house made of concrete, sharing a small room with all his four siblings. Some of his older mates were shot because they were part of criminal gangs. He attended school in a neighborhood nearby. He passed elementary school, and even high school, despite many adversities. At fifteen, he bought a gun and a motorcycle, two useful objects to survive in Buenaventura. He then started to work as *mototaxista*, transporting people for short distances within the neighborhood. He never acquired a driving license, though. No money for that. In 2017, age sixteen, he began working in the hardware shop of Claudia. I met him for the first time in 2019. He used to wear old, dirty shirts, and Nike shorts. His upper body was quite buff from carrying bags of cement. He still worked in the evenings as *mototaxista*, after spending all day in the hardware shop. "To get enough money for my studies," he told me.

After finishing school in early 2020, Alexander expressed his desire to study for a technical career. But during the COVID-19 lockdown, things turned tough, and he had to postpone his plans. Doña Sandra lost her job as a cleaner in a hotel for truck drivers run by one of Claudia's acquaintances. And Julio, Alexander's stepfather, fell ill. They spent all their savings for food. In 2021 he found a new job as a freighter in the port, then enrolled in an institute to become a port agent. He and Valentina, his girlfriend, moved to a new rental house. She works sporadically as tourist guide in her hometown in the rural Pacific. He sold the gun, and the motorcycle, and things seem to be going well in his life. He is in love. And he will have a good job soon, he said.

State Intervention

The Plan Todos Somos PAZcífico

In this chapter, I address the state-led development project Plan Todos Somos PAZcífico, launched by the Colombian state in 2014. One of the main goals of the project is the improvement of the water supply system of Buenaventura by means of the construction, monitoring, and repair of the existing infrastructure network. In what follows, I examine the political and technical vicissitudes of the plan since its launch. The PTSP, I contend, reflects two different yet interwoven practices of the Colombian state. First, it shows how material interventions of the state in marginalized regions (the so-called frontiers) respond to a specific form of state-building processes at the frontier. Following Simón Uribe, I understand this state presence as produced and sustained a through a relationship of "inclusive exclusion." Drawing on Agamben's reflections on sovereign power and exception, Uribe argues that the frontier, rather than lying outside state order, is constituted "through a relationship of inclusive exclusion through which state power is constituted and preserved" (2017, 10). While the PTSP evokes long-awaited promises of inclusion by means of improving and repairing the water supply system in Buenaventura, its delays, bureaucratic traps, and hierarchical structures reproduce forms of marginalization and perpetual exclusion. Although many people in Buenaventura make sense of the deficient infrastructures for water supply as a form of state absence, the state is, in fact, present, since it mobilizes high amounts of financial and managerial resources in order to repair these infrastructures.

A second form of state practice the PTSP reflects is what Pellegrino (2022) describes as "complying incompliantly": In this sense, the state, while failing to solve a problem, claims to have at least partially met its promises. An arrangement of representations and discourses, materialized in construction sites, figures, timetables, decrees, speeches, and meetings, serve as ways to demonstrate the compliance with the plan, even as the promise of a functioning water supply system is not fulfilled. Here, I follow Brian Larkin who points out that "infrastructures represent and are represented in the built forms; the protests that congeal around them; the sets of numbers, graphs, and tables by which they are administered; the budgets that undergird them" (2013, 186).

Although the PTSP was designed and planned to solve the problem of the deficient water supply system in Buenaventura, urban citizens cannot rely on functioning infrastructures. Indeed, at the time of this writing, the amount of time for which water is available each day has not improved significantly. Thus, I understand the deficient water infrastructures as a form of structural violence; it represents a deprivation of a vital public good and a violation of a constitutional right. In this chapter, I approach the PTSP ethnographically. In doing so, I define an "ethnographic site" within the "dispersed ensemble of institutional practices and techniques of governance" which constitute the state (Hansen and Stepputat 2005, 14). However, the wide institutional landscape of the Colombian state has complex institutional articulations at several levels, as McFee (2019) has shown. Hence, I also address the PTSP's embeddedness in wider interinstitutional cooperation, encompassing agencies, ministries, and municipalities. In what follows, I briefly reconstruct the institutional history of the PTSP and map the actors and institutions involved in the project. I draw here on various official sources (mainly laws and reports) and on interviews I held with state officials.

I further describe four key ethnographic encounters I had with the PTSP, which demonstrate how managerial hierarchy, racial prejudices, underfunding and cumbersome bureaucratic processes widely shape the project. The first one is the visit to the headquarters of the PTSP in Bogotá and the interview with an official who explained the formal structures, legal framework, and bureaucratic procedures of the PTSP. Following Hansen and Stepputat, I understand this apparently coherent, bureaucratic narratives as "the authoritative language of the state and the medium through which the state acquires discursive presence and authority" (2005, 8). I further contend that these representation practices are produced through technocratic arrangements of rituals, languages, artifacts, and bodies, and that they widely marginalize political contestation and claims by nonstate actors. This language is key to this form of state power, which is rendered technical rather than political: a paramount feature of the developmental state (Ferguson 1994; Li 2007).

Leaving the hermetic realm of bureaucratic language, I address in the second section of this chapter the racial prejudices articulated by mestizo officials beyond the "rationalist core" of the project. I thus aim to grasp the "halo of sentiments, affects, intentions and aspirations" of some PTSP officials, answering the call of Dominic Boyer to "humanize the expert" (2008, 45). Racism plays a fundamental role not only as a subjective affect but as institutionally anchored element and constitutive part of the Colombian state apparatus. The prejudices of mestizo officials toward racialized local experts, inhabitants and social activists reenact colonial narratives and reproduce difference. Everyday acts of racial discrimination, as anthropologists Jonathan Rosa and Vanessa Díaz (2020) argue, should not be understood as individual but rather as part of institutional racism. The institutionally anchored inequalities of the PTSP such as the exclusion of local expertise, the racial hierarchies and the regional differences are also enacted in discrete, mundane forms of racism.

In the third part I outline my visit to the Water Roundtables, which monitor state-led projects (at local, regional, and national level) to improve the water infrastructures in the city and which different state and civil society actors assemble. These very tense Water Roundtables evidence the disagreements that take place between grassroots organizations, local engineers, and PTSP functionaries. Whereas the central state convenes these periodical audiences to show the results of the project and allegedly open negotiations with other actors, the meetings turned out to be a technopolitical battleground after which the management of the PTSP would not change the project's timelines and procedures, though it would claim to have acted with transparency, including locals in the decision-making processes.

In the last part of the chapter, I describe an encounter with an engineer at a PTSP construction site and a conversation on the illicit connections made by the population to the water infrastructures. Following Ana Tsing (2012), I ask how both representations and material interventions of water infrastructures render informality and everyday material practices as excessive and undesirable.

As Ferguson's classical book on development shows, technocratic projects result in a "constellation that has the effect of expanding the exercise of a particular sort of power," while rendering things technical rather than political and introducing specific bureaucratic rationales (1994, 22). I argue that the presence of the Colombian state in Buenaventura through the PTSP enacts a specific form of state power articulated in a relationship of inclusive exclusion. This "particular sort of power" consists in the state presence and concomitant absence the project itself reflects in the leaky and ruined infrastructures and the failed attempts to repair them, in the racial prejudices rooted in state institutions and enacted in the everyday, and in the technical representations of the project and the neglection of a social and political history of marginalization both the city of Buenaventura and the Pacific region have endured.

The Plan

The National Development Plan, Todos por un Nuevo País (2014–2018; "United for a New Country"), of the second government of former President Juan Manuel Santos defined a development agenda and intervention strategy for the Colombian Pacific. In 2014 the government declared the region to be a top priority and created an institutional unit within the presidency dedicated to formulating public policy and development plans for the Pacific region (Gerencia del Pacífico). Since Buenaventura represents a critical site of national commerce due to the port infrastructures and economy, the government turned its attention to the city in order to solve the social and political problems that had arisen in the last few decades, such as violence and poverty.

In February 2014 a mass social mobilization took place in Buenaventura, during which locals and social activists from different organizations symbolically buried violence as a way of expressing their desire to see an end to the violence in the port city. In response, the central government opened negotiations with representatives of civil society and committed to making local investments to improve the provision of public goods. At the same time, and aiming to solve the security problems, the government militarized the city (Jaramillo 2020; Manos Visibles 2017). Furthermore, the presidency summoned local government officials and the private sector to a broad forum in October the same year. The forum, Buenaventura Próspera (Prosperous Buenaventura), sought to collect ideas and plans for a wider investment program in the port city, which was to be largely administered from the central government. On the last day of the forum, President Santos officially announced the launch of the Plan Todos Somos PAZcífico (Jaramillo et al. 2020, 148). With this project, the government aimed to close two development gaps in Buenaventura: the one between a modern and prosperous port complex and a precarious city, and the one between the Andean region and the Pacific region.

Initially, the plan committed US$400 million to finance the expansion and improvement of water infrastructures in the city of Buenaventura (Consejo Nacional de Política Económica y Social 2015). In 2015 the government announced that the program should be expanded to other (both rural and urban) areas of the Pacific region, though it did not increase the promised funding. This generated discontentment among social activists (Manos Visibles 2017, 34). In November 2015, through a law approved by the Senate, the government officially launched the PTSP, which would be financed through loans acquired at the World Bank and the Inter American Development Bank (Gobierno Nacional Ley 1735, 2015).

In general terms, the project is made up of three work packages: the improvement of water and sewage infrastructures in urban areas; the energization of rural settlements; and the construction and improvement of infrastructures of mobility. While the improvement of urban water infrastructures is prioritized and better financed than the other aspects, the project is not exclusively focused on these infrastructures, as was initially planned. In a way, then, promises were broken from the very beginning.

In terms of institutional framework, the PTSP was created as an entity within the National Unit for Disaster Risk Management (UNGRD), which, in turn, is part of the Ministry of Finance and Public Credit (Minhacienda). The PTSP administers an autonomous patrimony. The headquarters of the project are located in Bogotá, in the offices of the UNGRD. And though the program is focused on the Pacific region, the team is mainly formed by mestizo experts and state officials from the interior of the country. Indeed, the fact that most of the development projects directed to the region have been planned, designed, and executed from the city of Bogotá, the capital of the country, has been widely criticized by both grassroots organizations and academics (Leal 2015). During interviews, social leaders and local experts in Buenaventura complained several times about the arrogance and inefficiency of state officials who could not properly know "their territory."

Even though local officials and experts are employed by the PTSP (the so-called local links), the project has a strong hierarchical structure. Large parts of the team are based in the headquarters and have worked within institutions of the central state that are dedicated to formulating and executing development plans throughout the country. Most of the time, the language deployed within such institutions remains highly technical (Ferguson 1994). In fact, these development teams emulate practices, procedures, and representations of many worldwide development agencies (Rottenburg 2009).

In terms of management and execution, the program draws on a burdensome bureaucracy as one can clearly see in the organization chart (figure 7). Take the construction projects for water infrastructures, for example. In theory, municipalities are responsible for the formulation and design of construction plans for a certain piece of infrastructure work. The plans should then be submitted to the Ministry of Housing, City, and Territory (Minvivienda) to be evaluated. If adjustments need to be made, the plan is returned to the municipality and then back to the ministry. After eventual approval, it is finally submitted to the PTSP, which is responsible for the execution of the project and the subcontracting of a construction firm. The PTSP keeps oversight of the construction plans and prioritizes the works it considers paramount. These procedures take a very long time, since so many actors (the local state, diverse ministries, private firms, and the PTSP, among others) are involved. Disagreements, disinformation, and bureaucratic delays all complicate the execution of the projects. For that reason, in 2016 the PTSP introduced so-called facilitators to expedite the formulation and design of the construction plans at the local level, which was blamed for delays and faulty

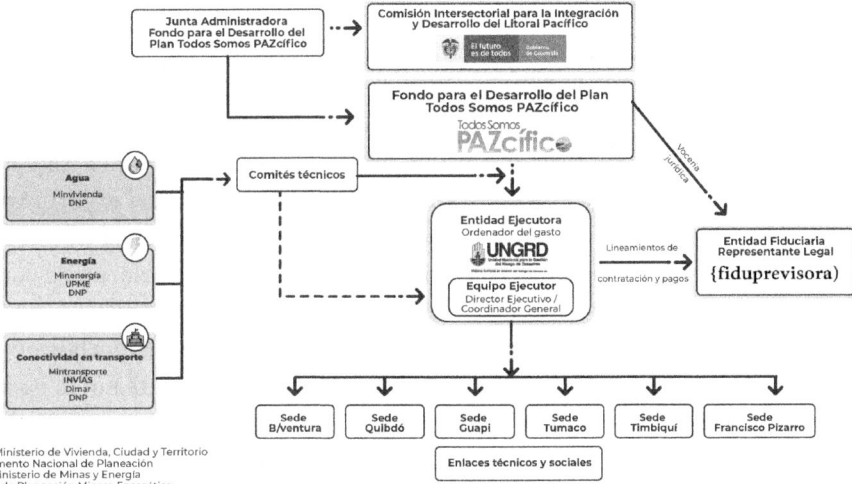

FIGURE 7 Organization chart of the PTSP

projects. However, these facilitators were met with skepticism by both local engineers and social activists.

In Buenaventura an assessment of the existing water and sewage infrastructures was formulated in the first decade of the 2000s. The report, titled Master Sewage and Water Supply Plan, was based on a comprehensive engineering survey and was the second comprehensive survey (after the one made in the late 1990s). The main aim of the survey was to identify the technical failures and weaknesses of the whole water supply system in the city. The report offered several suggestions as to how to intervene in the system in order to reduce losses and improve the flow of water (Acuavalle, n.d.). The work plan of the PTSP draws on this report.

When it comes to repairing the infrastructures, hydraulic engineers are tasked with replacing the pipelines, building water storage systems, and expanding the network. Flow rates serve as an indicator of the effectiveness of the repair and construction works. According to the Master Plan, Buenaventura's water infrastructure loses 70 percent of its water due mainly to leaks and technical problems in the intake. The list of priorities includes the measuring and repair of leaks; the rehabilitation of a twenty-seven-inch pipeline to replace the old main and leaky pipelines, the construction of which was abandoned in the first decade of the 2000s; and the building of two water tanks.

As Anand (2015) notes in the case of Mumbai, measuring leaks and water flows in deficient and obsolete water infrastructures is a very difficult and costly endeavor. For this reason, the PTSP and other state institutions have not addressed this issue yet, although local experts and activists have indicated that there is an urgent need to detect leaks and formulate a demand management plan. Indeed, the two prioritized construction works are the tanks and the twenty-seven-inch pipeline. While the tanks have been completed, the latter is still in construction; however, since the tanks will be supplied by the new pipeline, they are not in operation yet. Things at the PTSP have been constantly delayed.

A weak institutional framework as well as the uneven urban development plans formulated for Buenaventura during the twentieth century (chapter 1) have led to the wider malfunctioning of the water infrastructures in the port city. Infrastructures are highly political, and they age as a result of abandonment and precarious maintenance. However, the Master Plan does not consider these nontechnical, historical, and structural issues as part of the problem, which, as I argue, "de-historicizes" the politics of water infrastructures in the port city. The PTSP materializes a contemporary state effort whose main aim is to attend to a technical problem, not a problem resulting from historically produced racial and political inequality. The (social, political, and cultural) geographies of independent Colombia have drawn on colonial and modern imaginations that produced racialized landscapes, such as both the Pacific rainforests and urban worlds (Leal 2018; Restrepo 2013). The fact that the Afro-Colombian population of Buenaventura is deprived of a functioning infrastructural system of water supply is related as much to these historical processes as it is to technical and engineering issues.

Centralized and hierarchical organizations, institutional racism, underfunding, and burdensome bureaucratic procedures perpetuate this relationship of inclusive exclusion. The promise made by then-President Santos in 2014 that Buenaventura would have a functioning water supply system within four years has not been fulfilled. Similarly, the stated goals of the PTSP haven't been attained. Nonetheless, the effort *itself* (represented in reports, figures, discourses, and the presence of state officials in Buenaventura) gives the sense of effort and compliance, partially exempts the state from further accountability, and reveals a relationship of inclusive exclusion.

The Headquarters

In January 2020 I visited the headquarters of the PTSP, in the offices of the UNGRD, for the first time. After several attempts to get an appointment with the plan's director, I was finally invited to visit the headquarters, located in a modern business complex with offices and restaurants, hundreds of miles away from Buenaventura, in the north of Bogotá. To enter the compound, visitors must pass a security check and explain the reason for their visit. I waited for a while until the security guard could reach someone at the PTSP offices to confirm that I was expected.

The compound is a sort of dystopian, privatized city. Walled off from the public space, it hosts government offices, start-ups, shops, and restaurants in various buildings surrounded by urban gardens. Paved paths connect spaces within the compound, like in a shopping mall. Young white and mestizo people, elegantly dressed, walk around under the midday sun, chatting loudly. There are no street vendors, no traffic jams, no dust nor dirt. I walked toward the Gold Building, a very modern construction, wearing leather shoes and a jacket. After passing another security check, I went up to the fourth floor and entered the UNGRD offices. I was met by Beatriz, an official of the PTSP, and I introduced myself as a PhD student in political science and anthropology at a German university. I was told that the director, with whom I had an appointment, was occupied with other urgent activities and would not be able to give me an interview after all. Beatriz would be the one responsible of explaining to me how the project would be structured.

We entered a conference room. She opened her laptop and turned on the projector. Armed with a PowerPoint presentation, she presented the structure, history, and functioning of the PTSP, its management methods, internal structure, and current projects. The language of the presentation was highly juridical and technical. Several figures and maps purported to represent the PTSP as a whole, as a sort of institutional machine. The procedures seemed to be very clear, represented as transparent and logical. Depicting public institutions and processes in the form of mind maps gives the sense of the state as a neutral, well-structured, and functioning apparatus.

Although it was difficult for me to grasp and approach the cracks in her highly technical discourse, Beatriz was (unconsciously) reproducing a series of racial prejudices and geographical imaginaries on the Pacific while depicting the tensions and difficulties within the project. I noticed that her discourse contained adverse and prejudiced opinions of the population of Buenaventura, its local experts, and its local government. For instance, she stated that "institutional strengthening" was one of the most important features of the PTSP since it would be "non-sense to hand over a water supply system which people are not capable to maintain and repair regularly. *People should know* how to provide continuity of the service" (emphasis added). Historically, institutional weakness in the urban Pacific has been the main reason for the deficient provision of public goods. However, to reiterate that the region lacks both strong institutions and skilled personnel (in contrast to other regions of the country) suggests that local politicians and experts in Buenaventura are not capable of managing a modern water supply system, and further misrepresents the historical context of the politics of water supply in the port city and the region.

Beatriz also noted repeatedly that the PTSP's formal structure assumes the direct participation of local governments of Buenaventura in the formulation of the projects, but, considering "local mismanagement and corruption," she said the PTSP had to provide "facilitators" to speed up and promote the formulation and design of projects. She also stated that "those people" (*esa gente*) in Buenaventura, a pejorative phrase to refer to a group of persons, often oppose projects that have been designed as part of the plan, and that the projects had to be stopped, affecting the local population. She was referring to social movements and local activists, who, as I show below, have repeatedly criticized the PTSP. Indeed, there was a palpable hostility toward social movements and people from Buenaventura in her discourse.

Toward the end of the interview, I explained to her that one of my main interests was to understand both the tensions and negotiations between the different actors within the project. She showed little interest in responding. I felt that the question (and possible answers) would truly challenge the technical core of her presentation and go beyond the hermetic and congruent ways in which the state is desired and self-represented. The PTSP (as presented by Beatriz) would be a neutral state construct, contained in technocratic guidelines and based on laws, official documents, and clear structures; an answer to my question might have cracked this narrative. She answered vaguely, lowering her voice, and told me that I could verify that everything she said was true in a meeting I would attend the next day in Buenaventura. She said there are "frictions and conflicts with the community, because the truth is that *it is not an easy community*" (emphasis added). She also said that she could introduce me to Alberto, a PTSP officials who is often present in the "field," since he would be one of the people who continuously experience this type of friction. He would be the one "giving the face" of the state (Burnyeat 2022).

Racism

On Beatriz's suggestion, I met Alberto on the terrace of a hotel in the city center of Buenaventura. It was late evening after a stressful day during which we had attended several meetings. We each ordered a cold beer and took a seat on the terrace. I quickly understood that the conversation would take place outside the technocritical domains and the black box of the project. Alberto began by telling me about his life. His son, a student of hydraulic engineering in Europe, had been "traveling around the world working for development agencies." Through this very first story, he was trying to pull me into a confidential context of class and ethnic identity (Boyer 2008). I kept listening and let him talk.

He poured his beer into a glass and continued. As a civil engineer from Bogotá, he had worked on many infrastructure projects (state and private) throughout the country, mostly in marginalized areas. "I was always exposed to the violence of armed groups, to the corruption of local governments, and to hostile weather," he told me. "I am a warrior of infrastructure and construction," he added. His self-representation as a "warrior" offered a dramatic element—a modernizer who has fought to enter unruly territories which are difficult to dominate. He told me that he was a victim of countless extortions by armed groups, both guerrillas and paramilitaries, and that he had once been kidnapped for several days.

He told me in detail what it meant to work in such "wild territories"—he was mainly referring to the Amazon and the Pacific lowlands where he worked as an engineer. His depictions resonated with representations of both travelers and colonizers (*colono*). Indeed, these representations have played a crucial role in the constitution of "otherness" and the production of space in Colombia (see introduction herein; see also Serje 2011). Moreover, for Alberto, to "penetrate" territories means to know them firsthand.

"I am used to these kinds of people," he continued. "They are not easy at all." In general terms, he was referring to racialized Afro-Colombian people from Buenaventura. But he was specifically pointing to local engineers who are part of ASIB and who are in constant dialogue (and dispute) with PTSP officials. He assumed that I would agree with his opinions and that we would share a sort of ethnic complicity. He accused both local engineers and activists in Buenaventura of waiting for the termination of the operation contract with Hidropacífico, the private company providing the service, to "keep the business for themselves and make profit." He also said that they did not work hard enough—reproducing another racist pattern of Colombia and elsewhere—and that Black people were not reliable at all. The PTSP would not be as successful as expected because "Black people" would constantly cause conflicts, he claimed. "The general manager of the project is often upset about folks over here. But she doesn't give up, despite those people," he said. The general manager, a mestizo official with a long career within the Colombian civil service, is known for being a successful leader, sharp and consistent. PTSP officials refer to her as *la jefe* (the boss), a term that in Colombia points to someone holding intellectual and managerial authority, as well as the only one able to make crucial decisions. By calling her *la jefe*, PTSP officials sought to confer authority on their own observations. If "the people here" are difficult, it is *also* because *la jefe* says so. To invoke her frustration and steadfastness toward people in Buenaventura gives veracity to such an assessment.

At one point, Alberto started to use racist and pejorative language to refer to Afro-Colombians, slightly lowering his voice. He began to use phrases that I refuse to reproduce in this work. I was shocked. I kept drinking my beer and observed him, an overweight mestizo engineer, wearing an official uniform with the logo of the PTSP while reproducing representations of otherness in which a racialized, lazy, and corrupt Other emerges as a subject opposed the logics of progress, objectivity, and development. Of course, these views and this language cannot be found anywhere in official documents, laws, or speeches. However, it is evident that racial differences continue to be central to the everyday practices of the state. "The banal repetition of everyday actions and their mundane realities," anthropologists Sharma and Gupta (2006) note, "reproduce the state as an institution across time and space." Beyond the black box, racial prejudices seem to constitute social and material relations within and beyond the project.

The grotesque ethnic and racial prejudices Alberto reproduced during our conversation on the hotel terrace perpetuate and legitimize political, social, and spatial differences. Deprivation and exclusion from public goods are political processes materialized in the built landscape. In her work on the nineteenth and early twentieth century Colombian Pacific, historian Claudia Leal (2018) argues that a mestizo elite propagated discourses that depicted the landscapes of the region as racialized. Ideas of highly fertile yet harsh, inhospitable environments have been central to the representations of internal frontiers in Colombia such as the Pacific region. She further argues that the constitution and development of urban centers in the region was marked by racial dynamics (Leal 2018, 185–223).

The reproduction of racial prejudices by state officials points to the subtle, banal, and everyday representations which unfold in an underneath yet key realm of the state apparatus. It shows both how geographic logics of the Colombian nation-state are reproduced and the ways in which infrastructure projects are mediated and constituted through ethnic and social dynamics. In an article on the so-called street bureaucracies and the water supply system, anthropologist Nikhil Anand (2011) examines local clientelist networks in Mumbai that the population mobilize in order to secure connections and access to the city's public services. One of his informants, an engineer called Kerkar, suggests that connections in the Muslim neighborhood of Premnagar would be hindered by the laziness and negligence of its inhabitants. He conceives of them as coming from "outside," Anand asserts; further, according to the engineer, the Muslim neighborhood would always be "dirty," because "they don't work hard, nor did they keep their neighborhood clean" (Anand 2011, 556). Kerkar, Anand notes, both ignores and reproduces an urban reality:

the historically produced, ethnically driven exclusion of Muslim neighborhoods from public service systems.

Racist assertions and actions, as Anand shows, do not merely reproduce personal beliefs or prejudices. They are rather an integral part of
institutional racism. Although I did not attend internal meetings of the
PTSP in Bogotá, I can infer that the tensions between the mestizo leading
group and local actors was referred to in racial terms. When social activist and local experts reclaimed and generated tensions, demanding state
efficacy in the project's progress, they would be depicted as backward,
aggressive, and lazy. The project is hierarchical in nature because it was
planned by the national government and monitored by the creditors—
the World Bank and the Inter American Development Bank. Local actors
are rather included pro forma in the decision-making processes of the
project, as the next section well exemplifies.

The Water Roundtables

As part of the accord signed between the central government and the
Strike Committee in 2017, so-called Water Roundtables were established
to periodically discuss and monitor the progress made by the different
state institutions to improve the water infrastructures in Buenaventura.
The meetings take place every three or four months in an auditorium of
the municipality. Different state institutions, as well as grassroots organizations, send representatives to attend the gatherings. I was officially
invited to one of these meetings by PTSP officials. At the entrance of
the auditorium, I met a group of activists and state officials I had talked
to before. We were chatting and drinking coffee, waiting for the meeting to begin. Representatives from the Superintendence of Residential
Public Services (Superintendencia de Servicios Públicos Domiciliarios),
the Ministry of Housing, City, and Territory (Minvivienda), Hidropacífico, the SAAB, and the PTSP and even the mayor of Buenaventura all
attended the meeting. Although the environment was quite tense, everyone was conversing politely. An agenda had been circulated in advance
indicating that there would be several presentations.

A young mestizo state official from the Superintendence of Residential
Public Services was the first presenter. He began by introducing the most

recent figures on water supply coverage in the city, according to data gathered by the service provider, Hidropacífico. A projector displayed figures on the screen. After the official started reading the statistics, several people began shouting at him. He stated that around 80 percent of the inhabitants in Buenaventura had a regular connection to the water supply system. "That is not true! You are lying!" a social activist said loudly. The atmosphere became quite tense. A local engineer shouted: "The state has to provide reliable data, this is scandalous!" The state official seemed intimidated. He apologized and asserted that the superintendence had gathered information from the provider and that, in case the data were truly misleading, they would conduct a survey in the field. Social leaders stressed that without reliable data, projects could not be implemented effectively. However, the superintendence plays only a minor role in the politics of the construction, maintenance, and repair of the water infrastructure system. This national institution rather regulates the billing and cost recovery procedures of operators. Nonetheless, it represents the central state and is meant to publish figures regarding water and sewage supply coverage.

The next speaker was a higher official from Minvivienda, namely the deputy of the water supply section within the ministry. With an arrogant and condescending tone, this mestizo, upper-class higher official stood at the front and began by stating that Buenaventura was one of the most important and beloved territories for the ministry and for himself. The audience laughed, unveiling a certain irony in his assertions. A city with one of the most precarious water supply systems in the country could not be a "priority" for an institution such as Minvivienda, a social leader told me after the meeting. The official then said that he was not there to *rendir cuentas* ("render account") but rather to "work together with the people of Buenaventura in order to continue with the improvements of the water infrastructures in the city." The audience laughed louder. After decades of low investment, institutional weakness, and (infra)structural violence, this banal assertion of an official of the central made people laugh. At that point, the atmosphere became even more tense.

For the next two hours, the official presented the state of things and progress of the different projects that were supposed to be executed in Buenaventura (most of them led by the PTSP). He used the symbol of a traffic light to illustrate his point. Next to the three huge circular lights, the PTSP construction projects were listed: the completed ones (green); the ones in the process of implementation (yellow); and the ones that had not yet begun (red). Even though there was a clear imbalance in the progress of the different projects (most of them were listed next to the red light), the official seemed to be optimistic about the progress made by the PTSP. He then showed pictures of the opening event of the wa-ter tanks—though neither of the tanks were yet connected to the water networks and would remain off the grid until one of the main pipelines was rehabilitated. The official represented the water tanks as a completed project, even though they were not yet contributing to a better function-ing of the water infrastructures. In fact, the tanks should have been listed next to the yellow light.

The representation of material arrangements, official documents, and tables generate certain forms of visibility, regardless of the practicability and technical functioning of infrastructures.[1] The tanks constructed by the PTSP, placed in a highly visible place next to the main road at the entrance of Buenaventura, exist in a range of representations that fosters a "treacherous" visibility. Yet these tanks in Buenaventura are not yet connected to the water infrastructures and remain off the grid. However, they can be marked off as a completed project, as something successfully built. This is related to the fact that pipelines are mostly buried, out of sight for most people. But by making infrastructures visible (two huge tanks placed in a prominent location), the state visibly demonstrates its alleged compliance. Presenting the tanks as a completed project while, in fact, they remain disentangled from the rest of the network both gener-ates a sense of progress and a creates a state effect (Mitchell 1991).

Another issue that arose during the meeting was the accord between the Strike Committee and the state. The PTSP is financed by a loan of the World Bank and the Inter American Development Bank, and the funders placed some conditions on the loan regarding the implementation of the plan. Even though the accord between the central state and the Strike Committee signed back in 2017 (see chapter 3) did not include the PTSP

---

1. Brian Larkin points to a "poetic mode" of infrastructures, whereby "form is loosened from technical function." For example, "a pipe may not be attached to an effluent disposal system, but it is attached to techniques of regulation, audit, and administration" (Larkin 2013, 225).

(which was planned and launched years before), both state officials and members of the Strike Committee understood it to be part of the efforts made by the state to improve the water infrastructures in the city and thus as, at least indirectly, part of the accord. A member of the committee complained several times about the fact that, in the meetings they held with the PTSP, officials of the banks were often present. The "shuffling institutional arrangement" of the PTSP would heavily encumber the implementations of the accord. "We signed it with the state, not with the development banks," he added. The many institutions involved in the projects would challenge the progress of the projects due to blurry articulations and shared responsibility. These claims were widely disregarded by mestizo officials.

Toward the end of the event, Alberto (the PTSP official I had talked to in the hotel), presented a brief report on the activities. During the presentation, social activists and local engineers pointed to several inaccuracies in the report and vehemently criticized the project's management. Alberto acted "professionally," reacting calmly to all of the comments and criticisms. The same person who, just days before, had spoken to me about Afro-Colombians and Black people in a pejorative way was now masking his animosity through diplomacy and highly technocratic language. Indeed, the technocratic language of the presentations, accompanied by statistics, reports, work plans, and "traffic lights" status markers, served as a way of representing and validating the "progress" made by the PTSP. However, under the surface and beyond the "rational core" (Boyer 2008), other affects, discourses, and facts were sustained and reproduced by state actors.

After more than three hours, the meeting came to an end. The group of social activists, local state officials, and experts left the auditorium and gathered at the entrance of the building. I approached them and began chatting. "Now you see how things work," one of the activists told me. "As a researcher, you have to be aware how the state is cheating on us, and you should write about it." I felt overwhelmed. If state officials such as Alberto had seen me joining the group of social activists and local engineers, they might think I was "on their side." But in a way, I was. In fact, not only did I sympathize with their positionings and goals, but they were key for me to understand and conceptualize the proceedings of the state, to understand what happens beyond the black box of the PTSP.

Without their insightful remarks during the meeting, I would not have necessarily noticed the inconsistencies and misleading representations state officials were displaying.

After an hour or so, some activists, local engineers, and I were still standing in a circle and talking about the meeting. The sun was lowering over Buenaventura. The extreme heat had receded, and we felt a breeze blowing in from the sea. The others kept criticizing how things were presented and how burdensome bureaucratic proceedings were. However, the atmosphere was no longer tense. In fact, everyone was sort of hopeful. "You have to put pressure on state institutions and insist," Nestor said while lighting a cigarette. "Then things may work out."

Regularization

In January 2019 I was sitting next to engineer Jairo Hernández in a cab going from a construction site to the city center of Buenaventura. We had begun our interview walking through the muddy soils of the construction site of Loma Alta, surrounded by cement mixers, heavy machinery, and steel rods. Hernández explained to me the technical details of the water tanks the state had built. Equipped with modern technology, the tanks could store huge amounts of water and serve as a backup to the supply system. Due to heavy rains, the rivers where the intakes are installed sometimes become turbid and the supply has to be interrupted. The water stored in the tanks would solve the problem, he explained to me. Suddenly, it began raining and the workers had to stop working. We walked to a shelter next to a huge billboard advertising the PTSP (figure 8). "The next thing to do is to rehabilitate the twenty-seven-inch pipeline to connect the tanks," he said, "but bureaucracies in Colombia are so burdensome." In fact, the tanks had been built within a year but were not yet connected to the network.

Besides being a consultant of the construction firm, Hernández is also part of ASIB, a local guild and important actor in the politics of water infrastructure in the city, which I closely examine in chapter 3. He seemed very familiar with the recent history of the water infrastructure system. As an Afro-Colombian and an ASIB member, he identified with the "territory and its people," he told me several times during the interview. As

FIGURE 8 Billboard of the PTSP

a consultant, he supervised the projects carried out by the PTSP and oversaw what "those people coming from the capital are doing over here in Buenaventura."

After standing and chatting with me under the shelter for around an hour, Hernández had to leave for an appointment in the city center. He offered to continue the interview in the cab. I agreed. Luckily for me, we got stuck in a traffic jam and had plenty of time to chat. During the interview, he told me in detail about many aspects of the techno-political framework that sustains the water infrastructures in the city: from the state of the water networks and the need for new water storage tanks, to the loan taken out by the central state with the World Bank and the Inter American Development Bank and finances of the PTSP, and to the occupation of public posts and the response of civil society to the PTSP. His language shuttled between technical, ethical, and political realms, and was less clinical than the language used by Beatriz, the official in the headquarters of the PTSP in Bogotá. In chapter 3, I return to Hernández's criticisms of the project. Here, however, I want to address the Demand Management Plan formulated as one of the projects of the PTSP.

While sitting in the cab, I asked Hernández about his thoughts on the everyday informal practices deployed by the population to access the centralized water infrastructure system. I was curious to know his opinion on the illicit connections, the domestic infrastructures of water storage, and the tampering of water meters (a phenomenon I address in chapter 4). In his response, he suggested that the illicit connections and not paying water bills was a kind of "citizen irresponsibility" on the part of the population. He argued that these connections and homemade infrastructures would depress the water supply system due to the leaks they generate. Hernández underlined the need to "educate people" in a "culture of rational water use." According to him, 80 percent of users didn't pay for the service. For this reason, no one, whether they have a licit connection or not, has access to water twenty-four hours a day, he said. When the system improvement projects were implemented and users "regularized," Hernández continued, the time of water supply would increase. To repair leaks meant, among other things, to prevent illicit connections and to "educate" people.

After having talked to many social activists and local engineers who advocate for local communities and legitimize illicit connections to pipelines as well as the construction of water storage systems, I was surprised that Hernández was accusing local people of acting irresponsibly and blaming them for the leaks in the system. After I asked about irregular connections needed to store water, another PTSP official assured me that the project would not enter "into such minutiae" and would only be focused on "improvement works so that all users could be formally connected to the pipe networks." He pointed out that a formalization of the water supply system would mean an improvement for the conditions of the population, allowing a regular and continuous access to the resource. In fact, education programs were not officially part of the PTSP.

Nonetheless, one of the main projects which should be carried out by the PTSP is the so-called Demand Management Plan (Plan de Gestión de Demanda). This plan consists of a wide survey of pipelines and users in order to effectively govern the networks, allowing the state to "see" (Scott 1998). ASIB members have emphasized the urgency of implementing this plan. However, their views on the plan sharply differ. While some see it as a technical procedure to identify and repair the many leaks affecting the system's pressure, others, like Hernández, view it as a means to "formalize" connections and control consumers. Due to the lack of investments and the weak institutional framework that sustains the water infrastructures in the city, informal pipelines and nontraceable networks have been appended onto the centralized system. Originally, it was intended that the survey would be conducted by both Hidropacífico and the SAAB and would be executed through a "georeferenced topographic location of the networks, as well as the length, diameter and material of each pipe section and the location and description of all the network accessories ... including material and diameters" (contract between City of Buenaventura and Hidropacífico, 2001, 7). However, due to a lack of resources and a diffuse distribution of responsibilities, it was never conducted.

Back in the taxi, while waiting for the traffic jam to clear, I looked out of the window and saw a poor neighborhood next to the road: a neighborhood with disastrous infrastructures and many water tanks installed on the rooftops of the dwellings. Hernández kept talking. Once the survey was available, the obsolete and dysfunctional pipes, which represent a great majority of Buenaventura's water networks, would be replaced, he said. "The service provider will be able to bill more," the engineer told me. "Because of the network survey. The company will be able to have reliable information on where people are illegally connected. If I have fifty fraudulent connections from this street down, I can cut off the water supply up here and stop the supply." He said that new pipes to be installed in Buenaventura were made of high-density polyethylene, which would replace the existing PVC (polyvinyl chloride) pipes. The Master Plan states that HDPE is the "material with the best performance, with the lowest leakage rate curve of all materials" (2014, 74). It is a material that has recently become popular for water supply systems thanks to its versatility to adapt to difficult terrain, its stiffness, and that it's both lightweight and heat resistant. An additional benefit—from the perspective of the supply provider, at least—is that an irregular connection to an HDPE pipe is almost impossible since, unlike PVC, it is not easy to pierce.

Although the replacement of the existing PVC pipes is far from being a reality, it exemplifies the logics of a development project such as the PTSP. As I show in chapter 4, the sociomaterial practices of storing water and improvising connections to the centralized water infrastructures of the city represent coping mechanisms deployed by the population in order to access a vital resource the state fails to supply properly. Certainly, if a "regularization" of water infrastructures achieves an efficient supply, people won't need to deploy these practices. However, impeding the improvised sociomaterial practices by introducing rigid materials and surveillance practices could worsen the situation and lead to a complete disconnection of impoverished subjects from the system. Thus, the solutions formulated by the state to solve the problem of water infrastructures and regularize the system pose a danger to the affected populations.

Scalability and the Erasure of History

In an article on capitalism and global entanglements, anthropologist Anna Tsing (2012) addresses and conceptualizes scalability as a key feature of modernity. Models and designs of production that were to be replicated and expanded throughout colonized territories and beyond encapsulate and reify ideas and projects of the modern world. To "scale up" alludes to discourses and desires of expansion and replication. "Scalable" is that which is deployed and executed based on a precise design and whose operation draws on the ability to discard and cancel those elements that could generate "effects of transformation" (Tsing 2012, 507). In this way, it scalable projects pretend to be composed of "elements of the social landscape removed from formative social relations," and therefore autonomous, interchangeable, and replicable (513). Thus, the scalable makes use of mechanisms that transform the world and pretend, at the same time, to maintain—unaltered—its design, the very matrix of its intervention. For Tsing, it is a "formula that constitutes the dream we have come to call modernity" (513). And although Tsing's definition is based on examples that include forms of production and exploitation of resources in the nineteenth and twentieth centuries, it also applies to a general method of intervening in and constituting the modern world.

The arrangement of materials such as pipes and hoses, the technical aspects, the centralized water supply system, and the cost recovery politics of operators, among others, are crucial elements of a scalable design that aim to shape, transform, and govern water infrastructures worldwide. Indeed, supranational organizations such as the development banks and the United Nations have been focused on modernizing water supply systems in so-called developing countries around the world. Modern cities draw on very specific forms of infrastructure that mirror forms of governmentality and that, at the same time, are based on scalable models. The PTSP, in fact, responds to these precepts of modernity. Assertive public policy, well-defined development plans, and precise engineering are the necessary tools to scale up a functioning project of modern infrastructure.

What happens with the *nonscalable* elements that appear during and after interventions, and that destabilize the original infrastructure? The elements that are not part of the scalable and generate—for example, leaks in the project and pipelines? Although the scalable designs pretend to erase or expel heterogeneity and diversity that could disturb its functioning, these destabilizing elements often persist. Buenaventura's infrastructure landscapes are, among other things, constituted by piracy: irregular connections, self-made water storage systems, and tampering. Furthermore, local knowledge and political mobilization seems also to "disturb" the implementation of the intervention plan. Indeed, the PTSP widely considers these elements marginal and alien to its techno-political designs: It pretends to erase them, while it ignores its complexity and nonscalable functioning.

Irregular connections and pirate infrastructures certainly do damage the system. The more leaks there are, the worse the supply of water is for everyone. While people draw on these sociomaterial practices to "survive" amid a deficient supply system, they further contribute to its very deterioration. Nonscalable elements can be destructive, and although they point to a heterogeneity, they are not "productive" forces but rather arise from precarity. Urban inventiveness, creativity, and informality are forms of nonscalable improvisation which appear in the context of failed scalable projects, such as water systems (Simone 2006). The water mafias in Mumbai, the collection of rainwater in Quibdó, and the storage systems and pirate connections in Buenaventura are just some examples of the persistent unfolding of the nonscalable within precarious urban worlds.

However, these fragile systems do not exist beyond or separate from the scalable infrastructure projects; they are attached to them, as I show in chapter 4 by analyzing the water storage systems in Ciudad Blanca. As the PTSP seeks to expand and regularize users, pirate, nonscalable networks would likely be dismantled. And although the PTSP could scale up a functioning system and use it as an opportunity to overcome precarity, it will probably not do so, thus posing a danger to people living off the improvised systems. What will happen when users become regularized and cannot access free water through illicit connections? What if they cannot pay the bills? Will they be cut off from the system?

Other nonscalable elements that appear within the scope of the PTSP are the local activists and engineers (see chapter 3). This group of actors have articulated political and technical discourses which do not align with the plans and goals of the PTSP. This is mainly based on a historically grown mistrust of the central state. Their insights, remarks, and comments are seen as "disturbing" for the project managers and engineers. This is not to say that these local actors do not pursue the improvement of a modern water supply system based on scalable projects. On the contrary, they want to see an assertive state intervention. Still, they deploy a political discourse that aims to grasp and foreground the everyday life of the urban poor in Buenaventura. Social activists not only argue for a better water supply system but also bring to light the daily experiences of marginalized and racialized people. An alternative development plan, which has been formulated by social activists in the city, points to the necessity of generating sustainable livelihoods for people, building modern infrastructures, and including citizens in decision-making processes. The discussions, arguments, and tensions that emerge during the Water Roundtables evidence the frictions between a scalable project and the more complex social, political, and material webs already existing and unfolding in Buenaventura.

Another feature of the PTSP as a scalable project is how it ignores historical configurations of the state in the region. The developmental agendas toward the Pacific region have had very similar goals: to integrate the region into the state-building process and to close the gap between the Pacific and the country's interior. However, these attempts have broadly failed. This corresponds to processes of abandonment. In the case of the water infrastructures in Buenaventura, institutional weakness, lack of investment, and an urban development agenda that mainly focused on the port economies all led to a deficient supply system (chapter 1). Almost seventy years after the first urbanization processes began in the city, the PTSP presents its goals and "achievements" without acknowledging the structural problems that exist, as if acting upon a tabula rasa. This means that the plan not only fails to attain its goals but reproduces a specific set of relation while aiming to erase a history of exclusion, underinvestment, and violence.

Infrastructures of Peace

The wordplay of the label Plan Todos Somos PAZcífico aims to refashion the Spanish name of the region (Pacífico) by adding a Z, merging the concept of peace (*paz*) with the region's historical name. Todos Somos PAZcífico translates as "We are all PAZcífico," suggesting that *we* (a pronoun that encompasses the mestizo nation) identify with a marginal region affected by violence and inhabited by an Other, incorporating it into the corpus of the nation-state project by means of development and peacebuilding. Certainly, the pronoun could also be referring to the whole of the nation (including non-mestizo subjects). However, given that the project was planned, conceived, and executed from centralized state institutions, the name reproduces depictions of certain territories as marginal, abandoned, and relegated. Every single development plan seems to want to be seen as finally engaging with people historically abandoned, the "reverse of the nation" (Serje 2011).

Moreover, the idea that peace should be included in a development project responds to the wider political agenda and marketing of former President Juan Manuel Santos (2010–2018). From 2012 onward, the government and the FARC guerrilla held peace talks that led to a peace agreement signed in 2016 in the city of Cartagena. Scholars have shown how peace politics reached beyond the peace process itself and was used as a governmental approach to several issues (see McFee 2019; Burnyeat 2022). Peace-building became synonymous with development, a hopeful future, and an (economic and material) integration of marginalized territories. To ensure the smooth transition to a "post-conflict society"—as scholars, officials, and important actors labeled the time after the signing of the peace agreement—was one the main goals of the Santos government. This new Colombia would, it was hoped, be less violent and unequal, more inclusive and modern, and would have functioning and integrated infrastructures.

Anthropologist Austin Zeiderman (2020) examines the material dimensions of the construction of this post-conflict society through infrastructures. In this "new" Colombia, security and development would expand and be guaranteed to the whole of the population; infrastructures, conceived as networks to integrate territories and permit the circulations of people and goods, are meant to fulfill these dreams. However,

Zeiderman argues that "as a notoriously intractable armed conflict continues alongside periodic peacebuilding efforts, substances like concrete, and the construction projects they support, become material and symbolic resources in the struggle to control a deeply uncertain process of historical change" (2020, 500). And although the PTSP does not aim to connect territories or use large amounts of concrete, it seeks (or sought) to improve the living conditions of a population highly affected by armed conflict as part of a peacebuilding strategy. Yet the state-making process the peace policy of Santos put in motion in Buenaventura through the improvement of the water infrastructures was rather unsuccessful, while violence continued to proliferate.

In 2018 right-wing candidate Iván Duque was elected president. He represented a political segment that broadly rejected the peace accords. Former president and far-right caudillo Álvaro Uribe Vélez (2002–2010) led a political movement to vote against the peace agreement in a referendum held in late 2016 and was a fierce opponent of Juan Manuel Santos. Iván Duque was his candidate and protégé. During Duque's administration (2018–2022), the implementation of the peace process (which involves many institutions and a huge bureaucracy) slowed down in part because of underfunding. Violence reached new peaks while hundreds of social leaders, environmental activists, and former FARC members were assassinated.

With regard to Buenaventura and the urban Pacific, the National Development Plan of Duque's government (Pacto por Colombia) ensured the further financing of the PTSP. However, and since his government did not consider peace to be central to its politics, the name of the project seems to be misplaced. Peace was a promise that should be fulfilled through the building of infrastructures that would foster territorial integration and development.

In this chapter, I have engaged ethnographically with the PTSP and shown how the burdensome bureaucratic machinery, the slow progress of construction, and underlying institutional racism prejudices reproduce the state's inclusive exclusion. The state's infrastructural project, the main aim of which was to improve the water supply system in a city that has been historically racialized and marginalized, has somewhat failed. The PTSP, whose funding ended in 2023, has not attained its stated goals. Those living in Buenaventura are still exposed to an infrastructural violence since they are being deprived of a functioning system of water supply. PAZ was a rhetorical element of the Santos government that encapsulated the desires of building a post-conflict society, ideologically but also materially. The agenda of Duque's government, which broadly ignores peacebuilding processes, saw the reemergence of many of the unsolved problems of the Pacific region in general, and of Buenaventura in particular. The pandemic of COVID-19 worsened the situation of the water supply systems. Many spontaneous mobilizations took place in the city during 2021, and the city found itself near infrastructural collapse more than once (Acevedo 2021). In general terms, things have not progressed as planned. The water service continues to be highly deficient. Promises were not kept. No surprises there.

Claudia

Claudia grew up in a large family of peasants in a small village near Pereira, in the country's interior. Her family was hit by violence during the never-ending armed conflict in Colombia. One of her uncles, a small farmer, was killed by guerrillas in the eighties for not paying vacuna. They first kidnapped him, and even though his wife paid a ransom, he was shot on the neck. The military found his corpse sixty miles from their farm. That is one of Claudia's childhood memories. Luis, Claudia's oldest brother, became a *comerciante* (shopkeeper, literally: a trader) and moved to Buenaventura in the early 1990s to try his luck there. At age fifteen, Claudia moved to the port city to work with him. There she met Alberto, a friend of Luis. Even though she was much older, they fell in love and married in 1997. He was also a *comerciante*. They moved back to their hometown and opened a small supermarket.

In 2000 their first daughter, Antonia, was born. "I was still a teenager as I gave birth to her,"' Claudia told me with tears in her eyes. One Saturday morning in 2002, a brawl started in their supermarket after a man complained about a sim card he had bought there some days before, and which was apparently damaged. He was loudly shouting at Claudia as Alberto entered the supermarket and stabbed him in his back several times. The man died the same day and the couple had to flee. They moved to the city of Guapi in the southern Pacific region. There, they changed their identities and started a business from scratch and began trading with gold they bought from Black peasants in the town. Claudia flew several times a month from Guapi to the city of Medellín to resell the gold to bigger merchants. She took a small plane accompanied by her daughter, hiding small jars full of gold in a teddy bear. But things in Guapi got too dangerous due to the presence of several armed groups. In 2007 they had to move back to Buenaventura.

There, Claudia and Alberto opened a big supermarket in the very center of Buenaventura, built two hotels for truck drivers along the road, and rented a *tienda* (small grocery store) in Ciudad Blanca. When people started asking for products like rods, tubes, and screwdrivers at the *tienda*, Claudia and Alberto decided to expand the store to include a section of hardware products. True entrepreneurs. Things weren't going well in their marriage, though. In 2008, a few months after Claudia gave birth to her second child, the couple divorced. "He was a violent person, and a *mujeriego* [a womanizer]. It was horrible," Claudia told me while sitting in her living room late at night, chatting with a beer in her hand. Alberto managed to keep all the businesses for himself—businesses they had built up together. Claudia could keep only the hardware shop and a small motel. "I was truly heartbroken. I felt betrayed." The shop became prosperous. She found good assistants and learned a lot about plumbing and repairing, fields traditionally aligned with men and masculinity. She sued Alberto, with no success. Then she met Iván, a truck driver who was staying at her small hotel. "He is a very sensitive guy," she told me, smiling shyly. However, Iván eventually moved back to a small town in Tolima, in the interior of the country. Now they have a long-distance relationship.

In 2018 Antonia, Claudia's daughter, age eighteen, got pregnant. She was living in the city of Pereira, studying law. There she met her boyfriend and the father of the child. "He is a crook, and a horrible father," Claudia told me. After the romance and the unwanted pregnancy, he was jailed for drug trafficking. That same year Antonia gave birth to Juanito. Three women, Claudia and her two daughters, are raising Juanito in their house next to the hardware shop. They are always concerned that something could happen to him in such a violent city, and about the hardware shop, their only source of income. Very tough women, I remember often thinking.

CHAPTER 3

Reacting to (Infra)structural Violence

Local Experts and Social Mobilization

Buenaventura es el puerto principal de la nación
que en Colombia transporta la mayor de su provisión
pero esto no solo un puerto aquí también hay población
y llevamos años recibiendo discriminación
señor alcalde, usted debe entender
que el paro no es por usted
el paro es por un gobierno que no ve
lo importante que somos para el país abastecer
y vivimos junto al agua y estamos muertos de sed
presidente esas publicaciones por que las hace
dizque usted respeta el pueblo y su derecho a expresase
Nuestras marchas eran pacifica, con argumento y base
y usted nos mandó al ESMAD para que nos lanzaran gases
      —"LO QUE NOS MERECEMOS," EL TEACHER, 2017

Buenaventura is the nation's main port
which in Colombia transports most of its commodities
but this is not only a port here, there is also a population
and we have been receiving discrimination for years
Mr. Mayor, you must understand
that the strike is not because of you

the strike is because of a government that seems to be blind
about the role we play for the country's supply
we live next to the water, and we are dying of thirst
Mr. President, why are you posting that stuff?
You say that you respect the people and their right to express themselves
Our marches were peaceful, with arguments
and you sent the police to throw gas at us

— "WHAT WE DESERVE," EL TEACHER, 2017

Local rapper El Teacher released the song "What We Deserve" during the 2017 general strike in Buenaventura, which lasted for more than twenty days. During this time, several social movements, grassroots organizations, trade unions, ethnic movements, and locals took to the streets and blocked the entrance of the port, impeding its regular functioning. The lyrics of the song express the sentiments that motivated the local social movements to call a general strike.

This chapter addresses the waves of social protest and political mobilization in Buenaventura that arose in the 2010s in the face of a proliferation of everyday crime, the deprivation of public goods, and deficient infrastructure networks. Put differently, it examines the mobilizations and the articulation of political discourses as a response to the various forms of structural and infrastructural violence that the majority of the population of Buenaventura was suffering. I show how these movements articulate the interweaving and overlaps between everyday violence and infrastructure. Back in 2008, the very first gatherings of social leaders in Buenaventura from ethnic grassroots organizations, labor unions, and environmental advocacy groups culminated in the constitution of the Comité por la Defensa del Agua y la Vida en Buenaventura (Committee for the Defense of Water and Life in Buenaventura). The fact that water and life both feature in the name of this new group points to two crucial aspects of social mobilizations in the port city. First, the name adopts a terminology rooted in the ethnic movements that arose in the 1980s and was strengthened by a new political agenda on ethnic minorities constituted in Colombia during the 1990s (Restrepo 2013; Escobar 2008). The formation of a political assemblage to defend water and life (as well as the territory) is linked to spatial conceptions of Afro-Colombian peasants in the rural Pacific. As geographer Ulrich Oslender has shown, "aquatic spaces" in the rural Pacific encapsulate a "particular set of spatialized relationships that has been instrumental in the organizing structures of rural black communities" (2002, 89). Second, the concepts of life and water were not merely adapted to the urban context of Buenaventura but aimed to reflect a specific phenomenon that was (and still is) harming large parts of the population in the port city: the deficient provision of water and the high rates of violence such as homicide and forced disappearance. By co-articulating water and life, the movement aimed to make visible the interweaving of violence and water infrastructures (Manos Visibles 2017). This book is inspired by this conceptual endeavor.

I focus in this chapter on the social mobilizations that began with the constitution of the Comité por la Defensa del Agua y de la Vida in 2008 and ended with a twenty-two-day general strike in 2017 that totally paralyzed the activity of the port. In the aftermath and after tense negotiations, the central government and the Comité del Paro (Strike Committee), a new committee that emerged from within the former one, signed an accord that allowed for the allocation of resources and the implementation of developmental plans to attend the needs of the population in terms of education, health, and security as well as water supply and sewage systems. I also address a group of actors who operate within (and beyond) the landscape of Buenaventura-based social movements: ASIB. This group of professional engineers has played a significant role in the negotiations between the central government and the social movements in the city.

Initially, the members of the ASIB served as technical advisers to important social leaders during the first mobilizations in the city. However, during a series of protests and mobilizations between 2014 and 2017, several members of the organization actively engaged in the political happenings of the city. Due to the professional nature of their organization, they were able to contribute expert knowledge that was central to the negotiations with the government. Moreover, they have developed a positionality in terms of ethnic identity and class. The members of the ASIB represent what I call "local experts," experts who are politically engaged, ethnically identified, and locally based. Yet this figure is not representative of alternative forms of knowledge production or alternative ontologies (de la Cadena 2019), nor does it point to forms of cooperation between activists' experts and local communities (Carmona and

Jaramillo 2020) since they identify as an integral part of the local population. This figure rather emerges from the ethnic-political movements of urban Buenaventura as well as from the tensions and controversies that have arisen between the central state and the group of local actors (see chapter 2), and the pressing need to approach the technical domain of hydraulic infrastructures.

The social movements have been pivotal to the political negotiations, controversies, and tensions that have taken place in Buenaventura between the central state and nonstate actors widely representing the interests local communities. Social movements have not merely claimed the rights of *bonaverenses* to access water and preserve life in this precarious city but have both articulated alternative plans of urban development and enacted languages of expert scientific knowledge through the ASIB. Given that infrastructures are highly technical objects, the negotiations around them constitute what Michel Callon and colleagues (2009, 13–36) calls "hybrid forums," spaces where a variety of actors come together in decision-making processes permeated by technical scientific knowledge. The ASIB, as a close partner of the social movement, was central to the production and circulation of expert knowledge, contesting the assumptions, procedures, and plans of the PTSP and the central state. Although their incidence in these negotiations has been weakened and marginalized by mestizo experts, they have transformed theses hybrid forums in "spaces of contestation and resistance" (Carmona and Jaramillo 2020, 1088).

Another important feature of social mobilizations in Buenaventura has to do with the restriction posed by the multicultural agenda that considers Afro-Colombian subjects mainly rural. Because of this conception, urban social movements have recently rearranged their discourses in order to attract attention to Afro-urban realities, despite the legal framework that aims to define Black subjects as rural and traditional (Zeiderman 2018). Even though social protest has a long history in the port city, the multicultural agenda of the 1990s threatened to marginalize it. Yet the wide alliances forged in the early 2010s and their persistence put social movements back on the political stage.

I draw here on ethnographic material I gathered during many conversations and interviews I held with members of the Strike Committee and the ASIB. I enjoyed most of the periodical encounters I had with the social leaders and local experts, which contrasted starkly with my encounters with PTSP officials and engineers. The conversations with social leaders and ASIB members tended to be very pleasant since these people were enthusiastic about water infrastructures and political mobilizations in Buenaventura, and they were interested in sharing their knowledge with me. For them, alliances are key to making their movement visible and to strengthening their networks beyond the city: they perceived me as a Colombian scholar living and working abroad, who, in turn, could spread the findings of the research and generate both visibility and a positive impact on the city's future infrastructures. I also felt that ASIB members had a strong interest in sharing their expert knowledge with me and thus seeking validation on the contentious topic of how to improve water infrastructures in Buenaventura.

A Brief History of Social Mobilization in Buenaventura

The consolidation of the three main urban hubs in the Pacific region responds to historical processes linked to the extraction of natural resources (Tumaco), the expansion of a port (Buenaventura) and the political-administrative independence of a territory (Quibdó). As historian Claudia Leal (2018) has demonstrated in the case of Tumaco and Quibdó, socio-racial dynamics between a mestizo elite and Black population marked the power relations within these urban centers and determined the constitution and development of urban spaces and the distribution of public goods. Although the Pacific region has been broadly excluded from the modernizing projects of the country's interior and has served as an offshore territory for the extraction of resources, the urban centers were erected as "enclaves of modernity" amid the "savage" and "unruly" surrounding territories. However, these urban spaces coproduced differential racial geographies along with mestizo and the Black identities. Thus, the Black populations were rarely part of the governmental and economic power and played only a marginal role within the state bureaucracy apparatus. Hence, processes of abandonment, racial segregation, low rates of investment, institutional weakness, and a lack of resources led to the disastrous unfolding of urban spaces throughout the Pacific (CNMH 2015; Arboleda 2004; Almario 2007).

Against the backdrop of structural inequality, social mobilization in Buenaventura began to develop alongside the growth of the port economies and the processes of urbanization by the second half of the twentieth century. The first important strike in the city took place in 1964. During the 1950s, Buenaventura was hit by both an earthquake (1955) and a seaquake (1957), which worsened the already dysfunctional public infrastructure system (Almario 2007). Faced with the precarious provision of public services in terms of housing and infrastructure, unionists and social activists declared a general strike and blocked the entrance of the port for around four days, a form of protest that would be repetitive in the city. In response to the strike, the government of former conservative President León Valencia (1962–66) launched the Buenaventura Plan, a development fund that anticipated the construction of housing projects and a bus terminal, the expansion of the bridge connecting the island with the continent, and the improvement of the water supply system. Yet it wasn't until 1975 that construction work began to take place, in the form of public schools and housing projects. However, no improvements were made to the water supply system (Bonet Morón et al. 2018, 15–16; Jaramillo et al. 2020, 144). Radio stations and newspapers denounced the noncompliance of the government and pointed to the still-precarious living standards of the population.

In 1998 a second strike took place in Buenaventura. This time, union leaders called the general strike and were joined by more than forty-five grassroots organizations. The strike was prompted by the fact that public servants in the city had not been paid by the state for more than six months. However, the population increase at the time and the consequences of the privatization of the port had worsened the problems in the city. Poverty and unemployment rates had skyrocketed. After the protesters presented a document to the government with around one hundred demands, both sides agreed to the formulation of a development plan for the city. After three days of protest, the Integral Development Plan for Buenaventura, 1998–2000, was launched. The years after the strike were full of hope for social activists in Buenaventura, since they had successfully negotiated with the central state. However, the development plan turned out to be insufficient to improve the living conditions of the population. Despite the expansion of some supply lines, the water supply system continued to be dysfunctional and to have coverage of around 60 percent of the households. In the following years, the waves of violence in the rural Pacific caused mass displacement to the urban centers, which in turn led to disorganized forms of urbanization (Jaramillo et al. 2020; Bonet-Morón et al. 2018, Manos Visibles 2017).

Still, the 1998 strike benefited social movements in Buenaventura. It strengthened ties between organizations, achieved the massive mobilization of people in the port city, and drew the attention of the national press and several state institutions. These two facts were pivotal to the mobilization in the decades that followed (Jaramillo et al. 2020, 142).

The General Strike, 2017

During the first years of the twenty-first century, the onslaught of paramilitary groups in the rural and urban areas of the Pacific generated a new social and humanitarian crisis. Many forcibly displaced people arrived in Buenaventura between 2000 and 2004, fleeing from the many massacres perpetrated by AUC paramilitaries in the region (CNMH 2015, 63). In 2007, in response to this crisis, a group of activists formed the Comité por la Defensa del Agua y la Vida. The committee brought together unionists, environmental activists, ethnic-territorial organizations, and other social groups. According to Nestor Romero, one of the social leaders of Buenaventura and founder of the committee, it was then that a truly new form of social mobilization began to take shape, focusing on the issues of violence, water, and the provision of public services. In 2009, during a forum organized by social movements that addressed the negative impacts of infrastructural megaprojects linked to the port economies, a new umbrella organization was founded: the Comité Interorganizacional (Interorganizational Committee), incorporating a wide range of movements including the Catholic church (Jaramillo et al. 2020, 146; see Zeiderman 2016).

In 2010 Juan Manuel Santos was elected president. As part of his national development plan, his first administration (2010–2014) announced the construction of a new port terminal in Buenaventura as well as the allocation of huge amounts of funding for the Pacific region. In 2013 the Interorganizational Committee called a meeting that planned possible protests in the following months and years. "Basically, we were preparing the strike," a social leader told me about the meeting. Everyday crime in Buenaventura rapidly increased and intensified from 2010 onward. For grassroots organizations and social movements, this was another reason to take to the streets. "We were trying to draw the attention of the rest of the country. We were living in a state of constant crisis, amidst violence, deficient water and sewage infrastructures and an almost nonexisting health care system," the leader added.

In February 2014 the first massive mobilization took place when the Strike Committee was created. Diverse working groups dedicated to different issues were established. These were spaces of dialogue and discussion among a wide range of social activists and neighborhood organizations addressing the problems of security, education, employment, and infrastructure (Manos Visibles 2017, Jaramillo et al. 2020, 150–52). In response, the central government executed a so-called Shock Plan. This plan would militarize wider parts of the city and allocate an initial investment. Furthermore, an official document addressing the "structural problems" of Buenaventura was formulated, and further investments were planned.

In 2014 Santos was reelected for a second presidential term (2014–2018). His new government was aware of the importance of attending to the needs of the Pacific region in the face of the massive mobilizations in Buenaventura and the imminence of a general strike, which would block the port and significantly affect the country's economy. One of his first actions was the creation of a unit within the presidency dedicated to formulating public policy and development plans for the Pacific region (Gerencia del Pacífico), as well as the launch of the PTSP (see chapter 1). The promise of a drastic reduction of homicide rates in Buenaventura as well as the adequate provision of water generated hope. However, things did not unfold as expected, and the strike was seen, at least by social movements, as unavoidable (Bonet-Morón et al. 2018).

Between 2014 and 2017, and mainly due to the state's noncompliance, the strike was prepared. During these years, the Strike Committee discussed a list of several demands and formulated a plan of structural and priority solutions. According to members of the Strike Committee, during these years they aimed to put pressure on institutions by warning of an upcoming general strike unless the government implemented the accords signed in 2014. In February 2017, during a visit from the chief of the National Planning Department, who was announcing a new urban development program to position Buenaventura as an entry point for Colombia to the global Pacific, a group of social leaders announced that the strike would come soon. The fact that the government was trying to promote Buenaventura as a world-class city of commerce generated anger within the population (Zeiderman 2016).

During 2017 the organization of a general strike began, with the support of around eighty-nine grassroots organizations (Jenss 2020, 73). On May 16, 2017, a group of three hundred people took to the streets and blocked the main roads that led to the port. The Strike Committee set up an agenda of activities, including speeches, marches, masses, and cultural events. Moreover, the Strike Committee began to document the happenings of the mobilization. During the first few days, more and more people joined the strike. By the fourth day, the slogan *¡El pueblo no se rinde, carajo!* ("The people won't give up, damn it!") had spread and fifty thousand people had taken to the streets. On May 19 armed forces sought to violently dismantle large parts of the marches to allow the port to reopen; however, they were unsuccessful. And the next day, even more people joined the mobilizations.

The fact that the Santos government was perceived as a "government of agreements" due to its peace policy and the negotiations with the FARC fostered the establishment of a dialogue between the Strike Committee and a group of negotiators sent by the central government to Buenaventura. In general terms, actors of the local and regional government were not taken into consideration by the Strike Committee due to cases of corruption and mismanagement (Jaramillo et al. 2020, 155). However, overseers of the United Nations and the ombudsman office took part in the negotiations. For twenty days, tense negotiations took place between the two parties, during which the port economy was paralyzed. Finally, the parties agreed to a set of terms and signed an accord which included the allocation of a special fund for the city (Fonbuenaventura) and the constitution of further working groups to promote projects regarding public education, health care, mobility, water and sewage infrastructures, and security, among other things. The Water Roundtables constituted an essential part of the accord.

In the aftermath of the strike, social organizations became very visible and relevant in the political landscape of Buenaventura. Several social

FIGURE 9 Mural depicting Temístocles Machado

leaders even became public figures. In January 2018, Temístocles Machado, a prominent social leader who was opposed to the expansion of the port infrastructure to the neighborhood Isla de la Paz, was assassinated. In the tense atmosphere after Machado's assassination and the circulating death threats, social movements continued to fight for better living conditions in the city. Murals commemorating the strike, as well as music videos and written memoirs, began to circulate (figure 9). A website and social media accounts were set up by the Strike Committee and even the international press wrote about the port. In the many conversations I had in Buenaventura, people referred to the *paro* (strike) as a turning point in the political happenings of the city. Moreover, elections for the local government were held in 2019, during my stay in the city. Víctor Hugo Vidal, one of the most prominent leaders of the strike, was running for mayor (figure 10). In October of the same year, Vidal was elected, and he took office a few months later.

Public scholars, engaged academics, journalists, and leftist politicians have paid attention to the social mobilizations and political

FIGURE 10 Political banner of Víctor Hugo Vidal on an unfinished house

happenings in Buenaventura (Acevedo 2022). Consequently, the movement gained visibility across the country and even internationally. After
reports by Human Rights Watch (2013), North American Congress on
Latin America (Nicholls and Sánchez-Garzoli 2011) and the Centro
Nacional de Memoria Histórica (2015), the press, NGOs, and state institutions were depicting a mobilized community reclaiming its rights.
Yet less has been written about both the alternative development plans
and technical knowledge articulated by the movements. The image of
fed-up citizens whose rights were violated did not fit with the *active*
participation of social leaders in the production and enactment of expert knowledge.

The Engineers Association of Buenaventura

The ASIB was founded in 2001 as an engineers' guild. It was established
with the aim of fostering "the active participation of local experts in the
solution of the several problems the city was, and still is, facing," as Alexander, one of its founding members, told me in our first conversation
in a restaurant in the city center. He added that "most of its members
were born in Buenaventura and are the first generation of their family
to hold a university degree." And although Alexander did not allude to
the members' identification as Afro-Colombian, that was something that
became clearer in our next meeting and in conversations with him and
other members of the association. Engineers affiliated with the ASIB have
been employed as consultants for various public and private institutions,
working on the design, planning, and execution of infrastructure projects
in the city.

In the mid-1980s, the Association of Engineers and Architects of Buenaventura was founded. In the following years, internal disagreements
and a limited effect on local public policy led to the dissolution of the
guild. As one founding member told me: "Although we were not politized
from the very beginning, many of us had the intention to contribute to
local politics. At that time, we were young experts witnessing the disastrous situation of Buenaventura and really wanted to help. But the
association lost strength during the nineties." In 2001 a group of ten engineers decided to form the Association of Engineers of Buenaventura

(ASIB) with the idea of building local expertise in order to improve the conditions of public infrastructure in the city. From the very beginning, ASIB members were close to social activist groups. Bonds of friendship and cooperation were forged between these groups, as both became visible in the local political landscape after the massive mobilizations that took place in 1998.

One of the reasons why these groups joined forces was, as ASIB members told me, the fact that they "feel identified" with the "territory," namely the Pacific region. Hence, and in contrast to experts and institutions coming from the interior of the country, ASIB and the Strike Committee share a political and ethnic identity. I argue that the shared identification of both group of actors responds to three closely related phenomena. First, the ongoing unwillingness or inability of the central state to deliver its promises in terms of project planning and execution (mostly unsuccessful) has generated a general skepticism toward the promises made and the expertise deployed—which locals understand as "external" to their territory. During some meetings with PTSP officials I attended in Buenaventura, ASIB engineers and Strike Committee members pointed out that planning and designing projects elsewhere (in Bogotá) would both hamper the ability of experts to understand the dynamics of the city and reproduce the historically rooted differences between the Pacific and the interior of the country. One of the main purposes of social movements and local experts would be to regain epistemological authority over the problems in the city. However, this does not suggest that the projects carried out by the central government should be "replaced" by local authorities (which, in terms of funding, would be unrealistic), but that the advice, opinions, and interventions of local actors should be integrated into the project. Put differently, their "enactment of expertise," to borrow from E. Summerson Carr (2010), should be taken into consideration.

Second, the fact that members of the ASIB and the Strike Committee alike identify themselves as Afro-Colombians is related to the political and legal framework regarding ethnic minorities that was constituted in the 1990s in Colombia. In a long conversation I held with ASIB members about Ley 70 of 1993, a law that conceded rights to Afro-Colombian communities, they repeatedly stressed that the law has had a positive effect on the formation and expansion of grassroots organizations.

"Thanks to the Ley 70, we can reaffirm what we are: Afro-Colombians," one member told me. Notwithstanding this, ASIB members also criticized the conceptual framework of this political agenda on ethnic minorities, which has been mainly focused on rural communities. "Who are Afro-Colombians?" engineer Yeferson asked. Are they "only the ones living in the rural Pacific who work as fishers and miners? Or are *we all* Afro-Colombians, including the urban population?" In an important article, Zeiderman (2018) address this issue by examining the discourses deployed by ethnic Afro-Colombian movements (like the Proceso de Comunidades Negras) in spaces such as Buenaventura. He argues that these movements and grassroots organizations seek to "reconfigure the legal and political geography that limits their agency in an urban context" (Zeiderman 2018, 1121). Whereas the identification of ASIB members as part of an ethnic minority unfolded within a legal framework that in turn has enhanced the alliances with other political actors in the city, they, the ASIB members, apprehend and aim to expand the conceptual axioms of such a framework.

Third, ASIB members identify themselves as part of the working class since they are, as they repeated to me on several occasions, the first generation of professionals in their families. Likewise, social activists understand themselves as part of *el pueblo* (the people). It is noteworthy that the convergence of class and ethnic identification in Buenaventura is linked to both the political formations of port unions in the second half of the twentieth century and the legal framework toward ethnic minorities in Colombia in the 1990s. An alliance between the ASIB and the social movements was made possible through a shared identity and a long-standing political work of cooperation. Several activities jointly organized during the first two decades of the 2000s such as workshops, informative meetings, and evaluations served both groups to share technical and political knowledge. In the face of the massive mobilizations that began in 2013, the ties between the ASIB and the social movements further strengthened.

Although these organizations work hand in hand, they do not play the same role in the political landscape of the city. In fact, many ASIB members left Buenaventura in the 1990s to find jobs in bigger cities such as Cali and Bogotá and have had to participate remotely in the political happenings of the port city. For instance, many of them commute between

Cali and Buenaventura. In contrast, social leaders usually live and work in Buenaventura, carrying out their political work at different levels on a daily basis. Indeed, ASIB members don't consider themselves to be social activists but rather see themselves as "technical advisers" of the Strike Committee. "We want to be part of the solution," Venicio, one of the ASIB members, told me while sitting in a café on the seafront. "The work of the central state has been disastrous, and we need to mobilize expert knowledge with social activists to put pressure and propose solutions."

Some local engineers are also part of the PTSP, employed by the state as local links (*enlaces locales*). It is tacitly agreed between the PTSP and the social movements that, at least on a local level, ASIB members have to be employed by the plan. However, their role as local links is very marginal within the hierarchical organization and bureaucracy of the PTSP. While their main task consists in overseeing the progresses of the PTSP on site, as well as the compilation of technical reports, locally employed engineers do not directly take part in the decision-making process of the project. Nonetheless, this position permits them to gain insights into the functioning of the project, which, in turn, allows them to participate in discussions and advise social leaders with information gained firsthand. Some PTSP officials with whom I talked (directly or indirectly) accused ASIB members of not being committed to the project. They stressed that local engineers would be more focused on participating in local politics than contributing to the project itself. One PTSP official even said that the ASIB and the Strike Committee would be conspiring to gain posts once the system was municipalized again.

While ASIB members criticize the PTSP and other development plans led by the central state, they do not intend to block the project nor impede its implementation. They do not aim to delegitimize the efforts made by the central state to improve the water infrastructures in the city either. Yet ASIB members employed by the PTSP do not merely assume the role of employee: the one of local technical facilitators whose main role is to oversee the construction sites. They actively participate in local politics, attend to technical and nontechnical issues, participate in discussions, openly criticize the central state, and articulate discourses revolving around ethnic and class identity.

The case of ASIB points to the dynamics of state interventions in the Colombian periphery and shows the interaction between social

movements and a porous state apparatus. It also reveals a particular way
of enacting expertise, based not only on the authority conferred by university degrees and work experience, but also on their ethnic and territorial affiliations, their politics, and their firsthand relationship with the
social and material world they act upon (see Carr 2010).

Local Expertise

In this section, I conceptualize the ASIB as a group of experts which I
identify as "local." In doing so, I foreground a figure that is situated in the
interstices between the development apparatus and civil society. Anthropological literature on experts and expert knowledge have complicated
the division proposed by Levi-Strauss (1966) between creative and technical scientific knowledge (Harvey and Knox 2015; Heslop and Jeffery
2020, 285–86). As subjects who experiment in specific environments,
adjusting their skills to immediate problems marked by the rhythms of
the objects, people and nature, *bricoleurs* (the creatives) are linked to
experience-based expertise; on the other hand, scientists are endowed
with skills to solve universal problems everywhere, building upon knowledge. In their work, Harvey and Knox proposed the term "engineer-
bricoleur" to describe the Peruvian engineers they encountered during
fieldwork on a road building project. These engineer-bricoleurs, they
state, "engage the uneven, unruly, and unstable environments out of
which infrastructures are made" (Harvey and Knox 2015, 17).

I contend that the ASIB engineers fit this type of experts proposed
by Harvey and Knox. Furthermore, I add a political dimension to this
phenomenon. As *"activist experts"* (Carmona and Jaramillo 2020, 1091),
I address the engineers' positionality not only in technical but also in
political terms. Their claims to "know" Buenaventura firsthand refer not
only to their material engagement with the unstable environments of
Buenaventura where infrastructures are installed, expanded, and maintained but to their political commitment with the interests of the people
of Buenaventura.

Several times, ASIB members referred to their profession as *hacer
ingeniería* (doing engineering). By this, they mean a process of planning,
designing, and executing infrastructure projects considering social,

urban, and territorial (meaning environmental and topographic) specificities. They claim that to know these specificities firsthand enables them
to properly and effectively execute infrastructure projects, to be a proper
engineer-bricoleur attending to the inconsistencies of models and the
unpredictability of materials.

However, the lack of resources and tools, an unstable institutional
framework, and their marginalization from the decision-making processes of centrally planned and executed projects highly constrains their
capacity to act. The mobilization of resources for the improvement of the
water supply system in Buenaventura has been reliant on investments
made by the central state. This is due, in the first place, to the fact that
large amounts of money are required to improve infrastructural systems
which cannot be provided by the municipality given institutional weakness and financial constraints.

Some ASIB members told me that they had constant "differences and
technical arguments" with PTSP engineers and officials, since the latter
"do not know the territory" and assessed that "*doing engineering* in Buenaventura is not easy at all" (emphasis added). "This is not something that
can be done from a desk in Bogotá," Hebert, a member of the association,
told me. "We have an added value, and that is that we were born, raised,
and trained here," he said. He told me that they had hoped to train some
mestizo engineers who have come to work in the city but that they were
not taken sufficiently into account. The "special conditions" of the city,
I was told, mean that there are certain climatic, topographic, and demographic specificities that require "field experience," and experts must
"apprehend the territory."

ASIB members do not reject the projects led by the central state, nor
do they consider themselves to be the only experts who should work
upon the territory. Their requests are rather based on the need to "think
together during the planning and execution of the projects," as Hebert
told me. Participation, according to him, cannot be limited to the inclusion of a single local engineer, which has been the case with the PTSP.
One of the reasons local engineers are not more actively involved has to
do with their professional accreditation, as I was told by PTSP officials,
since most of them do not hold a master's degree. In these cases, as the
engineers themselves point out, social background is a determining factor. "I am the son of a dressmaker and a bricklayer," Reinaldo, another

ASIB member, told me. "It was not so easy for us to study. Our families had to go to great efforts to pay our studies." He further remarked that they did not need a master's degree to do the work, since they have worked for several years in the city gaining "firsthand experience," which would be much more valuable than university knowledge.

The very first encounter I had with an ASIB member was with engineer Yeferson, one of the oldest members of the guild. It was February 2020. At the time, Yeferson was working for the PTSP as a "local link." Furthermore, Yeferson had experience as director of the SAAB. He invited me to the offices of the PTSP in Buenaventura. There was a desk, a board, and some plastic chairs; besides that, the place was almost empty. Compared to the headquarters of the PTSP in Bogotá, the office was underwhelming, and it reminded me of pictures I have seen of small administrative enclaves of NGOs in the Global South.

Over the course of some three hours, Yeferson explained to me the technical details of the water infrastructure system by drawing a map on the board and writing down several statistics. He pointed to the necessity to prioritize certain construction projects such as the rehabilitation of the twenty-seven-inch pipeline and the Demand Management Plan. He seemed very interested in making intelligible the technical and managerial arrangements of the water supply system of the city. "You always need this kind of information to understand what is going on here. It is not only about engineering, but also about politics." During the presentation, he openly criticized Hidropacífico, the private operator, as well as the general approach of the PTSP.

He pointed out that the private operator of the water supply system would not understand the "local necessities" of the population. "There are several types of settlements in Buenaventura that need to attach to the centralized system and not only be focused on a cost-recovery strategy." Yeferson stressed that the unplanned growth of the city would pose several challenges for the design and planning of infrastructure projects and that these should be addressed on the ground (*en terreno*). The state would need to include the local population in the decision-making processes. "Engineering is not only about installing pipes," he continued, "but about negotiating with the intervened population." The hand-drawn map would be a mere "abstraction needed to understand the water

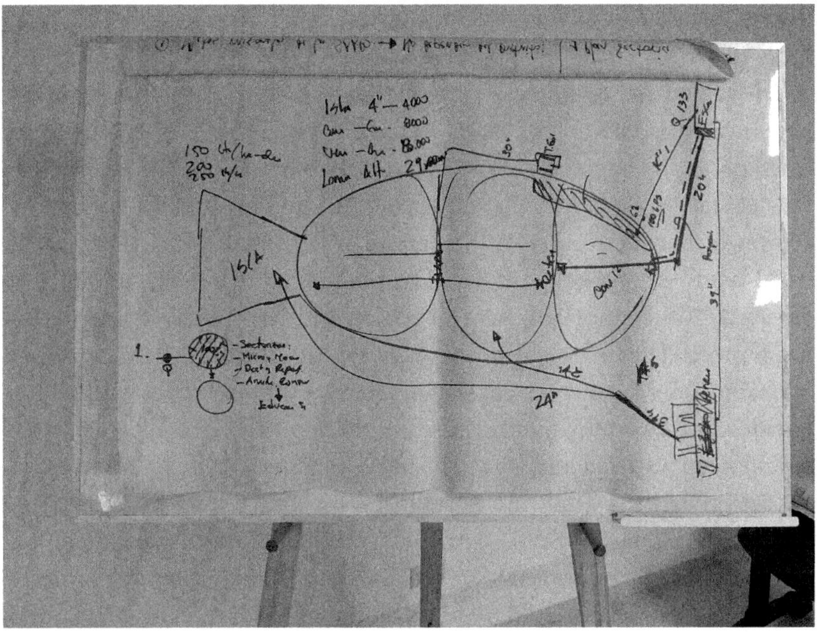

FIGURE 11 The "Fish Map"

infrastructure system. But you have to understand that there are people living there."

"It looks like a fish," I remember thinking after Yeferson finished drawing the map. "People here in Buenaventura draw it more or less like this," he told me (figure 11). The Cascajal Island represented the tail of a fish, and the body the continental zone. It was crisscrossed by lines and contained some drawings as well as numbers representing statistics. The drawing was accompanied by a narrative about the structure and the "state of affairs" of the water infrastructures. The engineer was speaking to me as an expert on a subject for which we shared a common interest (Boyer 2008). The lines through the fish represented the most important pipes in the city; the numbers stated the diameters of these pipes, the water that flows through them, and the volume of losses incurred in the system due to leaks. There were squares showing river intakes and water treatment plants, and rectangles showing storage tanks. The figures, lines, and drawings revealed an x-ray of a problem I already knew existed: the deficient water supply in the city as a public service (Appel et al. 2015).

"If we had the resources, we could guarantee the functioning of the system within a couple of years," Yeferson stated. By "we," he meant local experts and social activists. "We would for sure need the help from the central government. There is specific know-how that we don't have." However, cooperation with the central government (the PTSP, in this case) could only work if it were to be conceived of horizontally, he stressed. "We cannot only be a local link; we have to be a central part of the project." However, one of the main political decisions which should be taken, Yeferson suggested, was to terminate the contract with Hidropacífico and to "municipalize" the operation of the system again. They would need a strong and public institutional framework to build, monitor, and repair the water infrastructures. He then wrote down three big letters on the board—EPB—and loudly said: "Empresas Públicas de Buenaventura," or Buenaventura Public Company. Constituting a new, locally managed institution would be the starting point for a real change in the politics of infrastructure in the city.

After having spent several hours discussing the technical functions, projections, and politics of the water supply system, Yeferson took a seat and connected his laptop to a projector. On the screen, an old documentary on Buenaventura was projected. The documentary depicted the processes of urbanization in the city in the 1960s and 1970s, a time during which the city grew significantly. It showed internal migrants carrying their belongings through dusty streets in informal urban settlements, the makeshift houses on the seaside, and the port infrastructures. "Look, that is the way our ancestors settled down here; that is a very special form of urbanization." A social leader had made a pirate copy of the documentary, Yeferson told me. A barely audible voiceover narrated the recent history of the city, highlighting the rural-urban migration and the expansion of the port. The similarity between the rural and the urban forms of living became evident: People were building stilt houses on the seaside, fishing, and growing fruit and vegetables. In contrast, the modern port loomed in the background.

At one point in the video, a woman with a child was filling a bucket with water; Yeferson paused it. He stood up, approached the screen, and pointed to the stream from the which the woman was taking the water.

"This image encapsulates a story of deprivation," he said. "What you are seeing here is a vivid example of exclusion. People were forced to collect water from the surrounding streams and rivers." However, this would be how people came to inhabit urban places. The fact that impoverished urbanites have been disconnected for decades from the modern water supply system would pose several challenges for state-led programs. "Once you connect people to the system, new social dynamics emerge. We urgently need to include urban subjects into this process of transformation by informing them about the technical functioning of the infrastructures and the billing system behind it." People would not be used to paying for their water. "To act locally means to approach these people, to know the dynamics of their neighborhoods, to be open for negotiations." To work as an expert, he added, would also mean to be part of the urban dynamics, to know things firsthand.

By pointing to the structural inequalities of the city, Yeferson emphasized the need to understand specific urban dynamics. In his opinion, the PTSP would execute the projects from above, ignoring the history of the city and the local politics. The high rates of unemployment and poverty would greatly affect people once they were forced to pay bills. For that reason, social movements and ASIB members alike have developed a special development plan. This plan considers the economic integration of urban subjects by fostering the production of food through gardening and fishing in the river and the sea, as well as inclusion in the port economies. A long process of transformation should be put in place to effectively connect urbanites to centralized infrastructure systems.

Once the documentary ended, Yeferson asked me to go for a walk and see a settlement next to his office. We strolled through the neighborhood for around an hour. Yeferson identified almost every water pipe and supply line and pointed them out to me. We spotted several domestically installed water tanks and many leaks in the pipes (see chapter 4). The engineer stated that improvised connections to the water infrastructures would produce several losses. It would be crucial to know the history of every neighborhood to understand its material entanglements. "It is difficult to approach the very specific dynamics if you are not from here." Meticulous work would be needed to reduce the leaks in the system. A demand management plan could not only focus on figures and statistics but would also need to address the everyday life of urban people.

Indeed, leaks in the pipelines are part of wider political and economic processes. "We need local social workers, sociologists like you, and a group of politically engaged people to develop the Demand Management Plan." Also, engineers would be crucial to address a problem that is more than technical.

In a groundbreaking paper, urbanist AbdouMaliq Simone explores the relations between urban informality and state-led development programs. He argues that, in general terms, the many "unstable forces of informality" complicate the state-led efforts to improve infrastructure systems. State interventions that aim "to clean up or strengthen out mixtures of residence, commerce, and informal politics, have specific spatial implications that can limit the overall inclusiveness of existent urban economic activities" (Simone 2015b, 17). Indeed, the city is a heterogeneous composite of ways of life, histories of settlement, economic activities, and contestation. Acting in the name of improving the provision of systems for the poor creates a range of ramifications. Hence, the urban poor have to be considered in a broader range of social and economic interrelations. The role of local experts, as Yeferson asserted, would be, among other things, to take these interrelations into account.

While improvements in the water infrastructure system in Buenaventura therefore require the inclusion of local actors such as the ASIB members, PTSP and other state-led projects often ignore their political agenda. In fact, discussions about the positionality of experts seldom take place. The hierarchical organization of the project, the institutional racism, and the tensions between central state institutions and local actors are rooted in inequality and exclusion. To put in practice the plans formulated by local experts and social activist groups would require horizontal negotiations and debates.

A Productive Alliance

Over the course of the last decade, the productive alliance between social movements and local engineers in Buenaventura has deeply strengthened their capacity to act. While social movements in the Pacific region have been mainly linked to the new political and legal framework regarding the recognition of Afro-Colombians as ethnic minorities, social struggles in urban contexts have had to articulate discourses related to the rights of functioning public infrastructures. Although the social struggle in Buenaventura has had a long trajectory, the new political and bureaucratic approach developed in the 1990s has marginalized the discourses of Black urban subjects. As Zeiderman (2018) demonstrates, social movements have developed new strategies to approach urban issues. For instance, the social movement *Proceso de Comunidades Negras* has coined the term *afrourbano* to describe a new "ethnic urban subject" and address that subject's specific needs. Furthermore, the alliance between social movements and ASIB members has been crucial for understanding technical and managerial problems revolving around infrastructures, as well as for formulating development plans and articulating political discourses. However, the possibility of executing these plans has been constrained due to the lack of funds, the structures of the state-led projects, and the unequal geographies of the Colombian state.

Star argues that infrastructures are embedded within "structures, social arrangements, and technologies." Indeed, "people do not necessarily distinguish the several coordinated aspects of infrastructure" (Star 1999, 381). Furthermore, they exist in several registers and forms of representation. Technical know-how is needed to effectively address infrastructures. For the social movements I have discussed here, the articulations of their claims and political discourses revolving around water supply were contingent on a techno-political language and specific forms of knowledge. The alliance with ASIB members enabled a knowledge transfer and production which empowers them in their negotiations with the central state. The general strike of 2017 was based not merely on claims for better public infrastructures but on a wider understanding of hydraulic engineering and urban planning. Furthermore, suggestions, alternative plans, and proposals were formulated within the social movements. ASIB members' technical knowledge, as well as their local experience, broadly allowed for the formulation of claims and proposals to improve the water infrastructures. Yet these alternative plans have not been taken seriously by the central state.

As Appadurai (2001) has shown in the case of Mumbai, grassroots organizations articulate plans for a "governmentality from below." He argues that this kind of pro-poor activism rejects urban development expertise and relies upon conscious strategies of self-enumeration and self-surveying to negotiate with state bureaucracy at various levels and get access to public goods. In a similar vein, social movements in Buenaventura have formulated claims that interweave technical and nontechnical knowledge, and that also aim to develop a "governmentality from below." However, more than rejecting urban development expertise, local actors in Buenaventura propose to open spaces of horizontal negotiation and aim to interweave the development agendas formulated by the central state with their own claims of local needs.

Notwithstanding this, and as I showed in chapter 2, the hierarchical structure of state-led projects such as the PTSP, as well as everyday racism, creates disputes between the central state and local actors. The general mistrust of local activists and experts toward the central state limits the possibility of meaningful cooperation. Furthermore, because the improvement of water infrastructures requires a lot of money, local experts and social movements depend on centrally planned projects such as the PTSP. However, the termination of the contract with the private operator Hidropacífico in early 2022 opened up new possibilities for, at least at a municipal level, the gaining of control over the water infrastructures. Even though a public utility company has not yet been established, the SAAB has provisionally taken control over the operation and permitted the cooperation with local engineers.

In November 2020 I held a virtual follow-up conversation with six members of the ASIB. They seemed very interested in my research project and kept asking me questions about the impact of an anthropological approach to water infrastructures. They were interested in the university I work at and asked me whether further collaboration would be possible. "Doing engineering in our territory is quite difficult," one of them said. "We need to apply our know-how gained through firsthand experiences in the city, but we also need to strengthen ties and cooperate with several actors." While discussing the future projects of the PTSP and other state-led interventions, the ASIB members expressed their frustration: "We are all familiarized with the territory," Yeferson said. "We would be able to solve the problem of water supply within a couple of years. But sincerely, we are hamstrung." The ASIB members were willing to talk to me for hours and answer all my questions, even though it was Sunday afternoon in Colombia. The internet connection kept failing, but they rejoined the Zoom meeting every time. Throughout my research, they were key informants who helped me to understand the political landscape in the port city, as well as providing technical information regarding the water infrastructures. "You are always very welcome in our territory. And we are thankful that you decided to write about our city," Yeferson said. "And don't forget the fish and all the things I have told you about the water infrastructure. Remember that we all know things here firsthand."

Yeferson

Yeferson grew up in a stilt house, in the 1970s, he told me. He remembers his male acquaintances building whole house structures out of wood. "They tied up hoses to the shelves and connected them to the pipelines to access water," he said, always getting back to technical talk when narrating his life. In the 1970s, most dwellings were made out of wood and located on the seaside. Buenaventura was at the time still a small town, so different. People piled up alluvial materials to claim territory from the sea. "It is still the case," Yeferson continues, "but now things are tougher." In his childhood, he used to fish nearby. Now, the water is all contaminated. And the security situation has gotten worse.

Back then, some folks were violent in the neighborhood, he remembers. Brawls were quite common. "But there were rarely people carrying guns." He also remembers the social mobilizations from the seventies and eighties. His father used to be a freighter at the port, and a unionist. "We are the Black, working people," his father always told him. Yeferson was an intelligent child, and he always got good grades. Some of his older cousins decided to study. And he followed suit. In the 1980s, a regional university opened a campus in Buenaventura as part of a development plan, right after he graduated from high school. He enrolled in civil engineering. However, after a year or so, the program was shut down. The whole family moved to Cali in order to support Yeferson and other young acquaintances in their studies. They moved into a neighborhood of low-income housing the government of Belisario Betancur had just founded. "We were like twelve people living in a house for four," he told me. He had the best grades and was an honor graduate.

In 1989, at age twenty, he moved back to Buenaventura and started to work in a construction firm. "At the time I learned a lot about the public infrastructures in the city." He bought a house and got married a couple of years later. Then he worked for the municipality and nearly accompanied the social movement and the political happenings in the city. Things got very dangerous, and he decided to move back to Cali. As one of the few professionals in his family, he financially supported about seven people and encouraged the young to study. "It is very much important to study. For Black people from the Pacific, it is the only way to get out of poverty." He doesn't turn his back on his origins, he repeats several times. Nowadays, now that his contract with PTSP has ended, he lives in Cali and works as an independent engineer. He commutes to Buenaventura, where he has some projects, but he wants his two daughters to stay in Cali and go to university there. Perhaps a private one. Who knows? "Things change within one generation, dramatically," he said, smiling. "But the problem is structural. People in Buenaventura need better chances."

I met him the last time at a mall in Cali in August 2023. He was in a good mood. We had some coffee and a piece of cake. I was curious about his life, but he was still a bit shy, somehow aloof.

PART II

PART II

CHAPTER 4

Pirate Infrastructures

I turned the tap and put my hands under the faucet. No water came out. Only air and a very strange sound. I waited for a moment, thinking that it would maybe take a few minutes for the water to get from the pipes to the faucet. But I waited in vain. I knew about the water schedule in the neighborhood, but the water storage system installed in the rooftop of the house I was staying in had never failed before. I left my small room and looked for Claudia, my landlord and friend: "The water went out," I said. She apologized and climbed the stairs to a sort of attic. A few minutes later, she returned with a cracked plastic pipe in her hands. "The pressure damaged the pipe again. It needs to be fixed." She handed me a bucket and told me to go to the other tank, the one downstairs. There, I would be able to take "all the water I needed." She added that there would be water running from the tap later that day or, at the latest, the day after. I went to the other tank to wash my hands before taking my little notebook and making an entry in my field diary: *Buenaventura, November 19, 2019.* I wrote down what I had just experienced and sketched a drawing. I walked out into the dusty street and into the heat, and headed toward Claudia's hardware store. "What happened with the water?" I asked.

This chapter addresses the construction, maintenance, and repair of water storage systems and illicit connections in Ciudad Blanca. Due to the deficient water supply service, locals in Ciudad Blanca and elsewhere

in the city improvise small-scale infrastructures to store water and fill
the temporal gap of nonsupply. Although the systems work somewhat—
creating an effect of constant supply—they are very unstable and prone
to breaking down due to weak materials, improvised constructions, and
extreme weather conditions. I argue that the building, repair, and maintenance of these small-scale infrastructures represents a form of everyday
resistance to, and coping with, (infra)structural violence. Furthermore,
I understand these practices as ways of both coproducing the state and
negotiating its limits: by storing water, inhabitants generate an effect of
constant supply. At the same time, irregular and improvised connections
to the public pipelines aim to bypass the regulatory regimes of the state
and, in doing so, negotiate its limits. Academic literature on urban infrastructures has complicated the clear division of haves and have-nots,
addressing the myriad ways through which urbanites access public goods
(von Schnitzler 2016; Degani 2022; Simone 2015b; Anand 2017). I scrutinize here the ways through which urban subjects engaging with the
"cycle of breakdown, repair, and breakdown again," a key characteristic
of the small-scale water storage systems they are forced to build in order
to access water (Larkin 2004, x).

In Ciudad Blanca, water comes only for a few hours and then it goes
again. Consequently, people are forced to store water until it comes back
by building small-scale infrastructures. A domestic pipeline or hose leads
to a tank installed on the rooftop of the dwelling, which distributes the
water by gravity to the rest of the house during the hours of nonsupply.
It also happens that, due to eventual damage to the water infrastructures,
the supply takes more than two days to be restored. For this reason, people also collect rainwater as an alternative (Furlong 2014; Lawhon et al.
2018). In the most extreme cases, when the service is interrupted and
rainfall is also scarce, people are forced to buy bottled water in other
neighborhoods. Indeed, the rhythms of the water flows are highly unpredictable. As is depicted in the ethnographic vignette about the water
at Claudia's house, the constructions I address here are fragile material
assemblages; they are arranged by means of improvisation, are further
exposed to the sun, the rain, and the salt air, and face the challenge of
the irregular pressure with which water runs through the pipelines. Thus,
repairs and adaptations to these assemblages are a central part of the

sociomaterial daily practices in Ciudad Blanca and in Buenaventura more broadly.

Following Antina von Schnitzler (2016, 107), I understand infrastructures as a "political terrain" in which access to public resources is negotiated. Rather than a static and homogeneous distribution system governed by state entities, infrastructure represents an "accumulation of sociomaterial processes that are constituted through a relationship with bodies, discourses, and other objects [soil, water]" (Anand 2017, 13). The construction of small-scale storage systems and illicit connections emerge as a key site of these "sociomaterial processes" that constitute the water infrastructure system in the city. Being outside of what Graham and Marvin (2002) call an "infrastructural ideal," the people of Ciudad Blanca are force to create "pirate" systems of water storage and connection. As various authors have argued (e.g., Simone 2006; Larkin 2004; Degani 2015; Anand 2016), piracy is a central feature of the urban fabric in the Global South. According to Simone, piracy represents an appropriation of existing materials whose aim is to "multiply the uses that can be made of documents, technologies, houses, infrastructures . . . and the ability to put together different kinds of combinations" (2006, 358). Thus, the provision of water in Ciudad Blanca responds to the phenomenon of piracy in terms of appropriation, expansion, and alteration of the centralized water infrastructures in the city.

Several ethnographies on urban spaces in the Global South have addressed the ways in which infrastructure systems (re)configure the relationship between marginalized subjects and the state apparatus against the backdrop of contemporary economic deregulation and decentralization. For instance, Daniel Mains (2019) and Rosalind Fredericks (2018) have shown how the state, in the context of neoliberal policy, encourages active civil participation in urban infrastructure projects through institutional programs and nongovernmental organizations while redistributing labor and partially withdrawing from the public sphere. Tatiana Acevedo (2019) shows, in the case of Barranquilla, Colombia, how the state promotes the self-construction of electricity systems in marginal neighborhoods, providing citizens with the necessary materials and thus partially evading its responsibility to build infrastructure systems for the provision of public services such as electricity. This resonates with the state phenomenon of deregulation and the sharing of responsibilities by states, what Mbembe and Roitman (1995) call "do-it-yourself-bureaucracy." Other studies (von Schnitzler 2016; Degani 2015; Simone 2006) have pointed to the material alterations and appropriations of infrastructural systems as ways of negotiating between users and the technolegal regimes of state apparatuses.

The construction of water storage systems in Buenaventura by the population is not part of a state-led program and thus represents an improvised form of self-management in the face of the deficient provision of public goods. The state apparatus, in turn, continually promises an improvement in the supply systems and defers the fulfillment of its responsibility to the near future (see chapter 2). Through the construction and maintenance of storage systems and irregular connections, I argue, people of Ciudad Blanca articulate public infrastructures and, at the same time, redefine and negotiate the limits of the state. The coproduction of the state as the actor responsible for the supply of the continuous provision of public services becomes evident in the very construction of these storage systems, since storing and distributing water creates the *effect* of constant supply (Mitchell 1991). Coproduction refers to forms of sociomaterial articulation to the centralized infrastructures and other practices that enable the flow of water through the domestic pipes and hoses even in the hours of nonsupply. These storage systems are tolerated and ignored by state entities and understood as the solution to an immediate need (Anand 2015a). Meanwhile, the state defers its responsibility while formulating and executing development plans for the improvement of the water infrastructures.

I understand the irregular connections to the water system as a strategy that redefines the boundaries of the state, its governance, and regulatory regimes as payments are evaded and the water system is interfered with. Larkin writes that infrastructures "generate the possibility of their own corruption and parasitism," referring to the malleability of its materials, which, once altered, can evade the technical and legal frameworks within which they were planned and designed, as the example of illicit connection shows (2004, 289). Through these illicit material practices, payments and water consumption regulations are bypassed.

State officials constantly denounce irregular connections, arguing that they generate high losses in the system. At the same time, since the state cannot guarantee regular connections in all neighborhoods of the city, in practice these practices are grudgingly tolerated. This state-citizen relation resonates with the argument that the state incorporates citizens to its order through a relationship of inclusive exclusion. More than being expelled from the water supply system, marginalized subjects are permitted to access to it through irregular ways, being sometimes tolerated and sometimes punished. However, rather than examining how the state reacts to pirate connection, this chapter largely focuses on the dwellers' perspective, on how they deploy specific material practices and negotiate the limits of state control and regulation.

By both constructing storage systems and manipulating the public pipes, people seek to alter the flows in order to access water. Even though they are not able to control the flows, they materially negotiate their temporalities and rhythms. Consequently, this chapter underlies the *agency* of marginalized people in Buenaventura's urban landscape and their response to infrastructural violence. At the same time, it demonstrates its precariousness and fragility.

Ciudad Blanca

Ciudad Blanca is a poor neighborhood located in the continental area of Buenaventura. It was built from scratch in the 1990s as part of an urban housing project. Next to the neighborhood, there is a vía alterna, a parallel road that leads to the port, which was built in the first decade of the 2000s to improve the flow of trucks and avoid bottlenecks (see Melly 2017). The population of Ciudad Blanca consists mainly of internally displaced Afro-Colombians who came from the rural areas of the Pacific region in the 1990s and the first decade of the 2000s. Mestizo shopkeepers, truck drivers, and some Indigenous people also live in the neighborhood. And even though the housing project aimed to improve the living conditions of the population, a lack of public funding led to the decay of infrastructures such as roads, wires, pipes, and houses as well. The streets, for instance, are in very poor condition; some have cracked pavement, while others are not paved at all. Garbage is everywhere: plastic in all its forms, but also scrap metal from the car workshops of the vía alterna. Many people walk through, in, and out of Ciudad Blanca every

FIGURE 12 Rooftop water tanks

day: commuters, day laborers, truck drivers, shopkeepers, housewives, members of criminal gangs, police patrols. You can see and hear motorcycles all day long. Music blares from the loudspeakers installed in the front yards of the houses. The heat never subsides.

Ciudad Blanca, located in Buenaventura's mainland (*zona continental*), was built in the 1990s as part of a state-led social housing project. It was built next to the vía alterna, the second main road of Buenaventura that leads to the port, which was constructed to facilitate the circulation of trucks and commodities and to prevent a bottleneck of the principal road (Melly 2017). During the construction works of vía alterna (1999–2002), conflicts over the occupied, inhabited surrounding territories emerged, leading to selective assassinations and an increase in violent events (Lombard et al. 2021). Due to its proximity to the vía alterna, the social life of Ciudad Blanca is highly influenced by the "economies of the road": it has a number of restaurants, hotels, car shops, and truck parks (Harvey and Knox 2015). Most of the inhabitants of the neighborhood are informally employed in the transportation sector, a central part of the port economy. While men are mostly integrated into the informal economies of the road, most women are dedicated to housework. Young people like Yeison and Alexander tend to work for daily wages. Few people have formal employment contracts. Generally speaking, the income rates are low, and informal employment is high.

Buenaventura is marked by the segregation of a racialized majority—mainly Afro-Colombians—from the growing economies of the port. It is simultaneously caught in a perennial cycle of violence (Jenss 2021; Zeiderman 2016; Lombard et al. 2021). Ciudad Blanca, like many neighborhoods in Buenaventura, represents what anthropologist Daniel Goldstein (2012, 5) terms a "place of insecurity." These neighborhoods lack resources which should be provided by the state, such as security and infrastructures, and are "characterized more by fragmentation and unpredictability than by order and routine."

As part of my fieldwork, I lived and worked in the main hardware store of Ciudad Blanca for more than six months (figure 13). I stayed with Claudia, the owner, and her family during my research, when I rented a room on the first floor of her house and worked as a helper in her store. As an assistant in the shop, I actively participated in the sociomaterial practices of the neighborhood. I learned about the construction, maintenance, and repair of small-scale water storage systems, since local subjects mainly acquire the materials they need in the hardware shop. Moreover, I participated in conversations revolving around construction and repair which the clients regularly hold with the staff, mainly asking for advice.

During work, I held long conversations with Yeison and Alexander about urban infrastructures, local politics, the state, and the everyday violence in the neighborhood. I also visited their homes and got to know their life stories, their routines, and their ways of surviving in an impoverished, racialized, and hostile city. I learned about their life trajectories amid violence and poverty, but also of their resourcefulness, guided by a series of "practices, sensibilities, and tactics that allow them [and have allowed them] to adjust to the changing realities of the city" (Simone 2015b, 22; see also Han 2018). Both Yeison and Alexander are Afro-Colombians and victims of the armed conflict, whose families were forcibly displaced by violence from the rural Pacific in the 1990s. They are in their early twenties and work for a daily income in the hardware shop. Over time, they have learned about materials and construction—they can explain to customers how to fix a simple plumbing problem or how to assemble

FIGURE 13 The hardware shop

some pipes. They know the prices, the characteristics of the items, and the many ways to improvise with materials. Yeison lives in one of the adjacent neighborhoods, on the other side of the vía alterna. Through their storytelling, and amid a violent urban landscape under constant (re) construction, I learned a lot about the neighborhood, the everyday crime, and the water infrastructures. The many stories of material improvisation I wrote down in my field diary at the table in the hardware store resonate with that "quiet encroachment of the ordinary" proposed by Asef Bayat (1997): the subtle (sometimes silent) everyday politics of imagination and resistance that seek to forge and maintain livelihoods and ways of life despite marginalization.

Claudia, the owner of the hardware store, is from the interior of the country, like most shop owners in the Colombian Pacific coast. During fieldwork, she was one of my key people. Besides being my host, she protected me from the everyday dangers a foreigner is exposed to in Buenaventura. Paisas, mestizo migrants from the interior, play an interesting role in the city's economic and social dynamics. Like Claudia, many people from the interior migrated to the Colombian Pacific in the 1990s to try their luck with small businesses such as grocery stores, hotels, hardware shops, and restaurants. Most of them maintain commercial relationships with large traders in the interior of the country, facilitating

FIGURE 14 Assembling
the pipes

the circulation and movement of goods to the Pacific. In Buenaventura
these small traders enjoy a certain respect from the population, mostly
Afro-Colombian, as they generate employment and allow access to various products in areas such as Ciudad Blanca.

Claudia moved to Buenaventura after her brother Luis in the late
1990s. Coming from a family of peasants, she followed in the steps of her
brother as an entrepreneur. After working as an assistant in her brother's shop, she ran a hotel and a hardware shop with her husband and
their daughters. After she and her husband divorced, she kept the shop,

which has been a successful business for years now, despite the constant challenges. Claudia's recent past, her migration to Buenaventura and the key role she plays in the neighborhood as a shopkeeper is framed in the new social and economic patterns of the city. Due to waves of urbanization in the 1990s and the first decade of the 2000s, commerce gained an enormous relevance for the reproduction of life in Buenaventura and neoliberalism enhanced the import and circulation of commodities. Yet these were also the years in which violence and drug trafficking began to rapidly expand in the region (CNMH 2015).

Through social and commercial relations to the interior of the country, shopkeepers such as Claudia enable the circulation of commodities into the Pacific region. In Ciudad Blanca, Claudia became a key actor in the circulation of materials used to build, repair, and maintain local infrastructures. For me, the hardware store served as a sort of prism to apprehend the sociomaterial practices I address in this chapter. Shops in Buenaventura represent a node in the intense flow of materials, credit, money, jokes, and affections that sustain social and economic life in the port city.

Domestic Water Storage Systems

The first self-made constructions that I became aware of in Ciudad Blanca and the surrounding neighborhoods were the plastic and steel tanks installed on the rooftops of the houses, some of which were sold at the hardware store. At first, I assumed that these were tanks installed for the collection of rainwater as an alternative source of supply. Yeison and Alexander corrected me. They told me that the tanks are installed to store water that is supplied by the centralized supply system every other day and at different pressure levels. "You need water to live," Yeison told me, "so you have to store it for the hours when there is no service."

To do this, you have to extend the public pipe, first with a hose and then with another pipe that goes up to the top floor of the house, where a storage tank, made of plastic or steel, is installed. In most cases, the pipes and hoses are fixed to the outer walls, and exposed to sun, rain, and the salty air. The water collected in the tank can be distributed, by gravity, through an improvised assemblage of pipes and hoses to the different rooms of the house during the hours (or days) when the water supply is interrupted. Most of these systems have a buoy or float that, once the tank is filled, causes a stopcock to close so that water is not wasted. The designs for these constructions must be adapted to each house; they need to take into account its height, the location of the public pipes, and the average water pressure. There are different types of tanks, and prices vary depending on the size and the material. The largest, with a storage capacity of about 260 gallons and made out of PVC, are very expensive (130,000 pesos, approxi-

FIGURE 15 A recycled cylinder

mately US$30), given the low average income of the inhabitants in the neighborhoods. Tanks with a capacity of 65 gallons cost half as much. For economic reasons, most people buy metal cylinders or obsolete refrigerators that are recycled at the port for around 15,000 pesos (US$4) and, improvising a cement lid, turn them into water storage tanks (figure 15). This, however, makes the need for the construction and repair even more frequent and expensive.

The constant leaking of these domestic infrastructure arrangements poses difficulties to the population. One day, Antonio, a young man from the neighborhood, came to the hardware store with his water bill in his hand. He told me that he was being charged more than four times what he had consumed due to a leakage in his domestic pipe system. He now had a big puddle that was pouring into his house. Besides that, he had run out of water, since the water tank could not be filled. "Leaks are a nightmare!" he said, after buying tape to repair it. Leaks in the hoses and pipes that are connected after passing through the meter can be very expensive. Therefore, it is necessary to constantly check the constructions and repair and adapt them. However, the low and irregular income of the inhabitants does not allow them to always have the necessary items on hand to carry out construction or repairs. People sometimes repair leaks by using socks or old cloths. Moreover, the exposure of these constructions to sun, humidity, and rain makes them even more vulnerable to damage. These are not stable constructions or assemblies by any stretch, but improvisations mediated by precarious materials, low incomes, and people's capacity for inventiveness.

The small-scale infrastructures and the pirate connections to the pipe, rather than existing beyond the "beyond the realm of the state and urban planning," as Simone (2006) argues, exist as forms of articulation to the state-planned infrastructures. Yet this articulation to the state is mediated by the fragility and vulnerability of the materials used for the construction. Indeed, they make for an unstable system. "The tanks of the houses always have to be filled during the hours of water supply," Yeison told me as we walk through Ciudad Blanca. "You need a good distribution system in the house so that the water can be properly redistributed by gravity. You need good pipes and materials. These constructions are something difficult to achieve." For example, in Claudia's house there is a strong PVC pipe structure and two sixty-five-gallon tanks made of the same material. Usually, there is no water shortage in her house, since she has access to the best materials from the hardware store and has the necessary skills to make the installations. There are many people with far less stable arrangements. Some even decide not to build an elevated storage system at all in order to avoid the constant repairs and the expenses that this can represent. Jorge, a young man who used to work in the hardware shop once a week, told me that the tanks in his house were on the ground floor and had been built with a mixture of leftover cement. I looked at him in amazement and asked him how the water would be distributed from there to the other rooms of his house, since the water could not be distributed by gravity. "We use buckets," he told me smiling. "We carry the water to the sink, to the shower, and so on." Yeison told me that Jorge's family was very poor and could not afford to buy and constantly repair pipes and hoses.

The connections to the water infrastructure system must be made carefully to avoid leaks and losses in the system. The service provider is responsible for making a connection from the pipeline (called the distribution network) to the house, passing through a meter. From there, they use a polyethylene converter (called a PF, or pipe fitting) to connect the hose to the domestic pipe that supplies the tanks. To make these connections, a certain knowledge of plumbing is needed, which the inhabitants of Ciudad Blanca gain through practice and the advice they get from people with engineering skills such as Yeison and Alexander. The challenge is to be able to adapt the storage systems to the conditions and needs of each house, including the height and distribution of the spaces. As people expand their homes (by building additional floors, for example), the systems must be updated. The fragility of the connections and materials forces people to carry out periodic repairs and thus stabilize the storage systems.

After I offered him some money, Johnier, a young man who used to work for Hidropacífico, brought me to three different dwellings to show me the improvised forms of water storage systems. We first entered the dwelling of Doña Mirta, an old woman who had been forcibly displaced from the rural Pacific with her family in 2003. Johnier introduced me to her as a social researcher interested in water supply. She served us some Coke and invited us to take a seat before surveying the storage system. "Where I am from, the Yurumanguí River, water is everywhere. And here you need pipes and hoses and all these things. It's horrible." Johnier laughed and said that she should be thankful, that she must have one of the best water storage systems in the entire neighborhood. "You always have water, Doña Mirta." Perhaps unsurprisingly, the system had been installed by Johnier himself. Doña Mirta's nephew, a good friend of Johnier who lives in the United States and sends remittances once in a while, paid for the materials and working hours. The PVC hoses and pipes lead to the rooftop and are fixed to a lateral outer wall, protected by another removable PVC cylinder. On the rooftop, there is a huge cistern of concrete plated with bluish tiles. We climbed the stairs to see it. Johnier seemed very proud of his job. The shining tiles and the pure water in the cistern reminded me of a swimming pool at a luxurious club I visited many times during my childhood in the city of Cali. "You can store water for a couple of weeks. This lady is very lucky, I tell you. It is very expensive to build this, but her nephew really wanted her to have enough water, because of the river they come from." As I have noted in chapter 3, rural Black communities in the Pacific region inhabit what geographer Ulrich Oslender (2002) describes as "aquatic spaces," formed by social and material practices in and around river basins (and in some cases, the sea). Indeed, the scarcity of water in the urban areas of Buenaventura

generated social and cultural disruption for the migrated or forcibly displaced persons, as the example of Doña Mirta shows.

We then visited a mestizo family. The family's father, a shop owner,
died in 2009 due to a cancer that could not be properly treated in Buenaventura. The family then found themselves in financial trouble. The
storage system they had built in their house in 2005 when they moved
to Buenaventura to open a grocery shop was now falling apart. Many
leaks on the outer walls were visible. Cotton strips of old clothes were
used to repair them. Water poured out the pipes and hoses, generating
mold on the walls. Inside the house, the stench was unbearable. It was the
epitome of poverty and infrastructural breakdown. The fifty-gallon PVC
tank, which Claudia had given them as a gift, was only half-full. "When
they cut off the service, we have to ask the neighbors for some water," the
mother told me, smiling but embarrassed. In the tiny backyard, there was
another tank filled with rainwater. Dry leaves and dirt were floating on
the surface next to a plastic bowl. Before leaving, Johnier told me that the
rainwater would not be potable because of the dirt.

We then got on Johnier's motorcycle and headed to another neighborhood, located on Cascajal Island. We took the vía alterna, driving
at speed, zigzagging around trucks carrying American, German, and
Asian containers. At one point, we turned right and found ourselves in
Caracoles, a poor neighborhood next to an inlet and mangrove swamp.
Johnier used to live there in the 1990s, when he worked as a plumber.
For me, it was always risky entering new neighborhoods. "The neighborhood grew significantly in the 2000s as people from the rural areas were
displaced and came to the city," he told me. Then criminal gangs took
control over the entire settlement. The proximity to the sea turns the
neighborhood into a critical site of trafficking, since speedboats loaded
with cocaine can easily take off from the mainland.

We got off the motorcycle and went to Johnier's former dwelling. It
was a two-story house. The first floor was made of concrete, while the
second floor was only a wooden structure. "The water pressure in this
neighborhood is quite low. Tthat's why you normally need a pump to fill
up the tanks." We then entered the house, which Johnier now rents to
his aunt, and went to the garage. He showed me the motor pump. "The
storage system works well over here. It is stable. But the problem is that
you always need this fucking pump!" The water infrastructure system

in Buenaventura uses gravity to transport water from the source to the users. The source of the water, the Escalerete River, is located above the city. However, despite the gravity, the pressure drastically reduces due to the many leaks in the pipe network. At the level of the Caracoles, there is not enough pressure to lead the water to the tanks located on the rooftops. Some people need gasoline-run motor pumps to increase the pressure and fill the tanks. "But most people don't have the money for the pumps or the gasoline, so they fill tanks installed next to the pipelines using buckets." Johnier also told me that, when there is no supply, a municipal truck distributes water in the neighborhood. "But people here have also blocked the road leading to the port to protest when there is no water service, and the tank truck does not arrive." At this point, Johnier suggested that we should go back to Ciudad Blanca. It was getting darker, and it could become even more dangerous for me to be there.

Domestic Versus State Infrastructures

Anand (2011) argues that the physical conditions of water (the various reservoirs, the water's volatility and capacity for dispersion) exceeds the technopolitical regime of the state that frames and aims to govern the water infrastructures in the city. Thus, marginalized populations find alternative sources of supply in the face of deficient provision by centralized water infrastructures, such as wells or rainwater (see Furlong 2014; Lawhon et al. 2017). Certainly, some neighborhoods in Buenaventura are supplied by the surrounding rivers and rainwater. However, the water storage constructions in Ciudad Blanca and elsewhere point to a different phenomenon. These domestic, small-scale infrastructure systems reproduce the technologies and designs of the city's central water infrastructure, built and governed by the state. Rather than existing outside of state realms, these constructions are articulated with them. Put differently, the population coproduces public services through the construction of small infrastructure works on a decentralized, domestic scale.

Whereas these constructions are part of the wider assemblage of hydraulic infrastructures in the city and that don't operate *beyond* state-governed infrastructures, there are serious differences between the building practices of the state and these domestic constructions. The first

FIGURE 16 A dwelling in the neighborhood

difference is related to the building materials. People in Ciudad Blanca and elsewhere are forced to use fragile or even recycled materials that must be adapted in order to construct the storage systems. In so-called junkyards near the port, people buy obsolete refrigerators or metal cylinders upon which a cement base is built. Once put into operation, these informal tanks are highly prone to leakages and damage. Moreover, the water stored in them can be contaminated by chemicals. Indeed, these ways of precarious improvisation differ profoundly from state-led construction sites. Although improvised forms of construction and repair by public institutions may also be found on a small scale, the materials used by state institutions are much more robust and suited to the job.

Another important difference between makeshift small-scale infrastructures and centrally planned constructions is the predictability of water flows: while people in the neighborhoods are subject to irregular supply times and uneven water pressure, the state deploys tools and technologies for measuring and controlling water flows. Changes in pressure levels may damage domestic constructions or make them unable to store water. Indeed, the inhabitants of Ciudad Blanca cannot access information about pressure levels, so they cannot adapt to them. Another central difference is technical knowledge and expertise. On the one hand, citizens in Ciudad Blanca gain an empirical knowledge of plumbing (in some cases supported by people from the community who have some professional training in the area) and are forced to improvise. On the other hand, the state builds using technical and professional knowledge, with technologies and bureaucracies that allow a certain stability in the infrastructure works, less prone to damage.

The effect of the coproduction of a domestic infrastructure system with the state responds to the need of the population in the face of an irregular supply of the service. Using technologies comparable to those of the state, the population of Ciudad Blanca does not seek, in the first instance, to supply itself with water beyond the hydraulic infrastructure systems, but rather seeks to work with it. However, some practices also show how the population seeks to evade some state regulatory practices, such as service charges and the imperative to have regular connections to the system.

Hacking the Pipe

During the early days of my fieldwork working in the hardware store, I cautiously asked about the irregular connections to the water infrastructure system that are often installed by slum residents to access the public service. During my previous interviews and meetings with politicians and engineers of the city, I was told that this was a common practice in Buenaventura. Claudia told me that a PVC collar (a small device installed on the public pipelines to stabilize the hose connected to it) was one of the most frequently sold products in the hardware store. A few days later, Yeison took me on his motorcycle to show me the places where the pipes are buried a few meters below the ground, and where the hoses connected to them, some coming to the surface. We rode the motorcycle at dusk so as not to arouse suspicion. The light of the motorcycle illuminated the road and Yeison pointed out to me the hoses that came out of the ground, then followed the path where he suspected they ran under the surface until they reached the so-called mother pipe: one of the bigger pipes that cross the neighborhood. After we returned to the hardware shop, and while we were cleaning up and organizing the materials before we closed, I asked him whether all the people were illicitly connected to the pipe. "Not everyone. Some do it because they don't want to pay, others because they don't have any other choice."

Yeison told me that, in many adjacent neighborhoods, such as La Conquista and La Carolina, there are no regular connections to the water infrastructures and thus people are forced to make illicit connections. These neighborhoods, locally called *invasiones* (invasions), represent blank spots in the map of urban governance and policies and are irregular settlements on so-called vacant lots. As these settlements are not included in the Plan de Ordenamiento Territorial, a planning and development document and a matrix of urban policies at municipal level in Colombia, no connections are made to the infrastructure system. The process of recognition is slow and mediated by complex bureaucratic processes. Usually, people must inhabit these spaces of nonprovision for an indefinite period of time. For them, hacking the water networks represents a necessity for survival.

Most of the inhabitants of Ciudad Blanca (but not in the surrounding neighborhoods) have a formal installation to the service, which is provided, as in much of the city, only intermittently. These connections are mediated by a regulation technology: the meter. This arrangement inserts the subjects into a formal economy of payments, invoices, measurements, and claims. The service is provided by a private company (Hidropacífico), which is the entity in charge of bureaucratic mediations, through claims and petitions. In one of my visits to Hidropacífico's facilities in the center of the city, I spoke with several people from Ciudad Blanca who were standing in a long line in the midday heat waiting for answers to their claims relating to damages in the pipes or errors in the billing system. They expressed their anger with the company and with the bureaucracy involved. In fact, the company considers that its priority cannot be processing claims, as its general manager told me in a meeting in his office. He said that the priority was to maintain pressure in the system. "These people are very difficult. They have these irregular connections in their households, and nobody is made accountable for it. The system loses a lot of pressure because of these kind of connections."

Certainly, leaks generated by irregular connections are very frequent. One afternoon, Alexander took me on his motorcycle to the irregular settlement of La Carolina, which borders Ciudad Blanca. There you can see the clandestine connections to one of the principal pipes, made out of concrete. People perforate the mother pipe with drills or rods to insert hoses that lead to their houses, since the settlement does not have a regular supply. There are many leaks: water pools around the holes made to connect the hoses to the concrete pipe.

Even though people have regular connections in Ciudad Blanca, they also make illicit connections to the water infrastructures. Parallel connections to the supply lines bypass the meters and lead directly to the households. So as not to arouse suspicion, some days they let the water run through the meter so that it marks a certain consumption, while the rest of the time they supply themselves with the parallel hose. In doing so, they partly avoid the payment of the service and the high costs generated by possible leaks inside the house. These irregular connections, which I had been interested in since the day I arrived at the hardware store, represent a sociomaterial phenomenon that is inserted in the practices of construction, improvisation, and maintenance of these small-scale infrastructure system on a domestic scale. Since these kinds of connections are illegal, people did not talk openly about them. In cases where there is no other way to access the system (as in the neighborhood of La Carolina), inhabitants argue that they *"have* to hack the pipe," because otherwise they would not have water. In the cases in which parallel connections are made to avoid payments, however, nobody admits having such a connection.

The company also cuts off the supply service to those who have failed to pay their bills. To do this, they insert a silicone plug about two meters deep into the supply hose, obstructing the flow of water. Victor, a local plumber who works near the hardware store, removes the plug with a three-meter rod, which he has made for just this purpose. For 10,000 pesos (US$3), Victor can enable people to get their water supply back on, circumventing the state's regulatory policies. A Hidropacífico plumber with whom I spoke several times about this issue while we were riding his motorcycle around Ciudad Blanca told me that this used to happen in all the neighborhoods of Buenaventura, as people do not always have enough income to pay the bills.

Parallel connections are part of construction and maintenance practices on a domestic scale and represent a way to negotiate and redefine the limits of state control (in this case, of payment). The construction of infrastructure works for water storage represents a necessity and a *form* of inhabiting urban spaces. One hydraulic engineer who works for a small infrastructure project led by the municipality told me that people should be educated about "culture of consumption." Many inhabitants, according to him, built irregular connections that "depress" the system, resulting in lower pressure. "This is because the hoses are connected to the pipes in improvised ways. People don't understand anything about engineering," he added. State officials and experts often argue that responsibility for the leaks and, in turn, the dysfunction of the system lies overwhelmingly with the people.

In the face of a deficient water supply system, people introduce and reproduce sociomaterial practices to cope with inefficient infrastructures, resulting from public underinvestment, a weak infrastructural framework, and a recent wave of privatization. The construction and maintenance of these water storage constructions, as well as the irregular connections to the central aqueduct system, (re)configure the relations between subjects and the state, while the latter is coproduced, and its limits redefined. The constructions articulate to state technologies and infrastructures when it comes to the storage and distribution of water and, at the same time, they surpass the legal and material regimes that the state provides through irregular connections, thus redefining its limits.

Moreover, these small-scale domestic infrastructures are mediated through the fragility and volatility of the materials themselves (Bennet 2010). For Stephen Graham and Nigel Thrift (2007), the constant damage, rupture and decomposition of urban technologies and infrastructures produce significant moments of transformation.[1] The very phenomenon of repair itself involves a mobilization of techniques and resources that leads to a constant "learning, adapting and improvising" (5). Moreover, repair often aims not merely to restore that which is damaged but rather to improve upon it, innovate around it, and recycle unused material. These practices thus forge a heterogeneity of techniques and rhythms around the constructions necessary for the provision of water on a domestic scale. Hence, the improvised constructions in Buenaventura do not represent stable formations. They are not replicable

---

1. See also Jackson (2014).

solutions to a problem of shortage, marked by structured rhythms and procedures. They are rather the result of specific intersections: forms of improvisation and plumbing, linked to the circulation of money, weather conditions, house structures, and water pressure (Simone 2006). In the case of Ciudad Blanca, they are framed in a context of social and material vulnerability (Callén and Sánchez Criado 2015). These material practices are a strategy for inhabiting urban spaces marked by deprivation and poverty. A social activist told me during a walk we took in Ciudad Blanca that he did not want to encourage irregular connections to the aqueduct in the city but that, in the face of such shortages, people would have to access the resource in some way or another. "So I always tell people: 'if you find a way of hacking the pipeline, just do it!'" As long as the system remains inefficient, these constructions are a way of coproducing the state in its function of supplying public resources—just one more survival strategy in a hostile city like Buenaventura.

One afternoon, a man in his fifties arrived at the hardware store. He was consulting with Yeison about the tools he would need to split a pipe in his house to replace a broken connection. I saw Yeison sketching out a design of the connection the man needed to make to fix the pipe and connect it with two new hoses—one for the backyard and the other for the kitchen. Yeison spread out some items on the table and tried to offer the man a solution to his problem. Wilson, a local who had worked as a plumber for the public water utility in the 1990s, happened to be passing by and stopped at the shop. He also tried to help the man. With the pipeline and hoses, he simulated how he could assemble the connection; then he took the paper and made some changes to the design that Yeison had drawn. The man still seemed a little unsure if this would work, considering the conditions of his house and the places where the hoses and pipes passed through. Finally, he bought two PVC pipes and a pipe fitter and left the shop. I ran into him a few days later and asked him whether he was able to fix the problem. He told me that he had succeeded, but that the water pressure had broken the connection again, leaving him without water for several days. He explained that he had to wrap a rubber band around the hose to stop the leaks. "I will have to repair it once again. But only when I get paid, in two weeks. I cannot afford it now." He got on his motorcycle to go to work. "I'll see you over there at the hardware store," he called over his shoulder.

CHAPTER 5

Everyday Crime

Coping with Violence and the "Absent State"

The national press and the imaginary depict Buenaventura as a place of danger, a hub of endemic violence and terror. During my fieldwork in Ciudad Blanca, people constantly referenced the ongoing everyday crime they were exposed to. Violence in the city is part of the daily news and everyday chitchat. Indeed, the deficient supply of public goods and violence were some of the most important and persistent topics of conversation. Claudia, my host, regularly warned me of the violent events happening in the neighborhood and its surroundings. Talk of crime was everywhere.

At first, I wanted to avoid addressing violence as part of my research because I did not want my work to further fuel the popular representations of savagery and suffering in Buenaventura. However, within the first weeks of my fieldwork, I noticed that life in the neighborhood, including material practices, was entwined with everyday crime. Everyday crime was a haunting ghost constantly reconfiguring the geographies and temporalities of Ciudad Blanca. Like the state, it was marked by its "absent presence," its unpredictable appearances and harmful consequences. I argue that violent events in Ciudad Blanca alter the circulation of people and materials and at once jeopardize networks of trust and the products of "phatic labor" (Elyachar 2010). Moreover, I contend that everyday crime and murky patterns of violence reflect the forms of state-organized abandonment I have analyzed in the case of water infrastructures. By looking at the extortion experienced by shopkeepers, I stress the social and material vulnerability people are exposed to when crime pours into their neighborhoods.

The state, in turn, remains widely absent. It appears occasionally in theatrical forms, as I witnessed once during a military raid. Some residents such as Claudia draw on private communication with police officers to denounce alleged criminals in the neighborhood. When things get caliente, life in Ciudad Blanca is altered: people become frightened, and Claudia's hardware shop and other stores close for a while. But not only when things get caliente does violence affect mobility, the circulation of commodities, and the trust networks in the neighborhood. The murky patterns of violence and its immanence are constantly affecting the population. Who was killed last night? Whom can I trust? Like the flows of water, violence comes and goes in unpredictable ways, while the state seems unable to produce a stable security regime. In this chapter, I offer a detailed description of the everyday life of violence and how the population makes sense of it. I also address the coping mechanisms deployed by the shopkeepers to deal with extortion—a phenomenon affecting the circulation of commodities for the construction and maintenance of small-scale storage systems.

Violent Environments

"It has been quite caliente [in Ciudad Blanca] the last few days," Claudia told me. She was talking about the worsening of the security situation. "The guys visited me twice last week, they always want money." Later on, she told me that they had been asking for money once a month but that they come more often when it gets caliente. The money is to pay what they call *la vacuna*, the vaccine, a well-known form of extortion in violence-affected zones of Colombia (Moncada 2021, 64–72). It represents a form of illicit taxation collected by armed groups who pretend to provide security services for poor people, shopkeepers, and merchants throughout the country, profiting from a selective absence of the state in terms of security.[1] But in fact, Claudia told me, the vacuna only protects

---

1. Michael Taussig puts it as follows: "The *vacuna*, meaning vaccination—you pay a little to the guerrilla and you don't get a fatal, contagious disease and everyone is

the shop and her from the same guys collecting it in the first place—
they threaten and intimidate her (Moncada 2021, 19; Varese 2013). The
guys are also called *malandros, pinticas,* and *ratas* (Taussig 2003). These
are young, unemployed people—often armed, sometimes hooded—
claiming to work for a wider criminal organization, she explains to me.
Claudia believes they are acting alone. "But who knows?" she adds. Once
in a while she recognizes them walking by and takes pictures to send to
police officers via WhatsApp. Then one of the guys get killed and new
ones come to visit and ask for the vacuna. The state seems to be absent.
At least, it does not guarantee security in the neighborhood.

Claudia offers a wide range of products, from construction materials
to small infrastructural devices such as screws, pipes, and tubes. The
material circulations of these vital commodities into and within Ciudad
Blanca are mediated by the shopkeepers themselves, and by a series of
improvised practices including storage and surveillance, price speculation, transportation, and credits. Eduardo Moncada (2021), in his typifi-
cation of the responses to extortion, labels these ways of coping as "everyday resistance," in contrast to the phenomenon of vigilantism. While the
latter refers to forms of organized and institutionalized defense to combat extortion, everyday resistance is quotidian, improvised, and loose
coping practices (Moncada 2021, 64–72). However, the vacuna points
not merely to the victimization of shopkeepers and business owners but
to the exposure and fragility of sociomaterial relations and assemblages
in a context of precarity and scarcity.

Extortion, like other forms of crime in Buenaventura's neighborhoods,
is the result of the state's organized abandonment. Moreover, I argue that
crime jeopardizes what Julia Elyachar (2010) calls "phatic labor," a form of
trust-building among subjects that enhances the possibility of social, material, and economic transactions that reproduce and maintain both life
and value in the city. In Ciudad Blanca and elsewhere in Buenaventura,
trust, credit, knowledge, and financial transactions enable the circulation
of vital commodities and people in the cityscape. I argue that violent urban environments can constrain and alter the possibilities of building vital infrastructures at a domestic level in spaces of precarity because they
alter social and material relations (Simone 2006; Larkin 2013). Therefore,

happy; the cows stay put, the family stays whole, and everyone smiles at the clever
little joke of the *vacuna*" (2003, 91).

I address how organized crime interferes with the social, material and infrastructural practices of everyday life and how violence, therefore, constitutes a key feature in the infrastructures of the city.

Due to Buenaventura's strategic position for drug trafficking, a growing and expanding port economy, and devastating poverty and unemployment rates, as well as a partial (and intended) absence of the state, most of the neighborhoods of the city are stricken with violence (Nicholls and Sánchez-Garzoli 2011; Human Rights Watch 2014; CNMH 2015). Recently, scholars have demonstrated how violence is deeply intertwined not only with the surrounding illicit economies but with the port and the state-led development agenda itself (Jenss 2020, 2021; Lombard et al. 2021; Zeiderman 2018; Alves and Ravindran 2020). Several actors produce and coproduce violence in the city, including the state, the private sector, and neo-paramilitary groups. This book (and especially this chapter) contributes to the literature on urban violence in Buenaventura by developing a narrative of everyday violence that emerges from experiences during my fieldwork experience in Ciudad Blanca and that seeks a "bottom-up" perspective on this phenomenon (Taussig 2003). During my stay, I witnessed robberies, extortions, and assassinations in the neighborhood. Moreover, stories of crime, what John and Jean Comaroff (2016) call "crime talk," were constantly circulating in Ciudad Blanca through chats with people, the radio, and the yellow press. I contend that violence, in its callous, spectral, imminent forms, plays a constitutive role in the everyday life of Ciudad Blanca.

Although my main interests were the deficient infrastructures of the water supply system and the coping mechanisms used by a population facing scarcity and infrastructural breakdown, I also actively participated in chats revolving around violence. Besides carrying out several interviews with locals regarding the construction and repair, I witnessed how trust and credit played a vital role in the maintenance of productive relations between the shopkeepers and the population. Claudia told me several times that there were people she trusted because "you see their faces, hear their voices, how they treat you, and you know they are good people." Moreover, the frequency with which people attended the shop was decisive to build the relations of trust: "They come very often to the shop, so I trust them and give them credits." People's lower and inconsistent incomes and the compelling necessity of building and maintaining small infrastructure systems to ensure the access to public resources make these credits an immediate solution for this ubiquitous uncertainty (Simone 2015b).

A focus on phatic labor in Ciudad Blanca helps to understand the everyday practices that enable the circulation of commodities in the city. Extortion and violence appear as an opposite of sorts to phatic labor, interrupting and blocking communicative channels and circulation. Although extortion produces communicative channels while creating semiotic meaning (fear, terror) and increasing economic value (commodities get more expensive), these practices also generate a blockade or counterflow in the circuit of commerce. The "trusted people" to whom Claudia provides informal credits in the hardware shop are then harmed by the increase of prices, the irregular availability of certain commodities, and the uncertainty of the future of the shop.

In what follows, I describe the dynamics of violence in Ciudad Blanca from a bottom-up perspective in an attempt to understand extortion in everyday life. In doing so, I build on the experiences and semiotic articulations of local subjects, especially those of Claudia. By privileging the everyday experiences of violence, I do not seek to obscure or delegitimize other scholarly accounts on violence in the port city, nor do I pretend to define violence as something chaotic and spontaneous without structures supporting it. Rather, I seek to show how opacity and obscurity inform the ways in which violence operates in order to dominate and oppress those living in the margins (Taussig 1984). My focus on "ordinary violence" represents a vantage point to understand how material resources (public and private) are unevenly distributed at the urban margins of Colombia. Like water flows, flows of violence are murky and unpredictable.

Throughout my research stay in Ciudad Blanca, I noted that people avoided openly talking about their own experiences with violence. Several times, my interviewees referred to the "situation in the city" by using common phrases but denied having been directly affected by any experience of violence. It seemed to be something happening "out there." However, after some weeks, Claudia, her family, and employees at the hardware shop were talking to me about their experiences with crime in piecemeal fashion, often lowering their voices. Only after building trust was I able to hold conversations with them about this sensitive topic.

These conversations, which I reproduce here, were not recorded in audio. People feared leaving a record of their views on sensitive topics such as violence. Their voices could, for instance, be recognized by armed groups or others. Instead of recording the conversations, I kept a field diary in which I wrote the details with the consent of the people I interviewed. In some cases, they asked me to change some aspects or omit some details.

Everyday Crime

"Since I arrived in Buenaventura in 1999," Claudia told me while opening the shop one Friday morning, "violence has been everywhere in town." In 2015 the Colombia's National Center for Historical Memory published a comprehensive survey on violence in the port city. I was reading the survey during my research stay to understand what was happening in Ciudad Blanca, and I found several pages filled with maps and statistics, timelines, and the names of criminal groups.

Even though I found interesting descriptions of the development of violence in the CNMH report, which helped me to further understand what had been taking place in the city since the turn of the twenty-first century, I did not find it as useful for understanding Ciudad Blanca's everyday violence. "The *bacrim* doesn't play a crucial role anymore," Yeison told me, contradicting the CNHM report. I was astonished and wondered out loud: "So you don't think there are bigger structures of organized crime here?" He said, "There might be some structures, of course, but there are loose structures. People say there is one single big boss in Buenaventura. He may live abroad, somewhere in the United States. This is a fairytale. Can you believe that?" He laughed and continued: "Violence is everywhere, on every single corner of the city, so you only need to be hooded and say you are a member of a criminal gang, and everybody is *confused*. Sometimes you don't even need a gun."

Anthropologist Michael Taussig (2003, 18), who has been working in Colombia for many decades, was struck by a sentence he heard many times when people refer to violence: "¡En Colombia nunca se sabe!" (In Colombia you never know). Taussig's work on terror in southwestern Colombia aims to grasp the affects and experiences of the everyday violence people are exposed to. Storytelling depicts the opacity behind everyday kidnapping, extortions, and assassinations, he argues. In Ciudad Blanca, confusion, gossip, and rumors make sense given what people constantly experience. In fact, maps and statistics are useless when things have gotten caliente.

Claudia told me several times that she is constantly improving the security system of the shop. For instance, new fences had been built a couple of months before I arrived in Buenaventura. She uses different places (including her own house) to store some of the shop's stock, and she hides her cash in different parts of the shop. "The bad guys don't know how valuable things are, nor where my money is. There have been several attempts of robbery in the shop, but they always fail," Claudia told me, laughing. These attempts never take place during the day, when the shop is open, people are walking by, and customers are chatting with Claudia. It always happens at night. "I know them, I know the guys who have tried to rob the shop several times. There are *pinticas, delincuentes.*" "Aren't they the same ones who ask for the vacuna?" I asked, while struggling to move heavy bags of concrete from the shop to the old pickup truck she uses for deliveries. "No, no, the ones of the vacuna are better connected to the organized crime; these ones are only *rateritos.*"

Violence shapes language. In Colombia, there are many words for killing, for all kinds of felonies, for corpses, and for distinguishing between different categories of illicit actors. The bosses of organized crime and the drug trafficking organizations have several nicknames. *Pinticas, delincuentes* and *rateritos* are used for a different criminal stereotype: young, irrelevant "thugs," expelled by society, unemployed and impoverished (Taussig 2003, 9). They are often victims of the so-called *limpieza social* (social cleansing), a brutal necropolitical method carried out covertly by paramilitaries and police officers to impose "social order." "They might commit crimes on their own, but they always claim to be part of wider structures," Claudia told me as I took a break, exhausted from work I am not used to, and drink a Coke from the grocery shop next door. I was confused. I thought the ones asking for the vacunas might be *pinticas* acting on their own. "Yes, they are," Claudia continued after being interrupted by a customer complaining about the low pressure of the water system. She lowered her voice so as not to be heard by neighbors walking by. "The *pinticas* of the vacuna are more dangerous than the others, they carry heavy weapons, and even if they are not part of bigger structures, they are at least connected to them." When they come to ask for money, she is frightened.

Everyone in Colombia knows about the vacuna. People talk openly about it. In some violence-affected areas of the country, it has become normal. Claudia's brother Don Luis—who runs a grocery shop and a hotel in Caracoles, an even more dangerous neighborhood of Buenaventura— told me, while offering me a chocolate bar in his shop: "I have been paying the vacuna for almost twenty years now; for me, it is a kind of taxation. Sometimes I have to pay it twice a month." On the way back to Ciudad Blanca in Claudia's pickup, passing by the walled-off port, I wanted to know more about extortion. Night had started to fall as we entered Ciudad Blanca through its sneaky and dusty streets: at that time of night the city seemed more dangerous. "I don't have a big issue with the vacuna," Claudia said. "It's a kind of taxation, and since I evade some taxes charged by the state, it's fine. The problem is that you never know when they will come. At the beginning they were visiting me every three months, then they came once a month, and now, you cannot tell when they are coming. It's a surprise." I was shocked. But she just laughed loudly.

A few days later, Claudia received a written death threat. Very early one morning, she knocked on the door of my room. She was smiling nervously. She showed me a piece of paper containing a handwritten threat and a bullet stuck to the sheet with tape. It read: "Claudia. This is our last warning. We talked to you, but you played dumb. You got ten minutes to call this number: . . . If you don't call, we know that you have made a decision and we will have to proceed against you and your family. You either pay or you face the consequences" (figure 17). She told me that she had refused to pay the vacuna to a person who called her on the phone a few days earlier. She was not sure whether the note was from the same people who had called. She seemed confused. Then she called the number in front of me and arranged a meeting to pay the vacuna. I asked her whether I could come with her to witness the transfer. She just laughed and told me to stay in my room until she came back.

Interestingly, another coping mechanism Claudia deployed was denouncement. One rainy morning, while we were having breakfast in the shop, she showed me a WhatsApp chat with a policeman. There was a blurry picture of a young person and a message right under the picture that read: "¡Este es uno!" (This is one of them). The policeman reacted

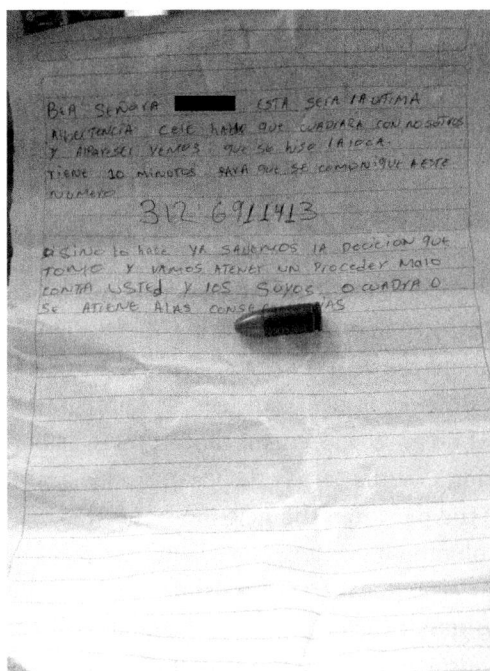

FIGURE 17 The death threat

with a thumbs-up emoji. The guy Claudia had covertly photographed was a *pintica*, a thug. She supposed that it was the same one who had recently called her several times. She hoped that he would get arrested or killed, she told me. He was allegedly not part of a wider criminal organization. "How do you know that he is not one of them?" I asked. "Because everybody knows who they are," she answered, grinning. Remarkably, then, the truth about violence in Buenaventura seems to fluctuate between secrecy (you can never know) and truism (everybody knows). Informal denouncement plays a twofold role for Claudia as a witness and victim of violence. On the one hand, it helps her to make sense of violence since she seems to recognize the perpetrators. On the other hand, she expects that the police will take action and improve security in Ciudad Blanca.

A pair of policemen on a motorcycle patrolled the neighborhood from time to time. They always stopped at the shop to chat with Claudia and sometimes with Ramiro, the owner of the grocery shop next door. Claudia and Ramiro gave drinks and snacks to the policemen. The conversations were mostly quite banal, revolving around family, the weather, and their jobs. They also all complained about the security situation.

"The military will come soon," a policeman once promised. Even though she did not fully trust the police (or the state), Claudia claimed that the "social cleansing" actions led by the police would at least free her from the thugs who don't belong to wider organizations and who were still bothering her.

A week after the last visit of the policemen, things became very caliente. It was January 2020, and a man was killed not far from the shop. A van of the Technical Investigation Team of the attorney general's office arrived. That day, three other people had been killed in Ciudad Blanca. I was frightened. "This is all about *ajuste de cuentas*," settling of scores, Yeison told me, making the violence logical and legible. Later in the evening, some *pinticas* had set up an illegal toll for motorcycles, asking residents for money and forcing Claudia to pay the vacuna once again. I locked myself in my room. The day after, the neighborhood was militarized. Soldiers from the Colombian national navy were stationed in front of Claudia's shop, heavily armed, eating snacks and joking. People went about their everyday business as usual, ignoring the military presence. Nobody wanted to act suspicious while the military "hunted" for the "thugs." The soldiers were stopping every young Black guy who was driving a motorcycle or walking by. The men were frisked, insulted, and intimidated. At one point, the soldiers went around patrolling, and we heard some gunshots. They captured more than five people, Yeison told me the day after.

From below, violence seems to be murky, and to affect people's everyday lives. By ethnographically reconstructing the violent events in Ciudad Blanca, I have sought to express the convoluted temporality and spatiality of violence in Buenaventura, drawing out the sense people try to make of everyday violence and fear by engaging with illicit actors and those who claim to bring order. The sentence "nunca se sabe!" (you can never know) grasps the states of uncertainty people are exposed to, alluding to the potentiality of illicit actors' organized connections and capacity for violence. Furthermore, it reveals the opacity through which violence operates. This resonates with Ben Penglase's (2009) study on Rio's favelas, in which he argues that criminal organizations create disorder, insecurity, and ambiguity through a "permanent state of emergence" and "public secrecy" as forms of domination. The unpredictable eruptions of violence amplify the fear and confusion of residents (*nunca se sabe*). At the same time, people attempt to make sense of violence through "public secrecy" in order of maintaining the "fiction of predictability" (*todo el mundo sabe*) (Penglase 2009, 59). In the meantime, the state appears only occasionally, contributing by default to the murky forms of violence.

Claudia's coping mechanisms as a shopkeeper both enable the continued circulation of commodities and are shaped by the irregular rhythms of the violent actors she is confronted with. Extortion does not merely block the system and jeopardize phatic labor but produces different coping mechanisms that broadly alter the sociomaterial relations in Ciudad Blanca. Claudia does not know with certainty when the guys will come for the vacuna, but she knows they will. Thus, she has to be able to respond quickly, deploying precious resources to develop coping mechanisms under constantly mutating conditions. However, the system remains unstable and threatens to collapse: "I don't know how long I can deal with this," she told me after that caliente day. "I think I am leaving this city soon." Without her hardware shop, things could get very hard for the residents of Ciudad Blanca. If new shopkeepers come, they must build trust from scratch.

On Adulteration, Interferences, and Resistance

Urbanist AbdouMaliq Simone (2006) asserts that "piracy" represents a key feature of urban life in the Global South because "production possibilities are limited." Hence, poor people appropriate existent materials of all kinds—"sometimes through theft and looting; sometimes through 'heretical' uses made of infrastructures, languages, objects and spaces; sometimes through social practices that ensure that available materials pass through many hands." Moreover, they aim to "multiply the uses that can be made of documents, technologies, houses, infrastructure, whatever, and this means the ability to put together different kinds of combinations of people with different skills, perspectives, linkages, identities and aspirations" (Simone 2006, 358). This phenomenon points to the ability (and necessity) of improvisation on the part of urban poor due to the limited resources available, public and private. Michael Degani coined the term *adulteration* to describe the same phenomenon in the Global South, where "adulteration makes a certain kind of otherwise insufficient city run. This is a 'para-industrial' city in which 'production possibilities are limited' and structural underemployment is the norm" (2015, 15). However, not only are "production possibilities" limited, but the circulation of technologies, infrastructures, and commodities are enabled and negotiated in different ways and at different scales. I argue that, alongside the social and infrastructural arrangements that might help to produce and reproduce life through improvisation, Buenaventura's lower class also must cope with interferences in the circulation of commodities and networks of trust, as the practice of extortion illustrates. Although these interferences also produce practices of improvisation (as I have shown in the case of Claudia's hardware store), these are more associated with conservation rather than adulteration. Thus, the aim to "protect" the commodities from robbery and extortion, and therefore enable their further circulation, is a coping mechanism designed not to "multiply the uses" of materialities but rather to limit their very circulation and availability.

But is this a form of resistance? In her work on prepaid meters in South Africa, Antina von Schnitzler (2016) shows how devices can occupy a political terrain of contestation and negotiation. By examining the sociomaterial practices deployed by users such as tampering and destruction, she points to the "political formations below the threshold of visibility of normative conceptions of political action" (von Schnitzler 2016, 6). In the face of biopolitical control through these devices, poor people develop coping mechanisms to access public services. In the same vein, Austin Zeiderman (2016) coined the term "submergent politics" to describe forms of political mobilization in Buenaventura, looking "beyond familiar frames of reference for other conceptual tools that can help us understand forms of cultural and political practice." In his work, Zeiderman focuses on the city's so-called intertidal zone, located at the boundaries between land and sea, which are particularly fragile in the face of legal and illegal capital expansion. Violence rates in these neighborhoods are the highest in Buenaventura. While organized crime and local elites aim to control key territories in the city through violence and infrastructural expansion, social and ethnic activist groups such as the Proceso de Comunidades Negras mobilize to resist eviction and claim civil rights despite the constant intimidation and death threats. Because in Buenaventura "politics in its various normative guises is impeded or prohibited by regimes of lawlessness and terror," political mobilization takes place in different registers and at different scales, as Zeiderman (2016, 825) shows. Zeiderman defines this as "submergent politics," meaning mobilization in "contexts of protracted precarity, remaining beneath the surface, rendered oneself concealed and undetectable," as activists are "forced to descend below the surface, to cover oneself or be covered over, to remain obscure and invisible" (825).

The coping mechanisms relating to everyday crime, infrastructural violence, and abandonment in Ciudad Blanca can be understood as a form of submergent politics too. Asef Bayat's (1997) term of the "politics of the informal people" also points to changes people can make in their everyday lives without necessarily aiming to undermine political authority. One of the main goals of these silent politics is to ensure the distribution of social goods and opportunities, such as land, shelter, piped water, and electricity. The hardship in Buenaventura (caused by violence, poverty, uncertainty, and structural unemployment) leads to the development of forms of resistance such as submergent politics, or the "politics of the informal people." The diverse coping mechanisms deployed by Claudia to protect the shop amount, in a wider sense, to an everyday strategy to ensure the circulation of commodities and the distribution of material goods in the face of illicit encroachment. Paying up, the adulteration of materials, the implementation of security systems, and denouncements are all ways to cope with la vacuna and enable possibilities of survival and reproduction of life in the city.

I left Buenaventura in March 2020 due to the COVID-19 pandemic, when President Iván Duque announced a strict lockdown. During the lockdown, I kept in contact with Claudia via WhatsApp. She complained about the measures of the government and told me that people could not survive without the hardware shop. "A lot of police are patrolling through the neighborhood, they are controlling every single corner, but I still open the shop for some clients," she texted me once. A wide range of commodities became unavailable. The general shutdown of the city threatened life even more than the virus itself. In a way, COVID-19 politics became another form of parasitical interference, perhaps even more dangerous than extortion. "There is no vacuna for this virus that I can pay," Claudia texted me with an ironic laughing emoticon. The fragility of materials, bodies, and life trajectories in Buenaventura makes urban subjects extra vulnerable to viruses and extortionists alike.

The organized abandonment by the state facilitates the presence of criminal organizations and the subsequent proliferation of violence. Several security policies designed for Buenaventura to "regain" control over the city have failed. Several social organizations have accused members of the military of having alliances with criminal gangs and drug trafficking organizations. While these connections cannot be proven, security is not guaranteed for large parts of the population. However, the intermittent militarization of neighborhoods, as in the raid I described in this chapter, points to the present absence of the state. The fragility of security regimes, the disputes over territory, and the murkiness of violence lead to a continuous blocking and interfering of social life and phatic labor, which makes the everyday much more difficult and unpredictable. Precarious forms of survival and resistance deepen the racial and social inequalities in the city. Consequently, the urban poor are forced to inhabit a sort of reverse side of the liberal city, while the city itself enters a negative spiral of informality and even more violence. The coping mechanisms I have addressed in this chapter respond to forms of seeing and inhabiting the city (co)produced by violence. Other possibilities, such as the right to political activism and mobilization, are restricted or even foreclosed. Buenaventura will remain plagued by violence unless structural, state-led reforms are made. Meanwhile, life will continue thanks to everyday ingenuity and the various forms of social, material, and political improvisation.

Yeison

In the mid-nineties Yeison's parents migrated from the Urabá region to Buenaventura. Located in northern part of the country, the Urabá region is known for banana plantations and the brutal violent dynamics of the internal war. During the eighties, many members of the leftist political party Unión Patriótica were killed by paramilitary forces in the wake of a frustrated peace process initiated by then-President Belisario Betancur. Due to violence, Yeison's family moved to Cali. His father was a backhoe driver, and he found a job in Buenaventura. He was precariously paid, and the family settled down in an informal neighborhood. Yeison was born in 1998.

In the late 2000s, the family acquired a piece of land in another settlement, and at the age of twelve, Yeison began helping his father with the construction of a small dwelling there. His father recycled metal rods from a junkyard next to the port. The rods were bent, and father and son spent hours hammering to straighten them out. "There was a mound of materials and implements next to the venue I vividly remember," he told me while cleaning his glasses. They saved money to buy cement, but they built the structures themselves. After having built two stable stories, the family moved in 2014.

Yeison always liked the traditional music from the Pacific. In high school, he joined a band and started playing marimba, a sort of xylophone originally from Africa and brought by enslaved people to the Americas. His capacities were restricted by a degenerative ocular disease doctors discovered when he was fifteen. Since the diagnosis, he has spent a lot of money for treatment. His biggest fear is becoming blind. However, he still plays marimba and regularly sends me videos of his concerts.

When he was twenty, his then-girlfriend got pregnant. It wasn't in the plans, though. One sunny afternoon, while having a beer in the hardware shop, he showed me a tattoo on his chest, with the name of his daughter and her day of birth. When talking about politics, he told me several times that he would identify himself as an Afro-Colombian from the Pacific region, even though his family is originally from the Atlantic coast. He has studied the legislation regarding ethnic minorities in the country and talked to several politicians and activists. "My life was always tough only because I am Black," he told me. "Violence is endemic here because people are Black. And it is the same story with water supply."

The same year his daughter was born, he started working in Claudia's hardware shop. He has always been skilled when it comes to plumbing and repairs, he told me. As an assistant in the shop, he learned even more. But he had bigger dreams, so he started to illegally lend money, a practice known in Colombia as *gota a gota* (literally: drop by drop). It consists of short-term loans with absurdly high interest. He sees himself as an entrepreneur. He and Alexander bought guns some years ago. Yeison still has his. He is concerned about his illness, about the fact that he might not be able to work in some years. "I do whatever I can to accumulate money. I have to take care of my daughter, and I won't be able to work in a couple of years," he said.

Conclusion

In this book, I have examined the interweaving of two key phenomena in the port city of Buenaventura: water infrastructure and violence. For that purpose, I have employed the concept of violence twofold. On the one hand, I have turned to the term "infrastructural violence" to point to processes of state abandonment, segregation, and oppression that have led to inefficient public infrastructures for water supply. Large-scale forces, crystallized over time, created the framework within which racialized populations were (at least partially) deprived from access to functioning public infrastructures. On the other hand, I have conceptualized violence as a quotidian phenomenon that appears in the form of assassinations, kidnapping, extortion, and forced disappearances. This is not to say that the insecurity and endemic violence people are exposed to does not respond to structural processes of oppression and inequality embedded in the long-standing Colombian armed conflict.

Overall, by addressing the myriad ways urbanites experience harm in the city in the context of dysfunctional infrastructures and everyday crime, I have used the concept of violence to examine social phenomena at different scales. Nancy Scheper-Hughes and Philippe Bourgois propose conceptualizing violence "as operating along a continuum from direct physical assault to symbolic violence and routinized everyday violence, including the chronic, historically embedded structural violence whose visibility is obscured" (2003, 318). My ethnographic engagement in an impoverished neighborhood allowed me to observe how life amid both dysfunctional infrastructures and everyday crime configures the relation between marginalized subjects and the state. However, this book not only addresses suffering as a consequence of (infra)structural violence but also identifies the coping mechanisms deployed by the population to deal with the inefficient provision of public water and the effects of everyday crime.

This book sheds light on the specificities of state intervention in the Colombian frontier by analyzing the inscriptions of infrastructure in specific geographies of the nation-state. Following Simón Uribe (2017) in his conceptualizations of the frontier as a space of exception, I argue that the state apparatus sustains a relationship of inclusive exclusion with the port city and its inhabitants. More than lying *outside* the state apparatus, the frontier is included into the civilizing project of the state by violent means (Uribe 2017, 9–10). Consequently, the state mobilizes huge amounts of resources while it fails at fulfilling the dreams of inclusion, (urban) development, and modernization. Simultaneously, the malfunctioning of these infrastructures awakens "feelings and memories of isolation, exclusion, and abandonment" (3).

Hydraulic infrastructures have been a "matter of concern" throughout Buenaventura's modern history of social movement and urban planning (Latour 2004). Indeed, social mobilizations from the 1960s on have reclaimed better infrastructure systems for the population. While the port economies and infrastructures were expanded and modernized and the population grew significantly, public infrastructures remained, throughout the twentieth century, highly precarious. However, the 1990s and the first decade of the 2000s marked a turning point for infrastructure in the city, making things even worse. This is related to several factors: the economic liberalization that led to the immense growth of the port economies and the volume of trade, prompting further infrastructural expansions and an urban development agenda that, once again, prioritized the port; the privatization of the port in 1993, which transformed labor relations and led to mass dismissals and the dismantling of the trade union; the new juridical framework (Law 142) that fostered the privatization of public utility companies owned by municipalities (Hidropacífico took over the operation of the hydraulic infrastructures in Buenaventura in 2001); and the rapid growth of the population and the emerging informal settlements as a consequence of mass displacement in the rural Pacific.

Parallel to the worsening of the social conditions of people in Buenaventura, violence became endemic in the city. The incursion of paramilitarism in the Pacific region and the further expansion of illicit economies in both its rural and urban areas marked the dynamics from the turn of the twenty-first century on. By 2010 the situation regarding poverty, violence, and infrastructure was alarming. At that point, the urban areas of the region—in particular Buenaventura—drew attention from the national press, state institutions, NGOs, and development banks. During that time social mobilization gained momentum in the city. New alliances were forged, and social protest began to shape the political landscape in Buenaventura beginning in 2013.

In anthropology, the study of infrastructures has proliferated in the last decades. In dialogue with geographers and science and technology studies scholars, ethnographers have sought to approach infrastructures as "integral and intimate part of daily social life" (Appel et al. 2018, 6). Infrastructures for the delivery of public goods have served as vantage points to scrutinize different forms of interaction and negotiation between subjects and the state. Tracking the history of the construction, expansion, and maintenance of these infrastructures reveals the differential provisioning that has developed within the context of liberal rule, modernity, and colonialism (van Laak 2018; Joyce 2003). In the case of Buenaventura, the production of a specific geographical entity, namely the Colombian frontier, has conditioned the development of these public infrastructures (Uribe 2017, 2019; Serje 2011). This book does not simply address the histories of the water infrastructures in Buenaventura as "archaeologies of differential provisioning" and inequalities (Appel et al. 2018, 3) but further illustrates the intermingling and dynamics between violence and infrastructure.

New Urban Geographies

In the 1990s the Colombian Pacific started to enjoy great scholarly attention within the social sciences and beyond. This interest coincided with the new legal and political framework regarding ethnic minorities in Colombia. Until that point, the region had played only a marginal role in both the national imaginary of the country and social studies. During the 1970s and 1980s, scholars accompanied the political process that brought together Indigenous and Black peasant movements seeking ethnic-political recognition (Restrepo 2013). Furthermore, the consolidation of Afro-Colombians as emerging political subjects through Ley 70 in 1993 led to a proliferation of literature on the region (e.g., Restrepo 2013; Almario 2007). Indeed, through the emergence of ethnic community councils and the concession of "collective territories," academics have imagined and projected onto the region new forms of conviviality, human-nature relations, and alterity (Escobar 2008, Oslender 2016).

Yet the expansion of the armed conflict into the region as well as the proliferation of illicit economies transformed the social, political, and even environmental dynamics. The timber industry and coca fields damaged large swaths of the rainforest; illegal goldmining contaminated the rivers with quicksilver; many young people joined armed groups; and a range of luxury commodities like gold jewelry, fashionable brand-name shoes, and expensive sound systems flooded the region (Taussig 2010). Massacres took place in many villages and settlements. Thousands of people were forcibly displaced. And the hoped-for future turned into a nightmare. The ethnographic accounts *My Cocaine Museum* by Michael Taussig (2010) and *De río en río* by Alfredo Molano (2017) brilliantly depict these social, political, and environmental transformations in the Pacific.

Many Afro-Colombians, imagined by both state institutions and NGOs as rural subjects practicing a sustainable economy based on gardening, fishing, and artisanal production in collective territories, had to abandon their rural territories and settle in urban areas such as Buenaventura. Grassroots organizations and social movements then faced new challenges and aimed to articulate a new "political subjectivity in urban contexts . . . to establish Afro-Colombian rights in (and to) the city, and to reconfigure the legal and political geography that limits their agency in an urban context" (Zeiderman 2018, 1121). The social mobilization I describe in this book reflects these efforts and challenges.

Despite the harsh urban conditions (and the many depictions of Buenaventura as a space of endemic violence, poverty, and underdevelopment), my fieldwork experience in Ciudad Blanca allowed me to witness a life *beyond* suffering, to witness the everyday strategies people use to inhabit a hostile city in productive ways despite their low incomes, mal-functioning infrastructures, and the everyday violence to which they are exposed (Robbins 2013). Many young people in the neighborhood told me about their dreams for the future in our conversations. Most of them hoped to run a shop and have a regular income in order to build a stable house and have a functioning water storage system. "I would be very happy if I could build a big cistern to store water," Yeison told me. "I could even share some water with my neighbors." Further, he said that he would build a wall to protect his house from criminals and that he might buy a gun. "Of course, leaving the city is always an option, but I really like Buenaventura and I see my future here."

Social research on urban centers in the Colombian Pacific (Buenaventura, Quibdó, and Tumaco) has been scarce. Few ethnographies on these cities have been published. Amid urban poverty, violence, and infrastructural breakdown, hope and alternative futures seem unreachable, and Indigenous ontologies and pluriverses seem foreclosed. In this context, Afro-Colombian subjectivity has to be reinvented and identity politics widely challenged. A new scholarly agenda on the urban Pacific should foster and enhance further discussions on race, marginality, precarious infrastructures, and violence. A dialogue with grassroots organizations and social movements would allow for the further conceptualization of the urban "from below" (Zeiderman 2018). The exceptionalities of the urban Pacific should not merely mirror dynamics of dispossession and suffering but should rather be apprehended "as sites of experimentation" in which scholars look at the "daily micropolitics through which new expressions of citizenship are negotiated" (Fredericks 2018, 25). Moreover, the urban Pacific should be a starting point from which alternative (Black) urban futures can be imagined and articulated. In this endeavor, ethnographic research is paramount. This book has sought to contribute to the studies of a Pacific region—a region that may have become tough and violent but in which hope must be retained.

Studying Flows

In the 1990s and the first decade of the 2000s, flow was used as a metaphor in scholarly literature to denote new geographies of movement and migration across transnational space. In violent environments, however, flows might represent something quite different, namely the harmful forces of unpredictable movements—of the state, of criminal gangs, of water engineers. Here, state–citizen relations are constantly reconfigured through violent means, affecting populations along the lines of race, class, and gender.

In the 2010s, infrastructural violence as an analytical lens gained prominence in academia, not only addressing forms of harm and exclusion as a consequence of both massive infrastructural projects and infrastructural warfare, but also approaching the everyday effects of disconnection and material marginalization (von Schnitzler 2016; Anand 2012). Everyday violence and infrastructure have seldom been addressed as interlocked phenomena. An exception is the work of sociologists Javier Auyero and Agustín Burbano de Lara, who explore harm in the urban margins of Buenos Aires by analyzing the "dearth of basic infrastructure and the profusion of various forms of violence" that jointly define "daily life in the poor neighborhoods of Argentina" (2012, 552). Their analysis, however, points to these phenomena as concomitant rather than entangled.

Addressing the overlapping effects of these two phenomena allows us to shed light on specific practices through which relations between the state apparatus and marginalized citizens are sustained and reproduced. Not only large-scale infrastructure projects and social mobilization but also everyday material practices at a local level elucidate the effects of this relation. Ethnographic explorations of affected subjects permit insights into the unstable rhythms and quotidian formations of violence and infrastructural precarity. On the other hand, looking at the technocratic approaches of the state apparatus and its history of marginalization allows academics to delve into the politics that produce and sustain these vulnerable cityscapes. Beyond that, examining the political mobilizations of subjects allows us to understand the correlation of forces and the formulation of urban alternatives by the population itself. At the same time, coping mechanisms such as the construction of small-scale infrastructures point to forms of politics Asef Bayat (1997) has defined as "quiet encroachment of the ordinary." *Violent flows* are harmful but also contested.

Buenaventura was conceived as an urban enclave of interests alien to the Black and racialized population that represents the majority in the city. This is linked to conceptions of the region as part of an internal frontier in Colombia. Specific spatial and material practices are tightly interlocked with colonial narratives, mappings, and other forms which aimed to apprehend these "marginal territories" and include them in the national and state order by violent means. Studying the specificities of infrastructural violence in these territories enriches the academic literature as it delves into specific mechanisms of state power. The production of racial geographies has been paramount to these phenomena. In contemporary Colombia, however, where minorities are constitutionally recognized, legally protected, and politically visible, it is difficult to find official narratives and discourses that overtly ascribe to (neo)colonial patterns. Yet racism informs institutional power and everyday interactions.

Ethnographies on marginal urban landscapes should pay special attention to the mundane, discrete, everyday appearances of violence in the form of infrastructural deprivation and everyday crime. Infrastructural violence does not only mean eviction or spectacular breakdown, nor the selective assassination of, let's say, social leaders. Violent flows are those that *come* and *go*, the forces that shape and form bodies and territories condemned to live at the margins of state and capitalism, in a silent, mundane manner. Violent flows have a historical origin in colonialism, in racial-driven urban planning and long-standing processes of state abandonment. You can see them: when gangs pour into the neighborhood and the water supply is cut off, once again.

Epilogue

Throughout my research stay in 2019, I saw several billboards in Buenaventura promoting Víctor Hugo Vidal as a candidate for mayor in the
next municipal election. Vidal was a prominent leader of the strike in
2017 and had been involved in social and ethnic activism for more than
thirty years, both in urban and rural areas of the region. For a short period of time, he was also a member of the municipal council. In 2019 the
social organizations that form the Strike Committee nominated Vidal as
a candidate for mayor. Even though activist groups tended to seek to remain outside the state apparatus, the municipal administration had been
overshadowed by corruption, clientelism, and mismanagement. Participating in the local government would offer an opportunity to foster the
implementation of the accords signed after the strike in 2017. However,
after announcing his candidacy, Vidal resigned his post within the Strike
Committee to keep the social movements and municipal government as
separate domains of politics in the port city.

In October 2019 Vidal won the mayoral election. He took office in
December for the period 2019–2023. As mayor, he actively monitored
central state activities. Even though the pandemic posed enormous challenges, Vidal was an effective leader. As far as the water infrastructures
go, the contract with Hidropacífico was not extended. For now, the SAAB
has taken over the operation.

The election of leftist Gustavo Petro in June 2022 as the new president of Colombia for the period of 2022–2026 opened up new possibilities for an agenda of social inclusion, environmental protection, and sustainable development to unfold. The new vice president, Francia Márquez, is a former social activist of Afro-Colombian descent who knows the grassroots and ethnic organizations in the region well. This government could design and implement new forms of intervention, articulated to the tools, needs, and discourses of social movements. A new geography of the Pacific could be drawn, and Buenaventura could be transformed into an inclusive city by means of expanding public infrastructures and including marginal subjects into urban projections and development plans.

In August 2023, after more than three years, I returned to Buenaventura. Things had changed dramatically, in Claudia's life, at least. After leasing the hardware shop to Yeison and Antonia, Claudia decided to sell it. Extortion had increased exponentially during the first half of 2023. Also, several conflicts had arisen between Yeison and Claudia. Apparently, the relationship between him and her daughter was not a healthy one. And he had a quite different notion of how to run a shop. "I have gathered experience for years; I have done everything: I have run hotels, *tiendas*, a hardware shop," Claudia told me. But the conflict with Yeison was too much. She found a buyer, a family from the country's interior that had recently migrated to Buenaventura, and sold it to them.

It felt strange—seeing the hardware shop only from the outside, with different owners inside it. My "field," the space from which I had experienced and witnessed the everyday life of people in Buenaventura, was "occupied" by others, by strangers. The field I had encountered was not there anymore. I felt nostalgic and relieved at the same time. How would everything have turned out if I had not met with Claudia, Yeison, and Alexander? Would I have gathered the same valuable data without them? Would I have been able to enter a neighborhood in Buenaventura? I like to think that I would have, but this book certainly would have been a different one.

This time, I visited the neighborhood with German photographer Marie Runge. I aimed to take some high-quality pictures of the pipelines, the concrete tank, and some improvised connections. I asked Alexander in advance if the security situation would be good enough to walk around the neighborhood and take some pictures. He agreed. And he was as kind as always, supporting me in my research. The sun was high, reaching its zenith, reflected back from the metal sheets of some dwellings, all but melting the asphalt. We visited the main pipeline running through the neighborhood. A pipeline full of moisture and leaks and illicit connections. Only the sound of crickets singing loudly penetrated the midday quiet. We then walked up to the big concrete tank, surrounded by an old rusty fence, the portier guarding it nodding to give us permission to enter. Once inside the venue, I noticed a guy gazing at us; he was wearing a cap and seemed suspicious. Alexander approached him. He was policing the area and asked what we were doing there. I felt panic rising up in me. He called his boss and held the phone out in front of me. I FaceTimed with a criminal; he wanted to see my face, but I couldn't see his. He had the frontal camera on, so I only saw a sidewalk. "What are you doing there?" he asked. I explained to him that we were carrying out research on water infrastructures for a European university. He said that we were welcome there and hung up. I was still full of fear, feeling my heartbeat all over my body. We sped up our pace and left the area. Then we walked for a couple of hours in the neighborhood, taking further pictures. Marie was afraid, and so was I, but we knew that this would be our only chance to take pictures, so we kept walking.

In 2022 things had improved in terms of security. The new peace policy of Gustavo Petro, called *paz total* (total peace), consisting of wide negotiations with all armed actors throughout the country, seemed to have positive effects on urban violence in Buenaventura. In October 2022, the two main gangs in the port city had come to terms after a negotiation, and no homicides were registered for more than twenty-two days. In December, President Petro visited the city for the second time, celebrating with social leaders and the population the beginning of a new era. But due to a lack of a legal framework, the *paz total* strategy in Buenaventura began to weaken. By mid-2023, videos of armed young men started circulating, and violence was on the rise once again.

As the sun set, we went to the restaurant where Doña Sandra, Alexander's mother, used to work. She wanted to meet me in person. She thanked me for being so kind and supportive to Alexander because I had paid him for being my research assistant. We then went to the house he rented with his girlfriend. On the patio of the small dwelling, a big plastic tank was connected to the tap to collect water, and three handsome puppies were playing on the concrete floor. We took a seat and chatted a while, feeling the salty breeze coming from the sea.

In the early evening, I met Yeferson, the engineer, and Nestor, the social leader, whom I knew from the time of my fieldwork. We reviewed the developments and changes of the water infrastructures in the city in light of a new central, progressive government. They seemed quite skeptical. The PTSP had still not met its short-term goals, even though the new general director had a better plan than the last one. "We expect more money to be invested. Otherwise, things won't change," Nestor said. The Demand Management Plan (Plan de Gestión de Demanda) was long overdue, Yeferson said. The ASIB, as a guild, insists on the necessity of carrying out this plan. Its members believed that the new government would put in much more effort, but the institutional framework would still be too weak and the bureaucracy too cumbersome. "We need to be heard," Yeferson insisted.

In the evening, we went back to Claudia's place and had dinner with her and her daughters. Then we had some beers, Marie and I sitting on an old sofa, Claudia on a plastic chair just in front of us. She began to talk about her life once again. The room was dark, weakly lit by a streetlamp. She began to tell stories I already knew, stories of violence both domestic and political, stories of enterprise, migration, and risk. Stories I have written down in this book. But why did she want to tell me all of this again? Perhaps to make sense of what had happened to her. I felt sad, knowing that I would be leaving the day after, but I also felt immensely thankful. For her protection, her stories, her time, her love. For being so engaging.

The day was over, and we went to bed.

ACKNOWLEDGMENTS

I wrote large parts of this book during the COVID-19 pandemic, which presented enormous emotional, practical, and intellectual challenges. Without the support of many friends and colleagues, completing this book would not have been possible. First, I would like to thank my supervisors, Stephanie Schütze and Claudia Zamorano, who read and commented on earlier drafts and provided invaluable guidance throughout the writing process.

As a junior researcher in the International Research Training Group (IRTG) Temporalities of Future at the Latin American Institute of the Freie Universität Berlin, funded by the German Research Council, I received generous funding and had the opportunity to participate in various seminars, colloquia, and academic events both within and beyond the project. The extensive fieldwork I conducted in Buenaventura was also funded by the IRTG. I would like to thank Ingrid Simson, Stefan Rinke, and Lasse Hölck for their support and encouragement. It was a pleasure to engage in discussions and dialogues on various topics related to Latin America with my colleagues at the IRTG. I am grateful for the many insightful comments and reflections on my work that I received from them. I would like to offer special thanks to Luis Kliche Navas, a brilliant political scientist who closely read several drafts of this book and helped me to refine the most important arguments, particularly those revolving around the state.

Without the openness, kindness, and support of the people I met in Buenaventura, this work would not have been possible. Several social activists and local engineers warmly received me in their offices, gave me long interviews, and assisted me in the challenging task of gathering data in a complex environment. Thanks to their expertise and patience, I learned much about hydraulic engineering, the history of water networks in Buenaventura, and the political landscape of the region. While their names must remain anonymous, my gratitude is immense. I would especially like to thank Claudia for hosting and protecting me for such an extended period in her home and shop in Ciudad Blanca. Her guidance through the field was key to the success of my research. The support of Yeison and Alexander, my friends from the neighborhood, enabled me to navigate a hostile urban environment. I am deeply indebted to them.

Further, I am very grateful to have become a part of the Laboratory for the Anthropology of the State in Colombia (LASC), a collaborative network of brilliant and generous anthropologists working on Colombia. Roxani Krystalli, Charles Beach, Erin McFee, Gwen Burnyeat, Valentina Pellegrino, Emma Shaw Crane, María Fernanda Olarte-Sierra, Sebastián Ramírez, and Alex Diamond all read earlier versions of this book and provided thoughtful comments and insights. I am also deeply thankful for their emotional and moral support. I would especially like to thank Erin McFee for introducing me to LASC and Gwen Burnyeat for patiently answering every single question I sent over WhatsApp. Thank you, Gwen, for your warm and thoughtful guidance. Without it, I would never have been able to publish this book!

I would also like to thank Andrés Guiot-Isaac, with whom I organized a virtual workshop on the state in Colombia and a conference at the Latin American Centre in Oxford. The academic dialogue we sustained over the past few years has been very fruitful and has contributed significantly to the realization of this book. I am grateful to my fellow panelists at the conferences I attended in recent years: the Latin American Studies Association in 2020, 2021, and 2024; the American Anthropological Association in 2019 and 2023; the Latin American Studies Association's conferences in 2021 and 2024; the Visions of the Future in the Americas conference at the University of Bonn in 2019; and the international colloquium Habiter les Villes Latino-Américaines at the École Nationale Supérieure d'Architecture in Paris in 2019.

Many scholars and friends alike read early drafts of this book and provided insightful comments. These include Julia Teebken, Rodolfo Espinosa, Richard Rottenburg, Luis Kliche, Laura Matt, Lorenz Gosch, Johannes Machinya, Faeeza Ballim, Georges Eyenga, Bronwyn Kotzen, Carolin Loysa, David Kananizadeh, Tiana Bakić Hayden, Sandra Rozental, Alke Jenss, and Gregor Dobler. Thank you!

The emotional support I have received from friends and family during this time has been paramount to getting through it all. I am deeply grateful to my mother, Ángela Lozano, for her unconditional love and support. I would also like to thank my friends abroad, with whom I maintain long-distance yet close and loving friendships: Joel Harf, Jessica Bigio, Jeremy Abadi, David Gómez, Javier Mardones, and Edrit Franquiz. I want to especially thank Jeremy Abadi and Mariana Quijano for hosting me in Cali during my several research stays, letting me feel at home. During the writing process, the beautiful, sunny midday walks through Neukölln with Saskia Rutz, my dear friend and neighbor, helped me clear my mind and continue writing. The wonderful moments I spent with Luis Kliche, Anna Wherry, Daniel Cuesta, Klara Faller, Vincent Kreusel, Juliana Dávila, Clemens Ruben, Julia Teebken, Sara Belleza, Marie de Lassance, Philipp Kandler, Gesche Wattenberg, Rodrigo Perujo, Mariana Vivian, Bram Daanen, and Wendy Bazán gave me strength to keep going. I am also grateful to my host parents in Germany, Andreas and Martina Flecken, and Franka and Gerd Zacher, who provided me with wonderful support throughout my time in Germany. Without them, I would never have completed this book. Although time has seen us follow different pathways, I am deeply thankful to Marie Runge for all her love and support.

This book is dedicated to my beloved friends Nicolas Hauptmann and Saskia Baumgardt, who have become like family to me.

Any errors remain my own.

BIBLIOGRAPHY

Acevedo Guerrero, Tatiana. 2019. "Light Is like Water: Flooding, Blackouts, and the State in Barranquilla." *Tapuya: Latin American Science, Technology and Society* 2 (1): 478–94. https://doi.org/10.1080/25729861.2019.1678711.

Acevedo Guerrero, Tatiana. 2021. "'The People Won't Give Up, Damn It!' Reclaiming Public Water in Buenaventura, Colombia." In *Public Water and COVID-19: Dark Clouds and Silver Linings*, edited by David McDonald, Susan Spronk, and Daniel Chavez. Municipal Services Project, Transnational Institute, and Latin American Council of Social Sciences.

Acuavalle. n.d. Plan Maestro Acueducto y Alcantarillado de Buenaventura.

Ahumada, Consuelo. 1996. *El modelo neoliberal y su impacto en la sociedad Colombiana*. 1st ed. El Ancora Editores.

Almario, Óscar. 2007. "¡Ay mi bello puerto del mar, mi Buenaventura! La larga historia del desencuentro entre el puerto y la ciudad y entre la región y el país." *Revista posiciones* 1:8–19.

Alves, Jaime, and Tathagatan Ravindran. 2020. "Racial Capitalism: The Free Trade Zone of Pacific Alliance, and Colombian Utopic Spatialities of Antiblackness." *ACME* 19 (1): 187–209.

Alves, Jaime Amparo. 2018. *The Anti-Black City: Police Terror and Black Urban Life in Brazil*. University of Minnesota Press.

Anand, Nikhil. 2011. "Pressure: The PoliTechnics of Water Supply in Mumbai." *Cultural Anthropology* 26 (4): 542–64. https://doi.org/10.1111/j.1548-1360.2011.01111.x.

Anand, Nikhil. 2012. "Municipal Disconnect: On Abject Water and Its Urban Infrastructures." *Ethnography* 13 (4): 487–509. https://doi.org/10.1177/1466138111435743.

Anand, Nikhil. 2015a. "Leaky States: Water Audits, Ignorance, and the Politics of Infrastructure." *Public Culture* 27 (2): 305–30. https://doi.org/10.1215/08992363 -2841880.

Anand, Nikhil. 2015b. "Accretion." Society for Cultural Anthropology, Theorizing the Contemporary. https://culanth.org/fieldsights/accretion.

Anand, Nikhil. 2017. *Hydraulic City: Water and the Infrastructures of Citizenship in Mumbai*. Duke University Press.

Anand, Nikhil. 2020. "After Breakdown Invisibility and the Labor of Infrastructure Maintenance." *Economic and Political Weekly* 55 (51): 52–56.

Aparicio, Juan Ricardo. 2012. *Rumores, residuos y estado en "la mejor esquina de Sudamérica."* University of the Andes.

Appadurai, Arjun. 1996. *Modernity at Large: Cultural Dimensions of Globalization*. University of Minnesota Press.

Appadurai, Arjun. 2001. "Deep Democracy: Urban Governmentality and the Horizon of Politics." *Environment and Urbanization* 13 (2): 23–43. https://doi.org/10.1177 /095624780101300203.

Appadurai, Arjun, ed. 2013. *The Future as Cultural Fact: Essays on the Global Condition*. Verso.

Appel, Hannah. 2012. "Walls and White Elephants: Oil Extraction, Responsibility, and Infrastructural Violence in Equatorial Guinea." *Ethnography* 13 (4): 439–65. https://doi.org/10.1177/1466138111435741.

Appel, Hannah. 2019. *The Licit Life of Capitalism: US Oil in Equatorial Guinea*. Duke University Press.

Appel, Hannah, and Nikhil Anand. 2018. Introduction. In *The Promise of Infrastructure*, edited by Nikhil Anand, Akhil Gupta, and Hannah Appel, 1–38. Duke University Press.

Arboleda, S. 2004. "Negándose a ser desplazados: Afrocolombianos en Buenaventura." In *Conflico e (in)visibilidad. Retos en los estudios de la gente negra en Colombia*, edited by Eduardo Restrepo and Axel Rojas, 121–38. Editorial Universidad del Cauca.

Asad, Talal. 1979. "Anthropology and the Colonial Encounter." In *The Politics of Anthropology*, edited by Gerrit Huizer and Bruce Mannheim, 85–94. De Gruyter Mouton. https://doi.org/10.1515/9783110806458.85.

Asher, Kiran. 2009. *Black and Green: Afro-Colombians, Development, and Nature in the Pacific Lowlands*. Duke University Press.

Asher, Kiran, and Diana Ojeda. 2009. "Producing Nature and Making the State: Ordenamiento Territorial in the Pacific Lowlands of Colombia." *Geoforum* 40 (3): 292–302. https://doi.org/10.1016/j.geoforum.2008.09.014.

Auyero, Javier, and Agustín Burbano de Lara. 2012. "In Harm's Way at the Urban Margins." *Ethnography* 13 (4): 531–57. https://doi.org/10.1177/146613811143 5746.

Bakker, Karen. 2014. *Privatizing Water: Governance Failure and the World's Urban Water Crisis*. Ithaca: Cornell University Press.

Ballestero, Andrea. 2019. "The Underground as Infrastructure? Water, Figure/Ground Reversals, and Dissolution in Sardinal." In *Infrastructure, Environment, and Life in the Anthropocene*, edited by Kregg Hetherington, 17–44. Duke University Press. https://doi.org/10.1215/9781478002567-003.

Ballvé, Teo. 2020. *The Frontier Effect: State Formation and Violence in Colombia*. Cornell Series on Land: New Perspectives in Territory, Development, and Environment. Cornell University Press.

Bayat, Asef. 1997. "Un-Civil Society: The Politics of the 'Informal People.'" *Third World Quarterly* 18 (1): 53–72. https://doi.org/10.1080/01436599715055.

Bayat, Asaf. 2010. *Life as Politics: How Ordinary People Change the Middle East*. Stanford University Press.

Bell, Kirsten. 2019. "The 'Problem' of Undesigned Relationality: Ethnographic Fieldwork, Dual Roles and Research Ethics." *Ethnography* 20 (1): 8–26. https://doi.org/10.1177/1466138118807236.

Bennett, Jane. 2010. *Vibrant Matter: A Political Ecology of Things*. Duke University Press. https://doi.org/10.1515/9780822391623.

Björkman, Lisa. 2015. *Pipe Politics, Contested Waters: Embedded Infrastructures of Millennial Mumbai*. Duke University Press.

Bonet-Morón, Jaime, Yuri Reina-Aranza, and Diana Ricciulli-Marin. 2020. "Movimientos sociales y desarrollo económico en Chocó, Colombia." *Estudios Gerenciales*, February, 127–40. https://doi.org/10.18046/j.estger.2020.155.3338.

Boyer, Dominic. 2008. "Thinking Through the Anthropology of Experts." *Anthropology in Action* 15 (2). https://doi.org/10.3167/aia.2008.150204.

Burnyeat, Gwen. 2018. *Chocolate, Politics and Peace-Building: An Ethnography of the Peace Community of San José de Apartadó, Colombia*. Studies of the Americas. Palgrave Macmillan.

Burnyeat, Gwen. 2019. "Chocolate, Politics and Peace-Building: An Ethnography of the Peace Community of San José de Apartadó, Colombia." *Maguaré* 33 (2): 323–28. https://doi.org/10.15446/mag.v33n2.88071.

Burnyeat, Gwen. 2022. *The Face of Peace: Government Pedagogy amid Disinformation in Colombia*. University of Chicago Press.

Callén, Blanca, and Tomás Sánchez Criado. 2015. "Vulnerability Tests: Matters of 'Care of Matter' in E-Waster Practices." *Technosienza* 6 (2): 17–40.

Callon, Michel, Pierre Lascoumes, Yannick Barthe, and Graham Burchell. 2009. *Acting in an Uncertain World: An Essay on Technical Democracy*. MIT Press.

Cárdenas, Roosbelinda. 2023. *Raising Two Fists: Struggles for Black Citizenship in Multicultural Colombia*. Stanford University Press.

Carmona, Susana, and Pablo Jaramillo. 2020. "Anticipating Futures Through Enactments of Expertise: A Case Study of an Environmental Controversy in a Coal Mining Region of Colombia." *Extractive Industries and Society* 7 (3): 1086–95. https://doi.org/10.1016/j.exis.2020.06.009.

Carr, E. Summerson. 2010. "Enactments of Expertise." *Annual Review of Anthropology* 39 (1): 17–32. https://doi.org/10.1146/annurev.anthro.012809.104948.

Castells, Manuel. 1996. *The Rise of the Network Society*. The Information Age: Economy, Society, and Culture 1. Blackwell.

Chalfin, Brenda. 2014. "Public Things, Excremental Politics, and the Infrastructure of Bare Life in Ghana's City of Tema." *American Ethnologist* 41 (1): 92–109. https://doi.org/10.1111/amet.12062.

Chatterjee, Partha. 2007. *The Politics of the Governed: Reflections on Popular Politics in Most of the World*. Leonard Hastings Schoff Memorial Lectures. Columbia University Press.

Chu, Julie Y. 2014. "When Infrastructures Attack: The Workings of Disrepair in China." *American Ethnologist* 41 (2): 351–67. https://doi.org/10.1111/amet.12080.

CNMH (Centro Nacional de Memoria Histórica). 2015. *Buenaventura: Un puerto sin comunidad*.

Comaroff, Jean, and John L. Comaroff. 2016. *The Truth About Crime: Sovereignty, Knowledge, Social Order*. University of Chicago Press.

Consejo Nacional de Política Económica y Social. 2015. Documento CONPES 3847: Plan Todos Somos Pazcífico. Departamento Nacional de Planeación.

Corbridge, Stuart, ed. 2005. *Seeing the State: Governance and Governmentality in India*. Contemporary South Asia 10. Cambridge University Press.

Cristo Bustos, Juan Fernando, and Guillermo Rivera Flórez. 2019. *Disparos a la paz: La historia desconocida de la implementación del acuerdo*. Bogotá: Ediciones B.

Das, Veena, and Deborah Poole. 2004. Introduction. In *Anthropology in the Margins of the State*, edited by Veena Das and Deborah Poole, 3–33. School for Advanced Research Press.

De Boeck, Filip, and Marie-Françoise Plissart. 2014. *Kinshasa: Tales of the Invisible City*. Leuven University Press.

de Certeau, Michel. 2013. *The Practice of Everyday Life*. University of California Press.

De Coss-Corzo, Alejandro. 2021. "Patchwork: Repair Labor and the Logic of Infrastructure Adaptation in Mexico City." *Environment and Planning D: Society and Space* 39 (2): 237–53. https://doi.org/10.1177/0263775820938057.

Degani, Michael. 2022. *The City Electric*. Duke University Press.

De Greiff A., Alexis. 2021. "Fragmentar carreteras sin dividir a la nación en Colombia, c. 1930: Una historia material del 'estado en acción.'" *Anuario Colombiano de historia social y de la cultura* 48 (1): 163–200. https://doi.org/10.15446/achsc.v48n1.91548.

de la Cadena, Marisol. 2019. "Uncommoning Nature: Stories from the Anthropo-Not-Seen." In *Anthropos and the Material*, edited by Penny Harvey, Christian Krohn-Hansen, and Knut G. Nustad, 35–58. Duke University Press. https://doi.org/10.1215/9781478003311-003.

Díaz Vargas, Álvaro Hernán. 2015. "Buenaventura: Ciudad—puerto o puerto sin ciudad." Master's thesis, National University of Colombia.

Edwards, Paul, Geoffrey Bowker, Steven Jackson, and Robin Williams. 2009. "Introduction: An Agenda for Infrastructure Studies." *Journal of the Association for Information Systems* 10 (5): 364–74. https://doi.org/10.17705/1jais.00200.

Edwards, Paul N. 2003. "Infrastructure and Modernity: Force Time and Social Organization in the History of Sociotechnical Systems." In *Modernity and Technology*, edited by Thomas J. Misa, Philip Brey, and Andrew Feenberg, 185–225. MIT Press.

Elyachar, Julia. 2010. "Phatic Labor, Infrastructure, and the Question of Empowerment in Cairo." *American Ethnologist* 37 (3): 452–64. https://doi.org/10.1111/j .1548-1425.2010.01265.x.

Escobar, Arturo. 1995. *Encountering Development: The Making and Unmaking of the Third World*. Princeton Studies in Culture, Power, History. Princeton University Press.

Escobar, Arturo. 2008. *Territories of Difference: Place, Movements, Life, Redes*. Duke University Press. https://doi.org/10.1215/9780822389439.

Esteyco and Findeter. 2015. La Buenaventura que nos Merecemos: Buenaventura Master Plan 2050.

Fedesarrollo-Cerac. 2013. Hacia un desarrollo integral de la Ciudad de Buenaventura y su area de influencia.

Ferguson, James. 1994. *The Anti-Politics Machine: "Development," Depoliticization, and Bureaucratic Power in Lesotho*. University of Minnesota Press.

Ferguson, James, and Akhil Gupta. 2002. "Spatializing States: Toward an Ethnography of Neoliberal Governmentality." *American Ethnologist* 29 (4): 981–1002. https://doi.org/10.1525/ae.2002.29.4.981.

Fernández, Felipe. 2022. "Construir y reparar frente al desabastecimiento: Estado, provisión de agua e infraestructura en Buenaventura, Colombia." *Revista Colombiana de antropología* 58 (2): 105–29. https://doi.org/10.22380/2539472X.2125.

Fredericks, Rosalind. 2018. *Garbage Citizenship: Vital Infrastructures of Labor in Dakar, Senegal*. Duke University Press. https://doi.org/10.1215/9781478002505.

Furlong, Kathryn. 2014. "STS Beyond the 'Modern Infrastructure Ideal': Extending Theory by Engaging with Infrastructure Challenges in the South." *Technology in Society* 38 (August): 139–47. https://doi.org/10.1016/j.techsoc.2014.04.001.

Gandy, Matthew. 2008. "Landscapes of Disaster: Water, Modernity, and Urban Fragmentation in Mumbai." *Environment and Planning A: Economy and Space* 40 (1): 108–30. https://doi.org/10.1068/a3994.

Gandy, Matthew. 2017. *The Fabric of Space: Water, Modernity, and the Urban Imagination*. MIT Press.

Garcia Ferrari, Soledad, Harry Smith, Francoise Coupe, and Helena Rivera. 2018. "City Profile: Medellin." *Cities* 74 (April): 354–64. https://doi.org/10.1016/j.cities .2017.12.011.

Gill, Lesley. 2016. *A Century of Violence in a Red City: Popular Struggle, Counterinsurgency, and Human Rights in Colombia*. Duke University Press. https://doi.org /10.1215/9780822374701.

Goldstein, Daniel M. 2012. *Outlawed: Between Security and Rights in a Bolivian City*. Duke University Press. https://doi.org/10.1215/9780822395607.

González, Fernán E. 2014. *Poder y violencia en Colombia*. Odecofi-Cinep.

Graeber, David. 2012. "Dead Zones of the Imagination: On Violence, Bureaucracy, and Interpretive Labor: The Malinowski Memorial Lecture, 2006." *HAU: Journal of Ethnographic Theory* 2 (2): 105–28. https://doi.org/10.14318/hau2.2.007.

Graham, Stephen, and Nigel Thrift. 2007. "Out of Order: Understanding Repair and Maintenance." *Theory, Culture and Society* 24 (3): 1–25. https://doi.org/10.1177/0263276407075954.

Graham, Steve, and Simon Marvin. 2002. *Splintering Urbanism: Networked Infrastructures, Technological Mobilities and the Urban Condition.* Routledge. https://doi.org/10.4324/9780203452202.

Guerrero, Tatiana Acevedo, Kathryn Furlong, and Jeimy Arias. 2016. "Complicating Neoliberalization and Decentralization: The Non-Linear Experience of Colombian Water Supply, 1909–2012." *International Journal of Water Resources Development* 32 (2): 172–88. https://doi.org/10.1080/07900627.2015.1026434.

Gupta, Akhil. 2012. *Red Tape: Bureaucracy, Structural Violence, and Poverty in India.* Duke University Press. https://doi.org/10.1215/9780822394709.

Han, Clara. 2018. "Precarity, Precariousness, and Vulnerability." *Annual Review of Anthropology* 47 (1): 331–43. https://doi.org/10.1146/annurev-anthro-102116-041644.

Hannerz, Ulf. 1996. *Transnational Connections: Culture, People, Places.* Routledge.

Hansen, Thomas, and Finn Stepputat. 2005. Introduction. In *Sovereign Bodies: Citizens, Migrants, and States in Postcolonial World*, edited by Thomas Blom Hansen and Finn Stepputat, 1–36. Princeton University Press.

Harvey, David. 2000. *Spaces of Hope.* Edinburgh University Press. https://doi.org/10.1515/9781474468961.

Harvey, Penelope, and Hannah Knox. 2015. *Roads: An Anthropology of Infrastructure and Expertise.* Cornell University Press.

Heslop, Luke, and Laura Jeffery. 2020. "Roadwork: Expertise at Work Building Roads in the Maldives." *Journal of the Royal Anthropological Institute* 26 (2): 284–301. https://doi.org/10.1111/1467-9655.13236.

Hoffmann, Odile. 2007. *Comunidades negras en el Pacífico colombiano: innovaciones y dinámicas étnicas.* Ediciones Abya-Yala.

Howe, Cymene, Jessica Lockrem, Hannah Appel, Edward Hackett, Dominic Boyer, Randal Hall, Matthew Schneider-Mayerson, et al. 2016. "Paradoxical Infrastructures: Ruins, Retrofit, and Risk." *Science, Technology, and Human Values* 41 (3): 547–65. https://doi.org/10.1177/0162243915620017.

Humans Right Watch. "The Crisis in Buenaventura." March 20, 2014. https://www.hrw.org/report/2014/03/20/crisis-buenaventura/disappearances-dismemberment-and-displacement-colombias-main.

Jackson, Steven J. 2014. "Rethinking Repair." In *Media Technologies*, edited by Tarleton Gillespie, Pablo J. Boczkowski, and Kirsten A. Foot, 221–40. MIT Press. https://doi.org/10.7551/mitpress/9042.003.0015.

Jaramillo Marín, Jefferson, Érika Paola Parrado Pardo, and Daniela Mosquera Camacho. 2020. "El paro cívico de 2017 en Buenaventura, Colombia: Protesta social y

transformación del poder político." *Análisis político* 33 (98): 136–66. https://doi
.org/10.15446/anpol.v33n98.89414.

Jenss, Alke. 2020. "Global Flows and Everyday Violence in Urban Space: The Port-City of Buenaventura, Colombia." *Political Geography* 77 (March): 102113. https://
doi.org/10.1016/j.polgeo.2019.102113.

Jenss, Alke. 2021. "Disrupting the Rhythms of Violence: Anti-port Protests in the City of Buenaventura." *Global Policy* 12 (S2): 67–77. https://doi.org/10.1111/1758
-5899.12878.

Joyce, Patrick. 2003. *The Rule of Freedom: Liberalism and the Modern City*. Verso.

Kaika, Maria. 2005. *City of Flows: Modernity, Nature, and the City*. Routledge.

Kockelman, Paul. 2010. "Enemies, Parasites, and Noise: How to Take Up Residence in a System Without Becoming a Term in It." *Journal of Linguistic Anthropology* 20 (2): 406–21. https://doi.org/10.1111/j.1548-1395.2010.01077.x.

Larkin, Brian. 2004. "Degraded Images, Distorted Sounds: Nigerian Video and the Infrastructure of Piracy." *Public Culture* 16 (2): 289–314. https://doi.org/10.1215
/08992363-16-2-289.

Larkin, Brian. 2008. *Signal and Noise: Media, Infrastructure, and Urban Culture in Nigeria*. Duke University Press.

Larkin, Brian. 2013. "The Politics and Poetics of Infrastructure." *Annual Review of Anthropology* 42 (1): 327–43. https://doi.org/10.1146/annurev-anthro-092412
-155522.

Latour, Bruno. 2004. "Why Has Critique Run Out of Steam? From Matters of Fact to Matters of Concern." *Critical Inquiry* 30 (2): 225–48. https://doi.org/10.1086
/421123.

Lawhon, Mary, David Nilsson, Jonathan Silver, Henrik Ernstson, and Shuaib Lwasa. 2018. "Thinking Through Heterogeneous Infrastructure Configurations." *Urban Studies* 55 (4): 720–32. https://doi.org/10.1177/0042098017720149.

Lea, Tess, and Paul Pholeros. 2010. "This Is Not a Pipe: The Treacheries of Indigenous Housing." *Public Culture* 22 (1): 187–209. https://doi.org/10.1215/08992363
-2009-021.

Leal, Claudia. 2015. "Conservation Memories: Vicissitudes of a Biodiversity Conservation Project in the Rainforests of Colombia, 1992–1998." *Environmental History* 20 (3): 368–95. https://doi.org/10.1093/envhis/emv051.

Leal, Claudia. 2018. *Landscapes of Freedom: Building a Postemancipation Society in the Rainforests of Western Colombia*. Latin American Landscapes. University of Arizona Press.

Lerma Bonilla, Lides Leonardo. 2019. "Análisis administrativo y técnico, del modelo de gestión públicaparala construcción de la vivienda de interés social, en el distrito especial de buenaventura: estudio de caso." Master's Thesis. Xavierian Pontifical University.

Lévi-Strauss, Claude. 1966. *The Savage Mind*. The Nature of Human Society Series. University of Chicago Press.

Li, Tania Murray. 2007. *The Will to Improve: Governmentality, Development, and the Practice of Politics*. Duke University Press. https://doi.org/10.1215/978082238 9781.

Linton, Jamie. 2010. *What Is Water? The History of a Modern Abstraction*. Nature/History/Society. University of British Columbia Press.

Lombard, Melanie, Jaime Hernández-García, and Isaac Salgado-Ramírez. 2023. "Beyond Displacement: Territorialization in the Port City of Buenaventura, Colombia." *Territory, Politics, Governance* 11 (7): 1324–43. https://doi.org/10.1080/2162 2671.2021.1908160.

Mains, Daniel. 2012. "Blackouts and Progress: Privatization, Infrastructure, and a Developmentalist State in Jimma, Ethiopia." *Cultural Anthropology* 27 (1): 3–27. https://doi.org/10.1111/j.1548-1360.2012.01124.x.

Mains, Daniel. 2019. *Under Construction: Technologies of Development in Urban Ethiopia*. Duke University Press.

Manos Visibles. 2017. *¡Carajo! Una narración de las movilizaciones sociales: Paros cívicos Chocó y Buenaventura, 2017*. https://issuu.com/manosvisibles/docs/paro -2017-paro.

Mbembe, Achille, and Janet Roitman. 1995. "Figures of the Subject in Times of Crisis." *Public Culture* 7 (2): 323–52. https://doi.org/10.1215/08992363-7-2-323.

McFee, Erin Katherine. 2019. "An Ambivalent Peace: Mistrust, Reconciliation, and the Intervention Encounter in Colombia." PhD dissertation, University of Chicago. https://doi.org/10.6082/UCHICAGO.1905.

Melly, Caroline. 2017. *Bottleneck: Moving, Building, and Belonging in an African City*. University of Chicago Press.

Menga, Filippo. 2017. "Hydropolis: Reinterpreting the Polis in Water Politics." *Political Geography* 60 (September): 100–109. https://doi.org/10.1016/j.polgeo.2017 .05.002.

Mitchell, Timothy. 1991. "The Limits of the State: Beyond Statist Approaches and Their Critics." *American Political Science Review* 85 (1): 77–96. https://doi.org /10.2307/1962879.

Mitchell, Timothy. 2014. Introduction. *Comparative Studies of South Asia, Africa and the Middle East* 34 (3): 437–39. https://doi.org/10.1215/1089201X-2826013.

Molano, Alfredo. 2017. *De río en río: vistazo a los territorios negros*. Aguilar.

Moncada, Eduardo. 2021. *Resisting Extortion: Victims, Criminals and States in Latin America*. Cambridge Studies in Comparative Politics. Cambridge University Press.

Moreno Monroy, Cindy Viviana Aurora. 2013. "Buenaventura a la deriva: Historia de un puerto en contravía de su pueblo 1945 hasta el presente." Bachelor's thesis, University of Valle.

Mosse, David. 2013. "The Anthropology of International Development." *Annual Review of Anthropology* 42 (1): 227–46. https://doi.org/10.1146/annurev-anthro-092 412-155553.

Müller, Frank I., and Julienne Weegels. 2022. "Illicit City-Making and Its Materialities: Introduction to the Special Issue." *Journal of Illicit Economies and Development* 4 (3): 230–40. https://doi.org/10.31389/jied.169.

Newman, Katherine S., and Rebekah Peeples Massengill. 2006. "The Texture of Hardship: Qualitative Sociology of Poverty, 1995–2005." *Annual Review of Sociology* 32 (1): 423–46. https://doi.org/10.1146/annurev.soc.32.061604.123122.

Nicholls, Kelly, and Gimena Sánchez Garzoli. 2011. "Buenaventura, Colombia: Where Free Trade Meets Mass Graves." NACLA, August 16, 2011. https://nacla.org/article/buenaventura-colombia-where-free-trade-meets-mass-graves.

Nieto, Carlos Eduardo. 2011. "El ferrocarril en Colombia y la búsqueda de un país." *Apuntes* 24 (1): 62–75.

Nissen, Mads. 2018. *We Are Indestructible*. GOST Books.

Nordstrom, Carolyn, and Antonius Robben. 1996. Introduction. In *Fieldwork Under Fire: Contemporary Studies of Violence and Culture*, edited by Carolyn Nordstrom and Antonius Robben, 1–20. University of California Press.

Offen, Karl H. 2003. "The Territorial Turn: Making Black Territories in Pacific Colombia." *Journal of Latin American Geography* 2 (1): 43–73. https://doi.org/10.1353/lag.2004.0010.

Ortner, Sherry B. 2016. "Dark Anthropology and Its Others: Theory Since the Eighties." *HAU: Journal of Ethnographic Theory* 6 (1): 47–73. https://doi.org/10.14318/hau6.1.004.

Oslender, Ulrich. 2002. "'The Logic of the River': A Spatial Approach to Ethnic-Territorial Mobilization in the Colombian Pacific Region." *Journal of Latin American Anthropology* 7 (2): 86–117. https://doi.org/10.1525/jlca.2002.7.2.86.

Oslender, Ulrich. 2008. "Another History of Violence: The Production of 'Geographies of Terror' in Colombia's Pacific Coast Region." *Latin American Perspectives* 35 (5): 77–102. https://doi.org/10.1177/0094582X08321961.

Oslender, Ulrich. 2016. *The Geographies of Social Movements: Afro-Colombian Mobilization and the Aquatic Space*. New Ecologies for the Twenty-First Century. Duke University Press.

Özden-Schilling, Tom. 2023. *The Ends of Research: Indigenous and Settler Science After the War in the Woods*. Experimental Futures. Duke University Press.

Palacios, Marco. 2006. *Between Legitimacy and Violence: A History of Colombia, 1875–2002*. Translated by Richard Stoller. Duke University Press. https://doi.org/10.2307/j.ctv1220mkn.

Pellegrino, Valentina. 2022. "Between the Roll of Paper and the Role of Paper: Governmental Documentation as a Mechanism for Complying Incompliantly." *PoLAR: Political and Legal Anthropology Review* 45 (1): 77–93. https://doi.org/10.1111/plar.12467.

Penglase, Ben. 2009. "States of Insecurity: Everyday Emergencies, Public Secrets, and Drug Trafficker Power in a Brazilian Favela." *PoLAR: Political and Legal Anthropology Review* 32 (1): 47–63. https://doi.org/10.1111/j.1555-2934.2009.01023.x.

Ramírez, María Clemencia. 2011. *Between the Guerrillas and the State: The Cocalero Movement, Citizenship, and Identity in the Colombian Amazon*. Translated by María Clemencia Ramírez. Duke University Press. https://doi.org/10.1215/978 0822394204.

Ramírez, María Clemencia. 2015. "The Idea of the State in Colombia: An Analysis from the Periphery." In *State Theory and Andean Politics*, edited by Christopher Krupa and David Nugent, 35–55. University of Pennsylvania Press. https://doi.org /10.9783/9780812291070-002.

Restrepo, Eduardo. 2013. *Etnización de la negridad: la invención de las "comunidades negras" como grupo étnico en Colombia*. Genealogías de la negridad. Editorial Universidad del Cauca.

Rhodes, D. G., R. Newton, R. Butler, and L. Herbette. 1992. "Equilibrium and Kinetic Studies of the Interactions of Salmeterol with Membrane Bilayers." *Molecular Pharmacology* 42 (4): 596–602.

Robbins, Joel. 2013. "Beyond the Suffering Subject: Toward an Anthropology of the Good." *Journal of the Royal Anthropological Institute* 19 (3): 447–62. https://doi .org/10.1111/1467-9655.12044.

Robinson, Jennifer. 2002. "Global and World Cities: A View from off the Map." *International Journal of Urban and Regional Research* 26 (3): 531–54. https://doi.org /10.1111/1468-2427.00397.

Rockefeller, Stuart Alexander. 2011. "Flow." *Current Anthropology* 52 (4): 557–78. https://doi.org/10.1086/660912.

Rodgers, Dennis, and Bruce O'Neill. 2012. "Infrastructural Violence: Introduction to the Special Issue." *Ethnography* 13 (4): 401–12. https://doi.org/10.1177/146613 8111435738.

Rodríguez, Enrique, and José Fernando Sánchez. 2002. "Imagen de región y procesos de construcción de ciudad en el Pacífico Colombiano: Los casos de Buenaventura y Tumaco." *Sociedad y Economía*, no. 2 (January): 49–71. https://doi.org/10.25100 /sye.v0i2.4190.

Ronderos, María Teresa. 2014. *Guerras recicladas: Una historia periodística del paramilitarismo en Colombia*. Aguilar.

Rosa, Jonathan, and Vanessa Díaz. 2020. "Raciontologies: Rethinking Anthropological Accounts of Institutional Racism and Enactments of White Supremacy in the United States." *American Anthropologist* 122 (1): 120–32. https://doi.org/10.1111 /aman.13353.

Rottenburg, Richard. 2009. *Far-Fetched Facts: A Parable of Development Aid*. Inside Technology. MIT Press.

Roy, Ananya. 2011. "Slumdog Cities: Rethinking Subaltern Urbanism." *International Journal of Urban and Regional Research* 35 (2): 223–38. https://doi.org/10.1111/j .1468-2427.2011.01051.x.

Safford, Frank Robinson, and Marco Palacios Rozo. 2002. *Colombia: Fragmented Land, Divided Society*. Latin American Histories. Oxford University Press.

Salazar, Boris. 2007. "Morir en Buenaventura." *Revista Posiciones* 1:66–73.

Sanford, Victoria. 2004. "Contesting Displacement in Colombia. Citizenship and State Sovereignty at the Margins." In *Anthropology in the Margins of State*, edited by Veena Das and Deborah Poole, 253–77. School for Advanced Research Press.

Scheper-Hughes, Nancy, and Philippe Bourgois. 2003. "Introduction: Making Sense of Violence." In *Violence in War and Peace: An Anthology*, edited by Nancy Scheper-Hughes and Philippe Bourgois. Blackwell.

Schindler, Seth. 2017. "Towards a Paradigm of Southern Urbanism." *City* 21 (1): 47–64. https://doi.org/10.1080/13604813.2016.1263494.

Schwenkel, Christina. 2015. "Spectacular Infrastructure and Its Breakdown in Socialist Vietnam." *American Ethnologist* 42 (3): 520–34. https://doi.org/10.1111/amet.12145.

Scott, James C. 1998. *Seeing like a State: How Certain Schemes to Improve the Human Condition Have Failed*. Yale Agrarian Studies. Yale University Press.

Serje, Margarita. 2011. *El revés de la nación*. University of the Andes.

Serje, Margarita. 2012. "El mito de la ausencia del estado: La incorporación económica de las 'Zonas de Frontera' en Colombia." *Cahiers Des Amériques Latines*, no. 71 (December), 95–117. https://doi.org/10.4000/cal.2679.

Sharma, Aradhana, and Akhil Gupta, eds. 2006. *The Anthropology of the State: A Reader*. Blackwell Readers in Anthropology 9. Blackwell.

Simone, AbdouMaliq. 2006. "Pirate Towns: Reworking Social and Symbolic Infrastructures in Johannesburg and Douala." *Urban Studies* 43 (2): 357–70. https://doi.org/10.1080/00420980500146974.

Simone, AbdouMaliq. 2015a. "Afterword: Come On Out, You're Surrounded: The Betweens of Infrastructure." *City* 19 (2–3): 375–83. https://doi.org/10.1080/13604813.2015.1018070.

Simone, AbdouMaliq. 2015b. "The Urban Poor and Their Ambivalent Exceptionalities: Some Notes from Jakarta." *Current Anthropology* 56 (S11): S15–23. https://doi.org/10.1086/682283.

Simone, AbdouMaliq. 2019. *Improvised Lives: Rhythms of Endurance in an Urban South*. After the Postcolonial. Polity.

Star, Susan Leigh. 1999. "The Ethnography of Infrastructure." *American Behavioral Scientist* 43 (3): 377–91. https://doi.org/10.1177/00027649921955326.

Swyngedouw, E. 1997. "Power, Nature, and the City: The Conquest of Water and the Political Ecology of Urbanization in Guayaquil, Ecuador, 1880–1990." *Environment and Planning A: Economy and Space* 29 (2): 311–32. https://doi.org/10.1068/a290311.

Swyngedouw, Erik. 2004. *Social Power and the Urbanization of Water: Flows of Power*. Oxford University Press. https://doi.org/10.1093/oso/9780198233916.001.0001.

Taula Catalana. 2016. "Informe de la visita de la delegación Catalana a Buenaventura." Catalan Bureau for Peace and Human Rights.

Taussig, Michael T. 2003. *Law in a Lawless Land: Diary of a "Limpieza" in Colombia*. The New Press.

Taussig, Michael. 1984. "Culture of Terror—Space of Death: Roger Casement's Putu-
    mayo Report and the Explanation of Torture." *Comparative Studies in Society and
    History* 26 (3): 467–97. https://doi.org/10.1017/S0010417500011105.
Taussig, Michael. 2004. *My Cocaine Museum*. University of Chicago Press.
Trovalla, Ulrika, and Eric Trovalla. 2015. "Infrastructure Turned Suprastructure: Un-
    predictable Materialities and Visions of a Nigerian Nation." *Journal of Material
    Culture* 20 (1): 43–57. https://doi.org/10.1177/1359183514560284.
Tsing, Anna Lowenhaupt. 2012. "On Nonscalability." *Common Knowledge* 18 (3):
    505–24. https://doi.org/10.1215/0961754X-1630424.
Tubb, Daniel. 2020. *Shifting Livelihoods: Gold Mining and Subsistence in the Chocó,
    Colombia*. Culture, Place, and Nature: Studies in Anthropology and Environment.
    University of Washington Press.
United Nations High Commissioner for Refugees. 2017. Colombia: Paramilitary Suc-
    cessor Groups and Criminal Bands (No. COL105773.E). Available at https://www
    .refworld.org/docid/591614014.html.
Uribe, Simón. 2017. *Frontier Road: Power, History, and the Everyday State in the
    Colombian Amazon*. Wiley.
Uribe, Simón. 2020. "The Trampoline of Death: Infrastructural Violence in Colom-
    bia's Putumayo Frontier." *Journal of Transport History* 41 (1): 47–69. https://doi
    .org/10.1177/0022526619888589.
van der Geest, Sjaak. 2017. "The Freedom of Anthropological Fieldwork." *Etnofoor*
    29(1): 101–12.
van Laak, Dirk. 2018. *Alles im fluss: Die lebensadern unserer gesellschaft—Geschichte
    und zukunft der infrastruktur*. S. Fischer.
Varese, Federico. 2013. *Protection and Extortion*. Oxford University Press. https://doi
    .org/10.1093/oxfordhb/9780199730445.013.020.
Vera, Juan Pablo. 2017. "The Humanitarian State." PhD dissertation, Rutgers Univer-
    sity. https://doi.org/10.7282/T3JQ13X1.
von Schnitzler, Antina. 2016. *Democracy's Infrastructure: Techno-Politics and Protest
    After Apartheid*. Princeton University Press.
Weizman, Eyal. 2017. *Hollow Land: Israel's Architecture of Occupation*. New ed.
    Verso.
Zeiderman, Austin. 2016. "Submergence: Precarious Politics in Colombia's Future
    Port-City." *Antipode* 48 (3): 809–31. https://doi.org/10.1111/anti.12207.
Zeiderman, Austin. 2018. "Beyond the Enclave of Urban Theory." *International Jour-
    nal of Urban and Regional Research* 42 (6): 1114–26. https://doi.org/10.1111/1468
    -2427.12661.

INDEX

Laak, Dirk van, 15
Lagos, 41
Landscapes of Freedom (Leal), 16–17
Larkin, Brian, 64, 84, 98, 146
Latin America: frontiers of, 20–21; North
    American Congress on Latin America,
    74n8, 124; politics in, 11; Spain in, 42–
    43. *See also specific places*
Leal, Claudia, 11–12, 16–17, 43, 56–57,
    95, 117
Levi-Strauss, Claude, 128
Ley 70 (1993), 125–26
Liberal Party, 70
local experts, 113–17, 128–34
local politics, 124–25

Machado, Temístocles, 122
Mains, Daniel, 145–46
Mann, Michael, 7–8
Manuel Vargas Front, 72
marginalized populations: access to, 28; in
    Buenaventura, 86; in Colombia, 11–12;
    exclusion of, 82–83; in frontiers, 18n11;
    infrastructural violence against, 186;
    ports for, 8, 114–15, 121–22, 182–83;
    public goods for, 33; racialization of,
    108–9; segregation of, 15–16; social
    activists for, 106; state institutions and,
    147
Márquez, Francia, 190
Marvin, Simon, 145
massacres, 45–46, 45n2, 72, 184
Massengill, Rebekah Peeples, 42
mass graves, 7
Master Sewage and Water Supply Plan,
    89–90
Mbembe, Achille, 146
Medellín: Bogotá and, 58, 61; socioeco-
    nomics in, 58, 61, 111–12; urbanization
    in, 39–41, 43
mestizaje, 11, 16n10
mestizo: Black people and, 55; in Colom-
    bia, 11; hierarchies for, 94; Leal on,

95; settler colonization, 42–43; social
    stigma against, 28–29; women, 28–29
Ministry of Finance and Public Credit,
    87–88
Ministry of Housing, 88–89, 96
minorities: Afro-Colombians as, 48,
    134–35; ethnic, 24, 114–15, 183–84;
    minority rights, 20
Molano, Alfredo, 184
Moncada, Eduardo, 167
mototaxistas, 82
mujeriegos (womanizers), 112
multiculturalism, 12
Municipal Development Institute (INFO-
    SPAL), 58–59
Muslims, 95–96
My Cocaine Museum (Taussig), 23, 35,
    184

National Center for Historical Memory,
    170
National Council for Economic and Social
    Policy, 61
National Development Plan. *See* Plan
    Todos Somos PAZcífico
National Front, 71
National Planning Department, 121
National Registry of Disappeared Persons,
    74
National Unit for Disaster Risk Manage-
    ment (UNGRD), 87–88, 91
neocolonialism, 17
neoliberalism, 51, 60–61
neo-paramilitary groups, 168
Newman, Katherine, 42
NGOs. *See* nongovernmental
    organizations
Nigeria, 24
nongovernmental organizations (NGOs):
    for Afro-Colombians, 184; in Bue-
    naventura, 7; in Colombia, 22–23, 124;
    FARC and, 45–46; in Global South,
    130; institutional support from, 25; in

politics (*continued*)
  activists in, 41–42, 99; of state officials,
  146–47; Strike Committee in, 98–99,
  115; of water, 80; of water infrastructure, 12–14, 33–34
Poole, Deborah, 19
ports: city points and, 75; in Colombia,
  6–9; in Colombian Pacific, 119–20;
  Colpuertos for, 59–61; development
  agendas for, 168; infrastructures of,
  16–17, 43–49, 72–75; for marginalized
  populations, 8, 114–15, 121–22, 182–
  83; port cities, 13–14, 24–28, 86–87,
  90, 92, 147–49; urbanization of,
  58–66, 117–19, 132–33; violence and,
  169–72. *See also specific topics*
poverty: Afro-Colombians in, 185; in
  Argentina, 186; Black peasants, 57–58,
  76, 112, 184; in Buenaventura, 35, 179–
  80; in Colombia, 111–12; deprivation
  and, 163; development policy for, 7n7;
  education and, 129–30; infrastructural
  violence in, 139–40; NGOs against,
  52; pirate infrastructure and, 105–6;
  unemployment and, 79–80; urban, 14;
  vulnerable neighborhoods in, 8; water
  and, 4–5
privatization, 46–47, 51, 60–61
Proceso de Comunidades Negras (PNC),
  135, 176–77
Proyecto BioPacífico, 20
PTSP. *See* Plan Todos Somos PAZcífico
public goods: in Buenaventura, 9; continuity of service with, 92; during
  COVID-19 pandemic, 49–50; deprivation of, 41; endemic violence and, 24;
  exclusion from, 95; invisible frontiers
  with, 7; for marginalized populations,
  33; politics of, 5–6; provision of, 26;
  public services, 145–46; public water
  management board, 54; resources for,
  55–56, 168–69; supply of, 80; water
  as, 12

public infrastructure, 43, 45, 135, 146
public secrecy, 78
PVC tanks, 68, 152–57

Quibdó, 56–57, 117

racialization: of Afro-Colombians, 149; in
  colonialism, 75; of marginalized populations, 108–9; race and, 12, 117, 186;
  racialized communities, 11–12, 21n15;
  racialized landscapes, 12, 90; racialized
  othering, 40; racialized populations,
  186–87; socio-racial dynamics, 117
racism: against Afro-Colombians, 16–17,
  29, 94–95, 124–26; against Black
  people, 117, 140; in Buenaventura, 4–5;
  citizenship and, 11; in Colombia, 11,
  85, 99; at Hidropacífico, 94; PTSP and,
  93–96; racial prejudices, 92, 95–96
rainwater, 152–53
refugees, 6–7
regularization, of PTSP, 100–104
resistance, to crime, 175–78
Restrepo, Eduardo, 48
Revolutionary Armed Forces of Colombia.
  See FARC
Robbins, Joel, 42
Rockefeller, Stuart Alexander, 9–10
Rodgers, Dennis, 7–8
Roitman, Janet, 146
Rojas Pinilla, Gustavo, 70
Romero, Nestor, 55–63, 119
rooftop water tanks, 148
Rosa, Jonathan, 85
rural Black communities, 115, 155–56
rural Colombian Pacific, 23–24, 72, 82,
  114–15, 149–52, 183–85

SAAB. *See* Sociedad de Acueducto y Alca-
  ntarillado de Buenaventura
Sabaletas, 22–23
Safford, Frank, 18–19
Salazar, Boris, 24

ABOUT THE AUTHOR

Felipe Fernández is an assistant professor of social and cultural anthropology at the University of Freiburg, Germany. He trained as an anthropologist and historian at the Freie Universität in Berlin and holds a master's degree and PhD in Latin American studies from the same university. His research focuses on infrastructures, state bureaucracy, and expert cultures in Latin America. His work has been funded by the Freie Universität in Berlin, the German Academic Exchange Services, the German Research Foundation, and the Humboldt Foundation.